tear here

The Complete Idiot's Guide to Etiquette Reference Card

Top 10 Dining Mistakes

1. Chewing or speaking with food in your mouth
2. Holding the knife like a dagger or the fork like a cello and putting cutlery, once used, back on the table
3. Putting purses, keys, gloves, etc. on the table
4. Finishing your meal before or after everyone else
5. Flapping the napkin to open it and putting it on the table before the meal has ended
6. Slouching, squirming, or tilting your chair
7. Picking or poking at your teeth
8. Leaving lipstick smears
9. Smoking—wait until the meal is over (and please, do not use your plate as an ashtray)
10. Buttering all the bread at once—tear off each piece and butter it before you eat it

Dining Calamities

➤ If you spill something, don't make a big deal out of it. Blot it with your napkin, and ask for another one.

➤ If you spill something on someone else, apologize, and offer to pay for dry cleaning, but let the other person handle the wiping and blotting.

➤ If you burp, touch your napkin to your lips, and say, "Pardon me," to no one in particular.

alpha books

Tips for Cool Kids

➤ If you are being ignored in a store, it's okay to say, "I think I'm next," or "Could you help me, please?"

➤ The drill for meeting new people is easy: stand up, make eye contact, say hello, and shake hands.

➤ If you get a really stupid gift, you don't have to lie. Just say, "Thank you," and/or, "It was nice of you to think of me."

➤ If you know you're going to be kissed, stick out your hand to shake. If that doesn't work, turn your head at the last minute, and take it on the cheek.

➤ If you want people to think you have good manners, say "please," "thank you," and "excuse me," and make eye contact when you speak to them.

Tips for the Workplace

➤ Gallantry will get you nowhere, except maybe into hot water.

➤ Don't worry about doors. First one there goes through first. Hold it only to keep it from hitting the person behind you, or if that person is carrying packages.

➤ It's taboo to hug and kiss in any business environment with the possible exception of the more creative and artistic fields, such as fashion or entertainment. When in doubt, wait for the other person to make the first move.

➤ When meeting someone, stand up, shake hands firmly without crushing, and don't start using first names until you are invited to.

Dealing With People from Other Cultures

➤ Gestures familiar to us, such as the "V" for victory sign or the "OK" sign, are considered vulgar and/or insulting in some other cultures.

➤ Be careful about sending flowers. White flowers in China, for example, signify mourning. Red roses in Europe signal romantic intentions.

➤ Propping your foot up so that others can see the sole of your shoe is considered flagrantly insulting in many parts of the world.

➤ When meeting someone in America, we smile, look 'em right in the eye, and stick out our hands to shake. In some places, this would be making three mistakes all at once.

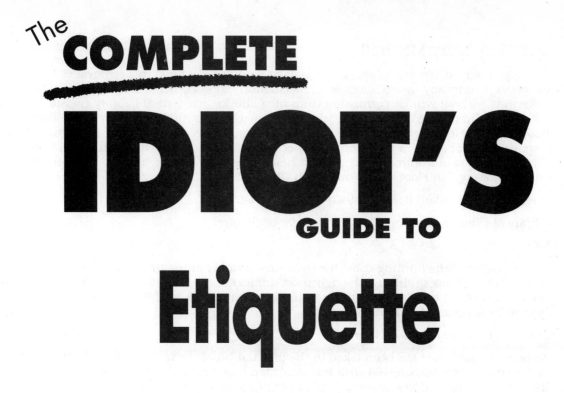

The COMPLETE IDIOT'S GUIDE TO Etiquette

by Mary Mitchell with John Corr

alpha books

A Division of Macmillan General Reference
A Simon & Schuster Macmillan Company
1633 Broadway, New York, NY 10019-6785

International Standard Book Number: 0-02-861094-6

Library of Congress Catalog Card Number: 96-084610

98 97 96   8 7 6 5 4

Interpretation of the printing code: the rightmost number of the first series of numbers is the year of the book's printing; the rightmost number of the second series of numbers is the number of the book's printing. For example, a printing code of 96-1 shows that the first printing occurred in 1996.

Printed in the United States of America

Publisher
Theresa Murtha

Editor
Nancy Mikhail

Production Editor
Whitney K. Ward

Copy Editors
Michael Thomas
Whitney K. Ward

Cover Designer
Mike Freeland

Illustrator
Judd Winick

Designer
Barbara Kordesh

Graphic Image Specialists
Brad Dixon
Dan Harris
Clint Lahnen
Ryan Oldfather
Casey Price
Laura Robbins
Marvin Van Tiem

Indexer
Tim Tate

Production Team
Angela Calvert
Tricia Flodder
Megan Wade
Christy Wagner

Contents at a Glance

Contents

Foreword

Our world desperately needs to hold on to the social traditions based on graciousness, courtesy, and kindness that have been passed down to us in the form of what is called etiquette. And we can do this while acknowledging and appreciating the changing tastes and styles of our dynamic contemporary society.

This book will help you to do both.

Our customers know that there are times when only "the right thing" will do, whether it is a gift, a formal invitation, or a letter of congratulation or condolence. They come to our stores to find just what they need—just the appropriate object or the correct bit of information—conveniently and pleasantly. This book offers the same sort of convenience. It is intelligently organized, brightly written, and most important, authoritative.

At Caldwell's, we have learned over the years that even successful and experienced people realize that, from time to time, they need information and advice on social and business etiquette. They can find it in this book.

The Complete Idiot's Guide to Etiquette is comprehensive, accurate, and fun to read. So read it in good spirits. And be kind to one another.

John K. Hunter
President
J.E. Caldwell & Co.

Introduction

Many baby boomers once thought the best place for an etiquette book was in the same bonfire as the bras.

Well, the times have changed, and so have we.

People for whom Woodstock defined—at least temporarily—an acceptable social ethic are now finding themselves in situations in which tact, appearance, what they say, and how they behave are critically important. They need to know more about the rules that make interaction with others not only inoffensive, but comfortable and smooth. In a word…etiquette.

Whether or not it's unfair, people will make character judgments about you based on how you handle social situations. This can also be a crucial factor when your superiors make decisions about how far and how high you can go in an organization.

Knowing the rules of etiquette sets you free from doubt and anxiety and allows you to approach things such as dinner parties, meeting new people, hosting gatherings, and responding to invitations and other correspondence with grace and confidence.

Once, these rules were learned at home, often around the dinner table. Well, families don't gather around the dinner table as regularly and formally as they once did, and parents don't set aside time for little lessons in "deportment," or manners.

Even those who have had a good grounding in etiquette need some updating in this rapidly changing world. A healthy supply of common sense and a knowledge of the traditions upon which much of etiquette is based are not enough. Some of the rules have changed or been modified, and they vary from place to place.

These are things that people do not know instinctively, no matter how smart they are. Somebody had to teach them. Somebody had to teach me.

The idea behind this book is to present the information you need to know about proper behavior, socially and professionally, in casual and formal circumstances, here and abroad. It is arranged so that it can be a quick reference guide as well as an examination of social behavior, generally and in specific situations.

Beyond Etiquette

Once, a foreign visitor at a dinner given by Pearl Mesta, "The hostess with the mostess," drank the water in his finger bowl instead of using it to cleanse his fingers. Mesta immediately followed suit, and the other guests took their cue from her.

Using the finger bowl as intended would have been proper etiquette, but it would not have been good manners.

Good manners come from the inside and do not change. Etiquette rules come from the outside, and they are constantly changing. The rules in school are different from the rules in the office. And the rules also change with time.

Good manners are based on kindness and respect, which transcend etiquette. In every human situation, there is the correct action, the incorrect action, and the appropriate action. This book is designed to give you the rules. Only you can judge whether to adhere to them verbatim. *Knowing* the rules is essential because it puts you in the position of knowing when it is appropriate to break or bend them.

Sometimes adhering strictly to rules is used as a weapon—which is the height (or depth) of bad manners. A person's feelings are *always* more important.

How This Book Is Organized

The book presents etiquette by category and is divided into six parts.

Part 1: Dining Etiquette. This section includes the most common dining mistakes, table settings, how to eat difficult foods, and tips that will help you approach the most daunting dining situations with confidence.

Part 2: Business Etiquette. The rules are different from social etiquette, as is the whole approach to the subject of manners. This part deals with what to say, how to dress, and how to react to various situations in the world of work.

Part 3: Correspondence. The pen is still powerful, the age of e-mail notwithstanding. In this part, we talk about the structure and style of letters and notes, appropriate stationery for different situations, invitations, and addressing people properly.

Part 4: Home Etiquette. Manners for children and young people are discussed here, as well as the problems and pleasures of home entertaining—everything from a casual get-together to a formal dinner.

Part 5: Saying the Right Thing. Here we look at how to deal with conflict and criticism. We also discuss meeting and interacting with people with disabilities and those from different cultures. How to handle the giving and receiving of compliments and gifts is also addressed.

Part 6: Fun and Games. This part deals with courteous behavior in the world of sports—everything from yachting to rollerblading. Also included are travel etiquette and tips on preparing for and surviving a wedding.

Conventions Used in This Book

There are several special items that are presented apart from the text. You will see them as boxed notes among the text. They are set apart for several different reasons.

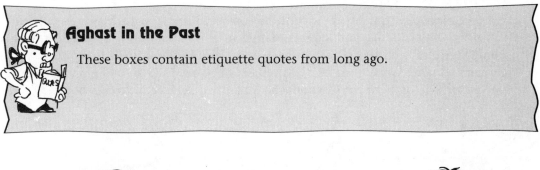

Aghast in the Past

These boxes contain etiquette quotes from long ago.

Did You Know?
These boxes communicate little etiquette facts and tidbits.

WDYS?
"What Do You Say?" boxes give tips on what to say when caught in a sticky situation.

Tip
"Tip" boxes illustrate etiquette how-tos.

Faux Pas
These boxes contain social blunder no-nos.

Dedication

This book is dedicated to our spouses, Daniel Fleischmann and Marjorie Matthews Corr, with love and gratitude for their support and forbearance during the writing of this book.

Acknowledgments

We cannot possibly number all the friends, colleagues, and family who encouraged us every step and word of the way to this book's completion. You know who you are, and we express our deep and sincere gratitude.

We were blessed with the specific contributions of Alison Douglas Knox, Esq., Thea Lammers, Oatley Kidder, and Kalinda Mathes from IISA; Lu Galloway and Scott Goldstein from Enterprise Rent-A-Car; Cathy Hagan and Maria Lynch from Tiffany & Co.; and John Hunter and Janet Weiss from J.E. Caldwell & Co. Nancy Mikhail of Simon & Schuster is a fine editor who brought a professional and reasoned perspective to the book.

Part 1
Dining Etiquette

Nowhere are your manners more on display than at the dinner table. And there are few aspects of social etiquette that people worry about more—for the most part, unnecessarily.

There is no reason in the world to be intimidated by the prospect of even the most formal dinner. It's all a matter of knowing the rules, and luckily, the rules are plain, no matter how fancy the meal.

Once learned, these rules will enable you to approach dining in public with confidence, and that means you will be able to relax and enjoy the meal and the company.

Dining with others can be one of life's most pleasant experiences. It is an experience that we can realize more fully when we know what to expect and what is expected of us.

Before we lead you to the table, however, let's take a few minutes to look at how the rules of etiquette and the attitudes of Americans toward etiquette have evolved over the years, particularly in the "New World."

Chapter 1

WHOSE A GUY GOTTA KILL TO GET A CORNED BEEF SANDWICH AROUND HERE!?

Etiquette in America— What Happened?

In This Chapter

➤ The tactless pioneers

➤ The American Ideal

➤ The era of conspicuous consumption

➤ The New Nobility

➤ Etiquette guides—yesterday and today

➤ Where we are now and why

Etiquette, of course, has evolved over time everywhere in the world. In America, that evolution took on a distinctively robust American flavor.

The Rough-and-Ready Pioneers

When the Americans, whose sinewy hands tamed a wild new continent and fashioned an industrial juggernaut, set out to acquire their own systems of courtesy and manners, they did so with characteristic vigor and a style that was by turns practical and quixotic, solemn and hilarious. These Americans came for the most part from Old World classes that were cut off from the customs of the "best" society, and many of them came to the New World because they despised the social rigors of European society. In the beginning, there was little time for contemplating the social graces. The struggle to conquer the wilderness was constantly renewed as American civilization marched toward the Pacific. Behind the westward-questing pioneers, the unceasing arrival of new hordes of immigrants kept conditions continually unsettled.

Also, there was the scarcity of women. In Europe, women were continuously in the majority, and they were the makers and the guardians of the traditions of courtesy. In early America, women were a minority and, in fact, so scarce that men tended to treat them with something close to reverence and to compete in exaggerated and often comical politeness for their attention. Women were to be respected and protected and, if possible, pampered.

Poor Richard and George Washington on Manners

Early on, minimal standards of civility were enforced by law. There were penalties for slander, lying, cursing, and even flirting. Strictures came from the government and the clergy, and advice came from the authors of almanacs such as *Poor Richard's Almanac*:

> Fish and visitors stink after three days.

> None but the well-bred man knows how to confess a fault, or acknowledge himself in error.

The few etiquette guides that were available tended to stick to the basics. A much-reprinted 18th-century guide for children warned:

> Spit not, cough not, nor blow thy nose at the table, if it may be avoided.

Adults were advised not to use the tablecloth to clean their teeth in George Washington's "Rules of Civility."

The Genteel South and the Robust North

But as leisure and wealth increased, something less basic began to be desired. The Southern plantation owner, sitting amid his productive fields and his black vassals, and the prosperous merchants and tradesmen of the Northern port cities, looked about for a standard of decorum and even elegance to serve as a reflection of their wealth and power. They looked about in vain, and ultimately looked back to England for the literature of civility.

The Literature of Civility

The English books that were imported were very often translations, adaptions, or outright plagiarisms of French works. France, since the age of chivalry, had been Europe's chief instructor in matters of manners. The bookshelves of the wealthy and the wannabees soon contained volumes dealing with specifics as to dress, dining, and deportment. In these publications, the earmarks of a gentleman were not only probity, or uprightness, but also valor, piety, and justice. The gentlewoman was modest, meek, chaste, and compassionate.

The habit of looking to England for printed politeness guides continued for about a half-century after the severing of political ties.

The "American Ideal: Not That Gentlemen Should Cease to Be"

As Americans marched into the 19th century, they discarded many of the social forms and practices of the Old World like a garment that no longer fits the form for which it was tailored.

England was bested in the War of 1812. America reached to the Rio Grande and the Pacific; waterways, like the Erie Canal, and railroads reached into the interior; new towns sprung up, and towns became cities; and the growth of industry rampaged across the landscape. Andrew Jackson, son of a destitute immigrant, moved into the White House in 1828 in the office previously held by the Harvard-educated Adamses and the powerful Virginia landholders.

Ordinary people believed they could make themselves into whatever they wanted to be. The idea was that any man could become a gentleman—not that gentlemen should cease to be.

From the 1830s until the Civil War, there was a flood of home-grown etiquette advice books. In these, we see a shift away from an emphasis on probity and valor, modesty and compassion, toward the view that etiquette is a set of rules to be learned. Americans did not want to be lectured to about character, chivalry, and morality. They wanted to learn the rules of behavior that would enable them to move comfortably in society.

Some of this advice came tongue in cheek:

> Always keep callers waiting, till they have had time to notice the outlay of money in your parlors.

5

And,

> Always whisper and laugh at concerts by way of compliment to the performers and to show your neighbors a sovereign contempt for their comfort.

And these books differed from those of the past in their overall attitude about how women should behave. The emphasis shifted from being meek, pliant, and weak. One advised bluntly that "Crying is no longer fashionable."

Americans were advised in journals and books to avoid "the stiff and stately pomp" of manners honed in European courts. Nathaniel Willis wrote in 1851:

> We should be glad to see a distinctively American school of good manners, in which all useless etiquettes were thrown aside, but every politeness adopted or invented which could promote sensible and easy exchanges of good will and sensibility.

He advised getting rid of "imported superfluities."

The Four Hundred—Rockefeller, Carnegie, Vanderbilt

After the Civil War came the era of the robber barons, the steel and railroad magnates, merchant princes, Napoleons of finance. Along came John D. Rockefeller, Andrew Carnegie, Cornelius Vanderbilt. *Scientific American* reported in 1866:

> There are more men in New York today whose annual incomes reach $100,000 than there were 25 years ago of those whose entire possessions amounted to as much.

A new nobility was created, putting to shame the old English "parchment nobility" in terms of wealth and extravagance. The most prominent leaders of this new nobility were called the "Four Hundred" in newspapers and magazines of the period.

The old simplicities of society were rent by these new plutocrats, some from the humblest beginnings. They burst upon the social scene with absurdities of conspicuous consumption and, in the process, rewrought the American social scene. It was a development viewed with alarm by some. E. L. Godkin wrote in 1896:

> We are about to renew on this soil, at the end of the 19th Century, the extravagances and follies of the later Roman Empire and of the age of Louis XIV.

Another observer lamented that "The sham aristocracy indulge in mushroom manners." Mushrooms are showy but of little consequence.

While the masses, of course, could not match the gyrations of the Four Hundred, they followed their activities avidly, mostly through "society" columns of the newspapers. The desire to learn "the rules" that governed the gatherings of these almost mythical figures became, perhaps, more widespread than ever. Magazines, particularly women's magazines, devoted space to "deportment departments." Newspapers began running etiquette columns, and advice to the lovelorn columns also often included advice on proper, or at least acceptable, behavior.

Conspicuous Consumption

The etiquette scribes of the "Four Hundred" period took the position that they were helping to instill a more aristocratic style of behavior, one that was more in tune with the improving fortunes of the middle class.

There was something of a backlash to all of this—critics who cried out against this wave of "artificial refinement." To these critics, *Appleton's Journal* replied in 1871:

> Is it not better to carry punctiliousness a little too far than continually to be sinning against those minor morals on which the pleasure of intercourse so much depends?

"Punctiliousness" was much in evidence. On crossing the street, a lady was to "gracefully raise her dress a little above her ankle." When bowing, the head was to be bent, and "a mere lowering of the eyelids" was rude. Formal calls were to last no longer than 15 minutes. One was never to "emphasize a point with a touch of the foot." Men were not supposed to smoke in the presence of women, and women were not supposed to smoke at all.

The dining room became an arena for conspicuous consumption, with what was described as a bewildering display of goblets, plates, and silverware. The etiquette of the ballroom was complex and severe. Formal introductions were imperative, and the style and form of the dances themselves were strictly proscribed.

The New Nobility

The etiquette strictures of the post–Civil War era began to loosen after the turn of the century:

➤ The pace of life began to mitigate against extravagantly ceremonious occasions.

➤ The possession of wealth lost some of its glamour and even the "best" families began to eschew ostentation.

➤ Women became more socially and financially independent and found other interests (particularly sports) besides the society scene.

The years after World War I saw an even more pronounced drift from what began to be seen, somewhat contemptuously, as "Victorian" manners. The "forbidden fruit" syndrome that accompanied Prohibition, the movies, the automobile, and the radio all had a profound influence, and finally, the Great Depression seemed to wash away the last of the old ways.

Although the American thirst for advice on behavior remained unquenched, its form was altered greatly. Emily Post and, to a greater extent, Lillian Eichler, gave advice that was practical and straightforward, much less doctrinaire and accusatory than the pronouncements of the etiquette doyennes of previous eras.

There seemed to be a national consensus that appropriate behavior could be simpler, more spontaneous, more genuine.

If anything, World War II reinforced this perception. The war years were years of a nation working together toward a single goal. The American heroes were the grimy guys in foxholes and the stout-hearted defense workers on the night shift. Rosy the Riveter symbolized the new attitude of and toward American women.

The Fit-In '50s and the Rebellious '60s

Nobody can claim that Americans were not concerned with correct behavior during the 1940s and 1950s. Good manners, fitting in, dressing right, and being part of the crowd were vitally important. Advice columns and magazine features on behavior remained popular, although the approach was perhaps more chatty than instructional.

Then came the 1960s, the hippies, the drug culture, long hair, longer dresses, denim, and disobedience. There was a pronounced decline in the popularity of books and magazine articles written on etiquette. Etiquette became a word seldom heard except in jest. In an era of rebellion, it was deemed unworthy even of protest.

But even during these years, when "being real" achieved something of a cult status, experts on etiquette emerged and were, if not honored, at least consulted. Letitia Baldrige was Jacqueline Kennedy's chief of staff at the White House, and Nancy Tuckerman was her staff coordinator.

Where We Are Now and How We Got Here

Through all of the changes and crises that molded American society over the years, there has remained a willingness and even an eagerness to accept information and advice about behavior. It has been called etiquette, manners, courtesy, or just "behaving yourself." But it has endured, a continuing reflection of the desire of an essentially good-natured and vital people to exist harmoniously with those around them.

And now, as America approaches the 21st century, this desire for knowledge and advice on behavior continues, but the wish to acquire information about etiquette is more sharply focused than ever before. Career-oriented people have come to realize that people skills equal or surpass technical skills in importance. The "social scene" is so often merged with the world of work. The arenas in which we are judged by our behavior are no longer primarily the ballroom and the dining room but the boardroom and the marketplace and, as our world shrinks, the international stage.

The Least You Need to Know

➤ In America, as elsewhere, the rules of courtesy change with changing times.

➤ The etiquette pundits have always stressed respect and kindness but have not always agreed on the details.

➤ These days, Americans are as interested as ever in learning about courtesy and behavior.

Shlurp

Table Manners—
The Basics

In This Chapter

➤ Ten most common dining mistakes

➤ A little list of no-nos

➤ Foods from hell

➤ American vs. continental style

Oh, the cruelty of cutlery, the gravity of gravy, the terror in a teacup.

Hey, lighten up.

Although there are very good and serious reasons for you to be concerned, even apprehensive, about the complexities of this thing called table manners, there is no reason in the world why you can't become a poised, informed, and even charming dining companion. It's mostly a matter of knowing the rules—most of which are based on plain common sense—and avoiding the most obvious mistakes.

THOU SHALT NOT—The Ten Most Common Dining Mistakes

While reading this list, you may find that you have been a sinner in the past without ever realizing it. Don't worry. Redemption is at hand. And you certainly are not alone. The sins detailed below made the "top ten" list only because so many people have committed them so often in the past.

1. *Cutlery*. Don't hold your fork like a cello or your knife like Lady Macbeth's dagger. Also, don't wave your cutlery triumphantly in the air to emphasize a point, and don't put silverware partly on the table and partly on the plate. Once you pick up a piece of cutlery, it should never touch the table again. Knives go on the plate, blade facing in and touching the inside of the plate. Only the handle should rest on the rim of the plate.

2. *Napkins*. Don't blot or rub the lower half of your face. Dab delicately. Don't flap your napkin to unfold it, and don't wave it around like a flag. It belongs unfolded on your lap. If you leave the table, place your napkin on the chair and push the chair back under the table. Gently. Watch the upholstery. Don't refold your napkin at the end of the meal; otherwise, an unknowing server might give it to another diner. Pick it up from the center and place it loosely on the table to the left of your plate.

3. *Chewing*. Never chew with your mouth open. Also, no matter how urgently you want to inject the perfect kernel of wit and wisdom at just the right moment, don't do it with food in your mouth. And don't gulp and blurt. Finish chewing, swallow, and smile philosophically, content in the knowledge that you could have said just the right thing, but had too much class to speak with food in your mouth.

4. *Appearance*. Remember what your mother said. Sit up straight. Keep your elbows off the table. If you have any doubt about where your hands belong, put them in your lap.

5. *Breaking bread*. This is a real bread-and-butter tip. Tear bread into bite-size pieces and butter each piece just before you eat it. Don't butter the entire slice of bread or the entire roll to get it ready for occasional bites during the course of the meal.

6. *Speed*. Take it easy. Gulping down food, whether you're at the Ritz Carlton or Gertie's Grease Pit, is not only unhealthy but unattractive. It can cross the line into rudeness when dining with others. Dining partners should have the same number of courses and start and finish each at about the same time. And it's just as bad to huddle over your soup like a hairy hermit while others are salivating for their dessert.

7. *Being picky*. If you have something trapped between your teeth, don't pick at it while at the table. If it's really driving you nuts, excuse yourself, go to the restroom, and pick to your heart's content.

8. *Lipstick*. It's bad form, especially at a business meal, to leave a lipstick trail behind. If you don't have a blotting tissue with you, make a detour to the restroom as you enter the restaurant or nab a cocktail napkin from the bar on your way to the table.

9. *Smoking*. Sitting in the smoking section of the restaurant doesn't give you the right to light up between courses. It affects your dining partners' taste buds and is a jarring note during any meal. Wait until the meal is over. And, please, do not use a plate as an ashtray.

10. *Purses, briefcases*. Keep them off the table. And this goes for keys, hats, gloves, eyeglasses, eyeglass cases, and cigarette packs. In short, if it isn't part of the meal, it shouldn't be on the table.

Did You Know?
The custom of "breaking bread" and taking only as much as you intend to eat originated centuries ago, when what was left of the communal loaf after a meal was given to the poor.

Once you pick up a piece of cutlery, it should never touch the table again.

A Little List of No-Nos

Having dealt with the ten biggest mistakes, we can move on to a list of little no-nos—things not important enough to make the BIG list, but worth noting anyway. Even though common sense and a sense of courtesy may keep you from committing many of these no-nos, they bear repeating.

➤ Don't salt or otherwise season your food before you taste it. This is particularly offensive when dining in someone's home and the cook is sitting at the table. It's also a bad idea in a restaurant, even though the chef can't be insulted because he's in the kitchen.

➤ Cut only enough food for the next mouthful.

➤ If someone at the table takes a pill, don't inquire about the reasons. If you must take medication at the table, don't comment about it. No explanations are necessary.

➤ Don't dunk. Doughnuts don't belong in coffee.

➤ Don't push your plate away, and don't push your chair back when you have finished eating.

➤ Never tilt your chair.

➤ Pass food to the right.

➤ Don't ask people where they are going when they leave the table.

➤ If you belch, cover your mouth with your napkin and say "Excuse me" to no one in particular.

➤ Never crumble crackers in your soup, or blow on any liquid that is too hot. Cool yourself until it cools.

➤ Put butter first on your bread plate or dinner plate, not directly on the roll.

! WDYS?

You are at a fancy dinner, and you are served something unidentifiable.

What do you say?

"I can't even guess what this is, but it looks wonderful. Can you clue me in?"

Don't Panic

Having spent so much time talking about mistakes, it is important to point out that nothing as diverse as dining with a number of other people will ever be achieved with perfect serenity. Things go wrong, and when they do, it is important to react calmly and, if possible, cheerfully.

Let's say you knock something over, break something, or drop something. The first thing to remember is: *Anybody can have an accident!* Stay cool. Downplay the incident as much as possible. If you spill something, blot up what you can. In a restaurant, call the incident to the server's attention—as unobtrusively as possible—and hand him your napkin if it has gotten wet. If the person next to you is a victim of the accident, let him handle his own damage-control. Apologize quietly and offer to pay for any dry cleaning bills.

Foods From Hell

"How do I eat this—never mind gracefully?" you say to yourself as you stare at the intricately tangled spaghetti on your plate. The following is a list of difficult foods to eat and how to eat them correctly. Remember, you *can* eat certain foods with your fingers. When in doubt, use a fork or spoon. If you already have your paws on the item, go ahead and eat it. Please, please, don't say, "Hey, they invented fingers before forks. Right?"

Artichokes require an attitude and a little digital dexterity. Pick it up, remove one leaf at a time, dip the soft end into the sauce, and pull (do not yank) it through your teeth to remove the edible part. Discard the rest. When you get to the heart of the matter, use a knife to scrape the fuzzy part off, and then proceed with the help of a knife and fork.

Avocados See list of fruits below.

Bacon can be taken in hand if it's very crisp. Otherwise, use a knife and fork.

Cake can be eaten with the fingers if it's bite-sized. If it's not, if it's sticky or comes with sauce or ice cream, both the fork and spoon come into play. Hold the spoon in your right hand to scoop up the dessert. The fork goes in your left hand and is used as a pusher.

Caviar should be spread on toast with a knife and eaten with your fingers.

Celery, pickles, and *radishes* are taken off the serving piece with fingers and placed on the side of your dinner plate to be eaten with your fingers.

Chicken and *fowl* require a knife and fork unless you are at a picnic.

Corn on the cob requires the use of both hands, even if you aren't on a picnic. Butter only a few rows at a time, and eat those before continuing. You won't encounter this food on formal occasions in America, and you won't encounter it at all in Europe, where it is considered food for livestock.

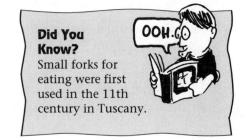

Did You Know?
Small forks for eating were first used in the 11th century in Tuscany.

Hard shelled crabs are treated like lobster (see below).

Lobsters require a number of strategies. Crack the shell with a nutcracker, and extract the meat with a seafood fork (that's the tiny little thing with the three tines). If you pull out a large piece, cut it with a fork. Pull off the small claws, and treat them as if you were drawing liquid through a straw. Eat stuffed lobster with a knife and fork.

Olives get the same treatment as cake, bacon, and celery. If the olive is pitted, eat it whole. If the olive is large and unpitted, hold it in your fingers and eat it in small bites, instead of popping the whole thing in your mouth and munching. As for the pit, kiss the palm of your hand, and deposit it on the edge of your plate.

Pasta comes in many different sizes and shapes. It's a good idea to avoid that business of twirling spaghetti with your fork in the bowl of a spoon. Instead, eat a few strands at a time, twirling them on your fork without the support of a spoon. Do not cut the strands with your knife. Small-sized pasta—ziti, penne, and the like—requires only a fork.

Aghast In the Past

"Don't, when offered a dish at a friend's table, look at it critically, turn it about with the spoon and fork, and then refuse it."

—G.R.M. Devereux, *Etiquette for Women*, 1901

Potatoes have a few different rules. Eat the inside of a baked potato with a fork. If you wish to eat the skin, cut it into manageable pieces with a knife and fork. Don't try to convert your baked potatoes into mashed food. Cut fries in half, and eat them with your fork only or a knife and fork.

Shrimp are eaten with fingers if the tails are left on. Shrimp cocktail is another story. These should be eaten with a seafood fork, in two bites if large. Better still, put them on a serving plate, and cut them with a knife and fork.

Tortillas are eaten from the end when using your hands, or they are cut starting at the end when using a knife and fork.

Fruits

The following is a list of difficult-to-eat fruits:

Avocados can be eaten with a spoon from their shells or with a fork when cut into pieces.

Berries should be eaten with a spoon if they are served with no stems attached. If served with their stems, hold the berry by the stem, and polish it off in one or two bites after dipping it into sugar or sauce.

Grapefruit halves should be sectioned so the meat is accessible without a lot of digging. Eat the sections with a spoon, and never squeeze the juice.

Lemon wedges should be handled carefully. You can secure them with a fork and squeeze with the other hand. If you pick up a wedge to squeeze between the fingers, use the other hand as a sort of squirt shield so that the diner beside you doesn't get an eyeful of lemon juice.

Oranges and *tangerines* can be peeled with a knife or fingers and then eaten by section with the fingers. If served on a plate in sections, use your fork.

Peaches should be halved, then quartered, with a knife. Eat the fruits of this labor with a fork. You can either eat the skin or peel it off with a knife or your fingers.

Pineapple is eaten with a spoon when served in small pieces and with a fork when sliced.

Watermelon, when cut into small pieces, is eaten with a spoon. Otherwise, use your fork. Put the seeds into the palm of your hand, and transfer them to the side of your plate.

Continental vs. American Style

In our shrinking world, we often see people using the continental or European style of dining, as well as the more familiar (to most of us) American style. Both are perfectly correct, and neither is preferable to the other. What's important is being consistent and being correct in whichever style you choose. Once mastered, the continental style proves to be far more graceful and efficient, so it is well worth learning. Children, by the way, often get the hang of this style of dining more easily than adults.

Some experts believe that, when knives and forks first became popular in Europe in the early 17th century, most people used them in much the same way as Americans do now. It was later that the upper classes in Europe began using what is now known as the Continental style and the practice spread—but not, obviously, to America.

WDYS?

The person sitting next to you has just commandeered your bread plate.

What do you say?

Nothing. Use the rim of your dinner plate.

American style. The knife is used for cutting only. It is held in the right hand (for right-handers) while cutting, and the fork is held in the left hand to help control the object being cut. The knife is then put down on the edge of the plate (blade facing in), and the fork is switched to the right hand to lift the cut piece to the mouth. The tines of the fork face upward when bringing food to the mouth. Hands are in the lap when not being used.

Americans are the only people in the world who use this basically inefficient style of dining.

Continental style. The knife remains in the right hand and the fork in the left. After the food is cut, the knife is used to push it onto the fork. The prongs of the fork face downward when the cut food is lifted to the mouth, unless the type of food—peas or creamed food, for example—requires a different tactic. The hands remain above the table from the wrist up when they are not in use.

Dining skillfully and enjoyably takes homework and practice. The good news is that it's not brain surgery, and anybody can do it. Most people take dining skills for granted until it's too late. But, just as nobody ever learned to ride a bike by reading a book, actual experience is necessary for you to become a poised, informed, and confident dining companion.

Bonne chance, and bon appetit!

The Least You Need to Know

➤ Appearance is as important as performance. Sit up straight. Keep your elbows off the table. Don't wave cutlery around or flap your napkin.

➤ Don't hurry or dawdle. Keep pace with the others at the table.

➤ Never chew with your mouth open or try to speak with food in your mouth.

➤ If you use the wrong piece of flatware, don't panic. Continue using it. Ask the server for a replacement when you need it.

➤ Once you pick up a piece of cutlery, it should never touch the table again. Put it *on* your dish, rather than leaning it half on and half off.

Chapter 3

Special Dining Situations

In This Chapter

➤ Banquets

➤ Buffets

➤ Formal dinners

➤ Business meals

Having dealt with the basics, let's investigate strategies for dealing with some special situations. These include banquets, at which as many as ten people are supposed to dine comfortably at a single round table; the buffet meal and the special etiquette it requires; the dreaded formal dinner; and the business meal.

Many of us learned about basic table manners around the family dinner table, and this, obviously, does not equip us to handle these special situations.

Braving the Baffling Banquet

It's an awards banquet or a wedding or the final function of a week-long conference at the Grand Hotel in a distant city.

The room is a sea of linen and candles. There are dozens of round tables, and each is supposed to seat—somehow—ten people. The place settings seem to be jammed together. One set of cutlery blends into the next. There are too many dishes and glasses, and far, far too many people. Stay calm. Continue to breathe normally. You can handle this, one step at a time.

First, find your table. Then, find the place card with your name on it. If there are place cards, never, ever, ever, rearrange them to suit yourself. This is a major breach of etiquette. Somebody gave considerable thought to the seating, probably considering factors such as familiarity and status—within the society, family, company, institution.

For example, it would be a bad idea to move your place card next to the host, just because you're friends. You're likely to unseat the guest of honor. (Tampering with the place cards is even more rude on private social occasions, because the host has given careful thought to the seating arrangement and will not be happy about being second-guessed by you.)

Before you sit down, introduce yourself to your dining companions if you don't know them, and say hello if you do. This is an opportunity to make a positive impression on your fellow diners by walking up to meet them and shaking their hands. On the other hand, you can always just sit down and start yelling your name across the centerpiece to people who, if they can hear it, won't remember it.

Enter your chair from the left side. Men, it is neither sexist nor theatrical if you draw out the chair for the woman on your right. Women, such a gesture should be accepted with grace.

The Place Setting

Now you are in your chair and confronted by a bewildering display of stuff. What faces you is not a malicious rebus designed to befuddle you. Think of it as a chart—a chart that will guide you safely through the meal.

First, look at the silverware, or flatware. Start at the outside, and move inward as the courses arrive. Accordingly, you can usually tell the number of courses to be served by taking a good look at the flatware. (At a very formal dinner, however, the server might replace the flatware before serving each course.)

Tip
Here's a good way to remember what belongs to your place setting at a crowded table. The first two letters of "drink" are DR. Think "drinks right." At a crowded table, your glass will be on your right and your bread plate on your left.

You'll probably see the following arrangement before you:

➤ Knives and spoons are on the right.

➤ Forks and napkins are on the left.

➤ Glassware/crystal are on the right.

➤ Plates, such as a salad plate or bread-and-butter plate, are on the left.

20

Now you are master of the universe, Arthur of the Round Table. As each course comes and goes, you will remain relaxed and confident. Having solved the place setting rebus, it is easy to remember certain basic rules of dealing with silverware:

➤ Once you have picked up a piece of silverware, it never touches the tabletop again.

➤ You do not "tip" or lean silverware against your plate. Instead you put the knife and fork, when not in use, right on the plate. The blade of the knife always faces you.

➤ The coffee/tea spoon goes in the saucer beside the cup.

Braving The Baffling Buffet

The buffet meal scene can resemble the Siege of the Bastille. Somehow, ordinarily sensible people seem to think the food will be taken away before they get some, or that others will take all of the food, leaving them to starve.

This irrational reaction results in the two major buffet blunders: approaching the table too quickly and putting too much food on your plate.

Approach

First, look at the dining tables. If there are utensils and/or plates there, you don't need to look for them at the buffet table. If there are place cards on the tables, do not shift them around to suit yourself.

See if there are one or two lines at the buffet. If there are two, there will be serving utensils on both sides.

Take your place in line. There are no gender privileges in the buffet line, so don't try to get ahead of others, and don't break up a couple or a group going through the line together.

Dishing

If one item is in short supply, go easy on it. At a restaurant or hotel, it is fine to ask to have a dish replenished. At a private party, don't ask.

Use the serving spoon or fork provided for that particular dish, and when finished, put it next to the platter or chafing dish. Leaving a metal spoon in a chafing dish could burn the fingers of another diner.

Don't overload your dish. Going back for seconds or thirds is perfectly acceptable. Don't bring back platefuls of food "for the table." That defeats the whole idea of a buffet.

Serving Stations

When there are serving stations, as at a brunch, remember that the attendant is limited in what he can do. Special requests are all right, if they are easily accomplished. For example, you can ask for scrambled eggs at the omelet station, but don't ask for "over easy" if there are no whole eggs in sight. And don't ask for ingredients in your omelet if you can see that they aren't readily available. Similarly, don't ask for an end cut of beef if you can see that there aren't any left.

Plates

In a restaurant, there should be plenty of clean, freshly polished plates available, thus eliminating the need to reuse a plate. Don't hesitate to ask a server to replace a plate or silverware.

In a private home, use common sense to determine whether you should retain your plate. In any case, don't scrape and stack plates when you are finished.

Aghast in the Past

"In refusing to be helped to any particular thing, never give the reason that you are afraid of it."

—Miss Leslie, *Miss Leslie's Behaviour Book*, 1859

Sitting Down

If people invite you to join their table as you leave the buffet line, accept graciously or say, "I promised Tom and his family I'd eat with them."

If you need to leave the table temporarily, be sure to place your napkin on the seat or arm of your chair.

Even though people at your table will be sitting down to eat at different times, it's still a good idea to generally keep pace with others at the table and engage them in conversation.

Standing Up

If you are to eat standing up, it is even more important to avoid overloading your plate. Circulate. One of the few—maybe the only—advantages of a stand-up buffet is that you can drift around and chat with a number of different people. For example, food at cocktail parties is often consumed while standing.

When you settle on a place to stand, make sure you are not blocking a path to the buffet table or anything else.

Going Uptown—Facing the Formal Dinner

Now that you have solved the mysteries of the banquet hall and the buffet table, let's move on to that most daunting dining dilemma—the formal dinner. Once again, all of its problems can be handled with grace and confidence if you know what to expect and how to react.

Before Sitting Down

Here, a lipstick trail is the red badge of discourtesy. Precautions should be taken before you reach the table. This is also the time to visit the restroom for hair repair and other finishing touches.

Did You Know?
The phrase "powder room" was originally used at formal balls in England centuries ago to designate the room in which servants attended to the wigs of the guests.

Remember to greet everyone before sitting down. Gentlemen must rise to greet late-comers. They may also rise when ladies leave and return to the table, although today's woman should not expect this.

A server will draw the chair for you. Enter from your left.

Napkins

Once seated, wait for your host to make the first napkin move. When the napkin is placed on the lap of the host, the others follow suit. Similarly, at the end of the meal, the host will be the first to place the napkin on the table to signal that the meal is over, having first made certain that everyone at the table has finished.

Large dinner napkins should remain folded in half and placed across your lap with the fold facing your waist. Never "flap" the napkin to unfold it.

If you leave the table during the meal, place the napkin on your chair. If the server does not push the chair back under the table, you should do so. The server may also refold your napkin and place it on the arm of your chair during your absence.

At the end of the meal, do not refold the napkin. Pick it up from its center and place it loosely on the table to the left of your plate.

Wine

Wine will be served during the meal. If you don't want wine, place your fingertips lightly on the rim of the glass when the server approaches to pour. Never, ever, ever turn your glass upside down. Say "I'm not having any today" (or this evening or tonight). The "today" sends a message: you don't disapprove of wine, and the others should feel no compunction about enjoying their wine.

Did You Know?
The custom of clinking glasses was originally a practice used to drive away evil spirits.

Wine is offered with the first (soup) course and will be poured from the right. Red wine (and brandy) glasses are held by the bowl because the warmth of the hand releases the bouquet. Red wine glasses may also be held by the stem, but white wine and champagne glasses are always held by the stem, so as not to diminish the chill.

Wait until your host has lifted the glass before you drink.

The Seven Courses

Once again, the number of pieces of silverware will indicate the number of courses you can expect, and the general rule is to start from the outside.

You may expect the formal dinner to consist of seven courses, in this order: soup, fish, sorbet (or palate cleanser), a meat or fowl dish, salad (often served with cheese), dessert, and coffee.

Courses are served from the left, removed from the right. Wine is poured from the right. (It helps to know from which direction they will be coming at you.)

Try to finish each course at about the same time as others around you. When finished with a course, hoist out the "I am finished" pennant. Do this with your flatware. Visualize a clock face on your plate. Place both the knife and fork in about the 10:20 position, with the points at 10 and the handles at 20. The prongs of the fork should be down, and the blade of the knife should be facing you. If you have been eating the course with the fork only, place it prongs-up in the same position when finished.

Finished Position.

You hoist out the "I am resting" pennant if you wish to stop eating temporarily during a course and don't want the server to snatch your plate away. In this case, the knife and fork are crossed on the plate with the fork over the knife and the prongs pointing down. The knife should be in the 10:20 position, as on the face of a clock; the fork prongs should be at 2 o'clock and the handles at eight o'clock, forming an inverted V.

Resting Position.

In fine restaurants, the servers are usually trained to recognize the "I am finished" and the "I am resting" signals.

Now let's look at how to deal with each course separately:

1. Soup

When eating soup, tilt the spoon away from you (dip the outer edge of the spoon into the soup first, rather than the edge closest to you). This diminishes dribble danger and looks more appealing. Sip from the side (not the front) of the spoon, making no more noise than a spider. Yes, you may tilt the soup plate (often, inaccurately, called the soup bowl) away from you to access the last of the soup.

Leave your spoon on the soup plate. However, if the soup is served in a two-handled bowl or bouillon cup, leave the spoon on the underlying saucer.

When eating soup, tilt the spoon away from you.

Tilt the soup plate away from you to access the last of the soup.

A two-handled soup cup.

2. Fish

Watch out. In fine restaurants, the fish course is often served with special fish knives and forks. In this case, hold the fish fork in the left hand, prongs down, as in the continental style of dining.

The fish knife is used to break the fish and push it onto the fork. The fish knife is held differently from the dinner knife because the fish is not actually cut. Rather, it is simply broken apart. Hold it between your thumb and your index and middle fingers—like a pencil.

If the fish is soft and boneless, you need use only the fork. In this case, leave the fish knife on the table. Hold the fork in your right hand, prongs up. The prongs can be either up or down when the fork is resting on the plate after you're finished.

Fish bones are removed with the thumb and index finger and placed on the side of the plate.

How to hold a fish knife.

How to place the fish on the fork.

! WDYS?

You are halfway through your entree, and you realize that you are using the wrong fork.

What do you say?

Nothing just then. Go ahead and finish the course with that fork. When the next course comes around, ask the server for a replacement: "May I have a new fork for this?"

3. Sorbet

While the serving of "ices" dates back to the Roman Empire, when packed snow was brought down from the mountains, the emergence of "sorbetto" was not seen until the middle of the 16th century in Italy.

These days, a sorbet is only served between the fish and meat courses. Although, it was once served between every course, to clear the palate of the distinctive flavors of each course, getting it ready for the next.

Go ahead. Eat the garnish, if it is served with one. Sometimes it is served with mint leaves, fresh herbs, or flower petals.

4. Meat and Fowl

Here you get more serious with your knife than during the fish course. But you will be using it more like a surgeon than a lumberjack. Place your index finger about an inch down from the handle, on the back of the blade, to help you press down firmly. Hold the fork in your left hand, prongs down. Spear the meat, and hold it firmly in place while you cut. Only cut enough food for the next mouthful.

It's okay to put a small amount of potatoes and vegetables on the fork along with the meat.

Knives and forks are held this way.

The meat knife. Place your index finger about an inch down the handle to help you press down firmly.

Hold the fork in your left hand, prongs down.

5. Salad

As with the fish course, you will use the salad fork and knife for this course, leaving the knife on the table if it is not needed. If cheese is served with the salad, place a small portion of cheese on your salad plate together with crackers or bread. Use the salad knife to put cheese on crackers or bread.

6. Dessert

When dessert is served with both fork and spoon, the fork is the pusher, the spoon is the eater.

Hold the fork in your left hand, tines down, and push the dessert onto the spoon in your right hand. Pie or cake requires only a fork. Ice cream and pudding require only a spoon. Leave the other utensil on the table.

7. Coffee

Be careful not to overload your cup with cream and sugar. Avoid swirling your coffee around too much, making a splash and puddle on your saucer. Don't slurp, but sip gently. If your coffee is too hot, let it sit for a while—don't blow on it. Lastly, don't leave your spoon in the cup. Place it on your saucer.

The formal place setting with cutlery, numbered in order of use.

Water goblet
11 Dessert fork
Champagne flute
10 Dessert spoon
White wine glass
Menu card
Red wine glass
Individual pepper shaker
Sherry glass
Individual salt shaker
9 Butter spreader
Bread-and-Butter plate
4 Fish fork
6 Dinner fork
8 Salad fork
Place card
Napkin
Place plate
7 Salad knife
5 Dinner knife
3 Fish knife
2 Soup spoon
1 Cocktail fork

The Business Meal

Business adds a whole new dimension to the dining experience, but dining also adds a whole new dimension to the business experience.

In other words, it's not just a meeting with food.

What happens around the dining table can form or harden opinions, dampen or heighten expectations, remove or deepen doubts:

➤ Can I work comfortably with this guy?

➤ She should have better sense than to do that.

➤ If he can't organize a lunch meeting, how can he run a department?

Setting up a business lunch or dinner requires careful planning and attention to detail. Everything from picking a restaurant, to seating, ordering, and tipping must be carefully thought-out in advance. Different rules and different strategies apply, and all of that is discussed in detail in chapter eight.

Although dining circumstances vary, you can handle them with more confidence by remembering the basics. Approach the experience with a positive attitude and a cheerful demeanor. Keep pace with the others. Watch your posture. Smile. When in doubt, do what your host does, or pick out the classiest person at the table and copy him or her.

The Least You Need to Know

➤ Knives and spoons are placed on the right, forks and napkins on the left. Liquids are on the right, and solids (such as the bread plate) are on the left.

➤ Use cutlery from the outside in.

➤ Use the side of your dinner plate for your bread if someone commandeers your bread plate.

➤ The gravest danger in buffet dining lies in overloading your dish.

➤ Never call attention to the dining mistakes of others or be overly apologetic about your own.

The Anatomy of a Restaurant

In This Chapter

➤ From maitre d' to busser—what role each person plays

➤ The art of toasting

➤ Using chopsticks

➤ Vegetarians

Since so many occasions for dining with others—for business or pleasure—occur in restaurants, it's helpful to understand how restaurants work.

The structure of a showy Las Vegas–type dining room is different from that of a casual California-style eatery, and both are different from that of a five-star French haute cuisine establishment. Accordingly, the protocol varies with the varying structures.

In this chapter, I will also de-mystify the tipping scene and talk about how to avoid getting burned while giving a toast. In addition, you'll learn the proper handling of chopsticks and how to deal with the sometimes touchy subject of vegetarianism.

Cast of Characters

When you go to a restaurant, staff members actually become your employees for the duration of the meal. Smooth dining is a team game. Knowing how your team works, what function each member performs, and how they relate to you and each other will greatly increase your chances of having an enjoyable experience.

Maitre d'/Host

Often, this is the person who will seat you.

The maitre d' is sometimes also the general manager of a restaurant and is often the owner in smaller establishments. The maitre d' is in charge of all floor service. His job involves staffing, coordinating reservations with seating, timing the flow of patrons with the pace of the kitchen staff, and handling special requests—like presenting an engagement ring or a birthday surprise.

Captain/Head Waiter

The terms are interchangeable, and not all restaurants have one. If one person takes your order and another serves, the first is generally your captain or head waiter. The second person in this instance is the *server*, explained below. The captain is the one to be consulted if there is a problem with the food or service.

Chef

King of the kitchen, he controls how food is prepared, presented, and served. Consult the chef if you have a special request concerning food. Your server can handle communicating a simple request like sauce on the side. For something complicated like a sugar-free, salt-free, wheat-free meal, you might want to make an appointment through the maitre d'.

Sommelier

Some restaurants have a sommelier, or wine steward. He is the one to ask which wine goes with the beef Bordelaise *and* the lobster. Sometimes, he will present and pour the wine as well.

Bartenders and Servers

These are the ones you have the most direct contact with, and they are under the supervision of the maitre d' or manager in most restaurants. Servers are also called by the horrible, however gender-free and thus, politically correct term, *waitron*.

Bussers

These are usually the first people who come to your table, pouring water and providing bread and butter. They also clear dishes and reset tables. If something is missing at the table, such as a water glass or a piece of flatware, let the busser know.

Each of these employees works to produce one result—a gracious and satisfied customer who returns regularly. Each, however, is motivated by different needs. The maitre d' wants everything to run smoothly, efficiently, and profitably. Servers, bartenders, and bussers are motivated by anticipated tips and recognition for a job well done.

Chefs are motivated by praise for their taste and creativity. If you visit one restaurant regularly, it pays to praise the chef when warranted. You can ask for the chef, in order to give personal congratulations, or send your message of appreciation through a server.

Tipping

Even if you use a credit card, carry some cash for tips. If you are a regular at a restaurant, or if you have gotten exceptional service and plan to return, it pays to take care of the maitre d'. A maitre d' who provides you with a great table for a special event or oversees a smooth-running business meal should receive ten to twenty dollars in cash, depending on the size of your group and the complexity of your special requests.

A captain or head waiter (the person who takes your order) should get five percent of the bill either in cash or specified on the bill if you use a credit card.

Your server should get at least 15 percent of your total bill, according to the level of service provided. Remember that your tip to the server usually is divided among the entire service team, which includes bartenders and bussers.

The sommelier should be tipped 15 percent of the wine bill if he performs special services (such as helping you choose the right wine for your meal).

Check room attendants get one dollar per coat. Add another dollar for a briefcase, boots, or umbrella.

Tip
Here is the technique for tipping the maitre d'. Fold a ten or twenty dollar bill in half, then half again and then half again so that the amount shows on both sides. Put it into the palm of your right hand, and shake hands with the maitre d'. The bill will smoothly, almost magically, disappear during the handshake.

Toasting

Toasting can make even a meal at the local diner a special occasion. It can bring a festive air to a gathering, and it has a way of bringing those present together.

Did You Know?
The toast originated during the Middle Ages, when people put a piece of scorched bread into a tankard of beer or wine because they thought it improved the flavor of the drink. The custom of putting a piece of toast in a drink is still followed in England—albeit rarely.

The host proposes a toast, often welcoming a guest to a meal, at the beginning of the meal. The toast may also occur in the middle of the meal, when the host raises his glass to the guest of honor on his right. If the host has stage fright, it is acceptable to have his or her spouse make the toast.

An example of an excellent toast is one that was given at a dinner for Nobel Prize winners in the State Dining Room of the White House. President Kennedy rose and said, "I think this is the most extraordinary collection of talent, of human knowledge, ever gathered at the White House, with the possible exception of when Thomas Jefferson dined here alone."

You don't have to be that clever. A typical welcoming toast might be: "I am so pleased that you all could be here to share each other's good company and this good food. Welcome."

At the end of the meal, before dessert, the same host might rise and toast the guest of honor: "I am so pleased that you could all be here to welcome my dear friend Florence, who's come all the way from Rome to visit."

Or: "It's wonderful to have Florence with us tonight. Let's toast a rare woman who looks at every situation in life as an opportunity to give of herself, to make things better, happier, more fun. To Florence."

Or, be even more specific: "I am particularly honored to have my mother-in-law with us tonight, jogging Jo Fleischmann—triathlete, pal, coach, and mom extraordinaire. To Jo."

One-word toasts, such as the Danish "Skol" and the Spanish "Salud," meaning "Health," are pretty much universally accepted as symbols of welcome. It's a nice idea to toast people in their native tongue, but be sure to learn the correct pronunciation beforehand.

Some examples:

Irish: Salante (SLANT tay)

Yiddish: L'chaim (leh KHY yim)

German: Prosit (PRO sit)

Japanese: Kanpai (kahn PI)

Toasting Blunders

Here are some things you should know about toasting:

➤ Do not toast yourself. If you are being toasted, just sit there, and afterwards, say thank you. Don't even put your hand on your glass, much less drink.

➤ Do not *read* your toast. If it is too long to commit to memory, forget it.

➤ Do not clink glasses. It's an old custom having to do with driving away evil spirits, and it's bad news for glassware.

➤ Do keep your toast short.

➤ Do toast the host in return if you are the guest of honor and are being toasted. You can do this as soon as his toast is finished or later, during dessert. Just keep it short.

➤ Do not tap the rim of your glass to get everybody's attention—it's tacky.

Tip
It has been said that toasts are like a woman's skirt. They should be long enough to cover the subject, but short enough to be amusing. That usually translates into about one minute.

➤ Do make a toast even if you're not drinking alcohol. Anything will do. It's the thought that counts.

➤ Do toast more than one person. For example, you might toast an entire family that has come to visit, or a whole team.

➤ Do not pre-empt. The host should be the first one to toast.

Tricky Situations

There are special guidelines when it comes to handling chopsticks and dealing with vegetarianism.

Chop Chop

In our shrinking world, you may find yourself in a situation in which politeness requires you to use chopsticks. Here's how:

1. Put the bottom chopstick in the web of your right hand between the thumb and index finger.

2. Use your two middle fingers to keep it steady. Hold it firmly but not too rigidly. This bottom chopstick will remain fairly stationary while you are eating.

3. Hold the top chopstick like a pencil between your thumb and index finger. This one does most of the moving.

You can hold the bowl or plate of food under your chin while you are eating until you feel really confident. There is nothing wrong with that, even after you have become an expert.

A good way to learn is to practice picking up popcorn at home.

In most restaurant situations, you shouldn't hesitate to ask for a fork. The Chinese invented the fork. (And now you know why.)

Bottom chopstick is placed in the web of your right hand between the thumb and index finger.

The top chopstick is held like a pencil between your thumb and index finger.

The top chopstick does most of the moving. The bottom chopstick remains stationary.

Vegetarians

If you are a vegetarian, you have a responsibility to let your host know in advance.

If you are planning a meal, and a guest tells you he is a vegetarian, you need to ask for a little more information. Some vegetarians don't eat eggs or dairy products, for instance, and others do.

If you are hosting a restaurant meal, tell the maitre d' that the guest is a vegetarian. Find out if there is a vegetarian menu. Ask for suggestions.

It's a good idea to ask guests you don't know well if they have any special dietary considerations. If you can't accommodate them, you can say something like:

"I've planned this party around my grandmother's meat lasagna recipe, but there will be plenty of salads and snacks available, or you can stop by later for dessert."

The key point is to not make a big deal out of it. A vegetarian can skip certain dishes and, if there is a question, simply say: "Everything is fine. I just don't eat meat." Saying things like, "I don't eat dead animals," is unnecessary, rude, and offensive.

In addition to knowing how a restaurant works, it is a good idea to get to know a couple of good restaurants really well. Become a regular. Learn the names of the key staff people, and engage them in conversation when convenient. After a while, you will be greeted more warmly and given special attention in these places. Also, you will feel more comfortable dining there and bringing guests.

The Least You Need to Know

➤ In general, tip 15 to 20 percent of the total bill in a restaurant, although 20 percent is becoming the norm.

➤ If you have a complaint, make it to the captain or maitre d'—quietly.

➤ When toasting someone, sincerity and brevity are the best policies. The drink used needn't be alcoholic.

➤ Don't spend an eternity studying the menu and interrogating the server, especially if the restaurant is busy.

➤ There's nothing wrong with requesting a fork in a Chinese restaurant if you prefer not to use chopsticks.

Part 2
Business Etiquette

Not only are the rules different in the world of business etiquette, the entire approach is different because the business world is structured differently from social or family worlds.

It is critical to understand this different way of thinking about relationships and behavior and how it applies to your dealings with your superiors, your colleagues, and your subordinates.

Knowing the accepted ways of doing things—what to say, how to dress, and how to react in various situations—is vitally important and becomes even more important the higher you rise in the ranks.

And management now values manners in the workplace as never before. More and more firms are organizing in-house training in etiquette for their employees. Career-minded executives are finding a connection between civility and success.

ON YOUR MARK!

Getting Started—The Corporate Culture

If you think it's nice but not necessary to know the rules of corporate etiquette, consider this. Success in getting, keeping, and advancing in a job depends 85 percent on "people skills" and only 15 percent on technical knowledge and skills, according to three separate research projects by Harvard University, the Carnegie Foundation, and the Stanford Research Institute.

So, it is vital to know the rules of business etiquette, and the first thing you should know is that these rules have a different foundation from those you may have learned as a child. Those rules evolved from the code of chivalry, which called for deference to others on the basis of gender and/or age. However, relationships in the business world (or corporate culture) have always been based primarily on rank, much like any military system. Rank, or the degree of power vested in different individuals, gives a business organization the structure it needs to function effectively.

How you behave in relation to persons of the same or different status varies with the kind of business and the style of individual businesses. Corporate and social behavior in a bank is more formal than in an advertising agency. And behavior in a newspaper city room makes an advertising office seem severely structured.

Don't worry. There are basic rules that will help you adjust to whichever business or professional situation you find yourself in. And behavior that is grounded in good manners—respect for others and concern for their feelings—will allow many inadvertent breaches of business or corporate etiquette to be forgiven (but probably not forgotten).

The Job Interview

The basics of corporate etiquette begin with the job interview. Sure, you're anxious. Here is a situation in which how you look, what you say and do, and your overall demeanor may have a critical impact on your future.

And the person opposite you seems to have all the advantages. Recruiters and interviewers take courses to help them develop sophisticated screening methods. The interviewer is on his home turf, and you are not. You are being measured against standards and guidelines that are clear as a bell to the interviewer, but not to you.

But you also have some important advantages:

> They (the company or organization) need someone, or they wouldn't be interviewing people.

> They are hoping you are the person they are looking for.

If you remember these two facts, if you know you are dressed properly, have a list of the points you want to make, and have a pretty good idea of what will be happening and how to respond, the situation won't seem nearly as one-sided.

Be Prepared

It's important to find out everything you can about the company before your interview. Read any reports or brochures you can find. Also, try to contact somebody who works at the company: a friend, acquaintance, or fellow college alumnus. Some source materials include:

➤ *F & S Index of Corporations and Industries*

➤ *Fitch Corporation* manuals

➤ *Moody's* manuals

➤ *McRae's Bluebook*

➤ *Standard and Poor's Register*

Some of the things you should find out about the company you are interviewing with are:

➤ The pronunciation and spelling of the name

➤ What the company does

➤ If it's a national or international company, as opposed to regional

➤ The size of the company

➤ The attitude toward women and minorities

➤ How long the company has been in business

➤ The general reputation

➤ The reputation for working conditions and environment

Before your interview, you should also find out everything you can about *yourself*. Take a long, honest look at yourself, and be prepared to talk about your traits. One way to help with this process is to list on a sheet of paper the important points about yourself:

➤ Education

➤ Volunteer work

➤ Honors and awards

➤ Interests, hobbies

➤ Why you want to work for this company

➤ What abilities you can bring to the company

The Interview

In general, it's a good idea to dress conservatively for interviews. However, dress can vary dramatically from company to company. Khakis and Docksiders might be the standard at one place, while wingtips and double-breasted suits are typical of another. When in doubt, it is perfectly okay to ask an employee or someone in Human Resources about appropriate interview attire.

Upon arriving for your interview, enter the room, smile, and make eye contact with your interviewer. Then, wait until you are asked to be seated. During the meeting, don't fidget or handle things on the other person's desk. Also, listen carefully to what you are being asked. Don't treat any question as unimportant. If a question is difficult, pause before answering. Compose yourself. Finally, at the end of the meeting, thank the interviewer cordially, and follow up with a note.

Bear in mind that your first interview with a company will probably be a "screening interview." The purpose of this interview is to screen *out* applicants. For instance, companies want to know if you're willing to relocate, if you have sufficient language skills, and if you fill other "requirements" or "prerequisites."

The interview will be held at the company site or by telephone. It's imperative that you arrive on time (but not early) and that you dress conservatively. If you are being interviewed by telephone, make sure that you have your materials on hand. If you don't, get the name and telephone number of the interviewer, and call back promptly. Whether you're being interviewed on site or by telephone, don't volunteer information you haven't been asked for.

After the screening interview (and perhaps other preliminary interviews) is your meeting with the hiring manager. This is the person who will make the final decision, and this is the interview that is the most unpredictable. The interviewer usually has no formal training in interviewing, may ask the wrong questions, and may be vague. He's casting around for enough information to let his intuition take over and help him make the decision. He may be looking for that "certain something" that he has not articulated in his own mind.

"So, tell me about yourself..." So...tell him about yourself. Be enthusiastic, but be honest, and keep it polite. Make eye contact. Talk about your strongest skills and your greatest areas of knowledge. Use positive, active language like, "I *enjoy* detail work. I am *committed* to excellence."

Business Attire

Never, ever underestimate the critical importance of attire within the corporate culture. What you wear says a lot about you, and you can damage or even destroy your chances of success in business by dressing inappropriately.

What do your clothes say about you? Do they say you have good sense and good taste? Do they say you have self-respect and that you have respect for those you are dealing with every day? People, particularly your superiors, are apt to conclude that the quality of your work will match the quality of your appearance.

Hint, Hint

If your organization has a dress code, observe both the letter and the spirit of the code. This is something you have to learn about right off the bat. Don't assume that a white shirt and striped tie will fit into any office situation.

A recent nationwide study by Levi Strauss & Co. and the Society for Human Resource Management shows that nine out of ten office workers now enjoy the freedom to wear casual clothing at least occasionally.

If there is no dress code, you can't go far wrong by studying how those in senior management dress. And don't be afraid to ask. It only means you care enough to get things right. Say to your boss: "I'm a little puzzled by the variety of styles I see here. What kind of dressing best represents the company?" Avoid extreme fashions. Don't buy things just because the fashion gurus say so. Think about what is good for you and your career, rather than what is "in."

Think Before Buying

Think in terms of your entire wardrobe. There are a lot of variables you have to take into account when choosing what will be in your wardrobe and what you will wear on given occasions. Here are some of the variables it would be wise to consider:

➤ *Regional variations.* Take climate and geography into account. An outfit that looks terrific in Vermont will look odd in Atlanta. The attire of a Wall Street broker might look downright funereal in Los Angeles. And colors! What might look fine in the easy sunshine of San Diego would have a jarring effect on Philadelphia bankers.

➤ *Business environment.* Think about the type of company you work for and the kind of work you do. If you are going to be tramping around a construction site with a hard hat on your head, you should not have high heels on your feet.

➤ *Type of occasion.* Consider the function. You don't wear elegant jewelry to a breakfast meeting, and you don't wear a polo shirt, even a $90 one, to a board meeting.

Did You Know?

The queen of England once gave the following advice to the prince of Wales: "Dress gives one the outward sign from which people can judge the inward state of mind. One they can see…the other they cannot."

Faux Pas

Skirts and trousers should not be so tight that they convey a message of sexiness. Exposed cleavage and miniskirts are not appropriate business attire for women, as tight "muscle" shirts or shirts that expose the chest are inappropriate for men.

➤ *Type of position.* Consider what you want your outfit to say about you. If you want it to say, "Your investment will be safe with us," don't dress in a way that says, "We're a friendly bunch of folks here."

Details

When it comes to dressing, the details are every bit as important as choosing the appropriate outfit. Careful attention must be paid to such details as shoes and jewelry. Sometimes it is the little things that people notice most and remember longest. The impression made by a carefully selected outfit can be ruined by one jarring detail, such as scuffed shoes or a missing button.

Faux Pas
Stay away from 100 percent polyester. It's called a "miracle fabric" because it's a miracle that anyone wears it. Polyester and wool or cotton blends are much more serviceable and usually look better.

Tip
There is no such thing as neutral clothing. Everything you put on communicates something, and your image is either working for you or against you.

➤ *Jewelry.* It shouldn't be obtrusive, and it shouldn't jangle. Avoid wearing rings on the right hand, and you will feel much more relaxed about shaking hands because you won't have to worry about rings digging into fingers. Wear a watch, even if your internal clock functions well. Business in the United States runs according to schedules and deadlines, and promptness counts.

➤ *Furs.* Don't wear them in the business world. They signal "pretentious" more than "successful."

➤ *Shoes.* They can shoot you in the foot. Fabric softener sheets give a quick shine and are easily kept in your desk or briefcase. If you wear sneakers to work, change both the shoes and the socks or hose when you get to the office. Feet tend to perspire more in sneakers, and the socks absorb odors.

➤ *Briefcases.* Keep your briefcase polished and clean. It should not be over-large nor should it be over-stuffed. If it's beat-up, get a new one.

Business Appointments and Functions

When attending a *business appointment,* take off your topcoat, and if someone offers to hang it up, surrender it gladly. If not, ask where you can put it, along with umbrella and galoshes on bad weather days. If there is no place to hang your coat, drape it on the back of your chair unless another alternative is offered to you. Just don't keep it on, and don't carry it around.

When you are in someone else's office, keep your suit jacket on. If someone suggests that you remove it, you may, or you may decide not to. Taking off your jacket is sort of invasive: it looks as if you are moving in. And if you do take it off, don't roll up your sleeves. Remember that you are a guest while in the office, and behave accordingly, even if you are working there for a short time.

Don't scatter things around. Keep files on your lap. Put your briefcase or handbag on the floor, or keep it on your lap. Don't put things or touch things on the other person's desk.

When attending a special *business function*, your invitation will often specify the appropriate dress for the occasion in the lower right-hand corner. If you have any doubts about what to wear, you can call the host or hostess.

Here are the definitions of two types of business functions as described on invitations:

➤ *Black tie formal* means different things to different people all over the country. The correct term for "tuxedo" is "dinner jacket." Black is always correct for men. White jackets are not. Women don't have to wear gloves, and never should shake hands in them.

➤ *Informal*, or *semi-formal* is slightly less dressy than black tie. Men should wear a dark business suit, a white shirt, and a dark silk tie with a quiet pattern. Women should wear a dressy suit in an evening fabric, a short cocktail dress, or a long skirt and blouse.

A Few Words on Complimenting

It is perfectly correct to compliment people on their appearance if the compliment is sincere. At the office, compliment the work, not the clothes. When giving or receiving a compliment, keep in mind the following points:

➤ Never ask people where they got their clothes or what they cost.

➤ Don't talk about what you paid for clothes or brag about designer labels.

➤ If someone compliments you, it's not necessary to return the compliment.

(BURP) Faux Pas

Don't give false compliments, and don't lie to people at social functions to be "polite." It is generally not necessary. For example, "You look fabulous," can sound hollow when a person says it too often. "It's been a long time since I've seen you," can be better than an insincere, "It's great to see you." People will detect your insincerity, no matter how good an actor you think you are.

The Least You Need to Know

➤ Researchers tell us that "people skills" are more important for advancement in the business world than technical skills or knowledge.

➤ Gender plays no role in business relationships. Rank does.

➤ When in doubt about how to dress, look at the people who are running your company.

➤ Before buying any piece of clothing, consider your position and the business environment, as well as factors such as climate, geography, and occasion.

➤ When complimenting someone, make sure you are sincere. When accepting a compliment, graciously say "Thank you." Don't argue the point.

Chapter 6

Introductions

In This Chapter

➤ How to make an introduction and how to respond to one

➤ What to do when you're not introduced

➤ What to do when you forget the person's name

➤ Tips on greeting people

This is the area of business relationships where so many people get off on the wrong foot and then shoot themselves in the other foot. Knowing the rules is critical. Knowing the rules will make you more relaxed and confident. This will come across when you are introducing people and will put them at ease.

The most important thing about an introduction is to "just do it." If you don't, people around you end up feeling invisible. It's better to attempt and botch someone's difficult name than to ignore it. Another thing to remember is that Americans expect three things when they meet people: eye contact, a smile, and a handshake.

Who's First?

The person who is being introduced, or "presented," is named last. Social etiquette is based on chivalry, so in a social situation, we defer to people based on sex and age. Business etiquette is different because it is based on hierarchy. Gender plays no role.

The rule is that persons of lesser authority are introduced to persons of greater authority: "Mr./Ms. CEO, I would like to introduce Mr./Ms. Junior Executive."

Again, remember eye contact. *Look at* and speak to the greater authority first; *look at* and speak to the lesser authority second.

Background Info

As you make the introduction, include a brief bit of information about those being introduced: "Jim just joined our Newark regional office."

You don't need to add the fact that Jim is a real good guy. When in doubt, be less personal rather than more personal.

Tip
When introducing anyone, particularly a public official, to a member of the media, make sure you include the affiliation of the media person so that the other person knows he may be speaking "on the record."

Providing a bit of information gives the two people being introduced some basis to begin a conversation. Never underestimate the power of sincere flattery: "Without Jim, our softball team would never win a game." Once they have begun talking, you can excuse yourself, depending on the situation.

There is an important exception to this "who's first" general rule. The CEO of your company is not more important than your client. A client is always more important that those in your company. The same goes for an elected official: "Mr. Muldoon, I would like to introduce Ms. Cooper, our chief executive officer. Mr. Muldoon is our client from Dublin."

Introductions at Business Functions

The host should meet and greet the guests at a business function upon their arrival. It's his job to make them feel welcome. If this is not possible or the host doesn't know all of the guests, he may appoint other greeters to represent him.

In this case, the greeter introduces himself and escorts the guest to the host. After he makes the introduction, he should move the guest along and introduce him to others or show him to the buffet table or the bar. The idea is to leave the host free to greet others.

It is not necessary to introduce a newcomer at a business/social function to everyone else. A good tactic is to introduce him to the closest group by saying his name first and then naming the others or having someone in the group name them.

Introducing Yourself

It is helpful to others and important for you to introduce yourself promptly and appropriately.

If you are at a business social function or with just a few people and you are not introduced, you should introduce yourself just as promptly as decently appropriate. If it looks as if the person who should introduce you isn't going to (he may have forgotten your name), you have to take over. Just smile, offer to shake hands with the nearest person, and say: "Hello. I'm Tom Engles. Jim and I are responsible for the Technec account."

In some situations, describing yourself in terms of what you do rather than by your title promotes conversation.

Don't interject endless details, such as how long you have been with the company or where you live.

Tip
Sometimes a title is all the information you need to give about a person, especially if the title is something like "Senator."

Responding to Introductions

How you respond to being introduced by others is just as important as how you make an introduction.

If it's an *informal* introduction, you can simply respond with, "Hello," or you can add a bit of information, such as, "I heard you speak at the seminar." In any case, keep it brief and friendly.

"How do you do?" followed by the person's name, is the best way to respond to a *formal* introduction. With this type of introduction, don't use the person's first name until he or she invites you to do so.

Tip
Think of the introduction as an equation. If you are formal with one, don't be casual with the other. Don't say, "Mr. Jones, I would like you to meet Tommy."

Tip
Avoid saying things like, "Margaret works for me." It sounds as if you are anxious to establish status. Try, "Margaret and I work together."

Greetings

There are very definite rules for the various aspects of meeting and greeting people in the corporate culture. Your mother was right when she gave you that advice about "first impressions."

Upstanding

If you don't rise to the occasion, you will sink in the estimation of others.

Everyone should stand up when being introduced. There was a time when women remained seated when new people arrived on the scene, but not nowadays. However, when newcomers arrive at a very large function, they are greeted only by those nearest them. If it is impossible for you to rise—if perhaps you are wedged behind the table—at least lean forward or rise slightly so as not to appear distant.

When someone comes to visit at the office, stand, and come out from behind your desk, unless the visitor is a co-worker or someone who comes into your office frequently in the course of the day. The frequency consideration comes into play even when a senior executive visits the office of a junior executive. If it's a common occurrence, there's no need to get up; however, you should certainly stop what you're doing and give your full attention to the senior.

Shaking Hands

A handshake leaves a very definite and often lasting impression, and in the business world, a handshake is the only truly appropriate physical contact for both men and women.

The proper shake:

➤ Comes with eye contact

➤ Is firm but painless

➤ Lasts about three seconds

➤ Takes only two or three "pumps"

➤ Starts and stops crisply

➤ Doesn't continue through the entire introduction

Begin with your fingers together and your thumb up.

Shake hands web-to-web, with a firm but not crushing grip.

Never offer only your fingertips, causing a weak, limp handshake.

Keep your fingers together and your thumb up. Slide the web of your hand all the way to the web of the other person's hand. Otherwise, he ends up shaking hands with your fingers. Also, shaking web-to-web effectively prevents the other person, no matter how strong, from crunching your knuckles.

You shake when...

➤ Someone offers his/her hand to you

➤ First meeting someone

➤ Greeting guests

➤ Greeting your host/hostess

➤ Renewing an acquaintance

➤ Saying good-bye

Tip

Here are a couple of tips to keep in mind regarding handshakes:

➤ Keep your drink in your left hand to avoid giving someone a wet, cold handshake.

➤ Don't rock or sway. Handshaking is not a tango.

Hugs and Kisses

In general, hugs and kisses are inappropriate in any business environment.

In fact, touching others in the workplace, whether they are of the same gender or not, is impolite, even if you feel that the other person is your pal. This includes patting on the back, putting your arm around someone, or putting your hand on their shoulder.

It is acceptable at a business/social function to kiss your spouse, if you happen to be getting along that day. Even then, keep it casual and cursory.

The Name Game

People wince inwardly when you mispronounce their names. It is a serious breach of business etiquette. If you don't know the correct pronunciation of someone's name, ask!

Tip

Don't address someone verbally by a corporate title, unless you happen to be speaking with the President of the United States, in which case you say, "Mr. President."

If you miss it, or are in doubt, ask apologetically for it to be repeated. Jokes or wisecracks about a person's name are not funny and are offensive.

If you have a name that is difficult to pronounce, help the person who is trying to pronounce it—and botching the job. You can smile and say: "It's a tough one, isn't it?" Pronounce it clearly without making a big deal about it. That just calls too much attention to the fact that the other person has made an error.

Coming Up Blank

It happens to everybody. If you are in a situation where it is up to you to make the introductions and you forget the name of the person to be introduced, say something like, "I remember our chat at the Cezanne reception, but I've forgotten your name for the moment," or, "Please tell me your name again. I'm having a temporary memory lapse."

Get the name, and go right ahead with the introduction. Don't make a big deal out of it by apologizing all over the place. Everybody has experienced mental vapor lock from time to time and will understand your predicament.

When you are introduced to someone, say the person's name, and repeat it during the conversation to imprint it on your memory.

If you are being introduced, and it seems that the person has forgotten your name, jump right in, extend your hand, smile, and offer your name.

Titles

Because so much of the corporate culture is based on rank and status, titles are vitally important. You can't refer to a *senior vice* president as a *vice* president or to the chief *operating* officer as the chief *executive* officer.

In the company of others, especially with people outside your firm, show your boss respect by addressing him or her formally as "Mr." or "Ms. Smith."

"Ms." is the appropriate address for a woman in business, regardless of what she chooses to call herself in her private life. "Mrs." and "Miss" imply social, marital, and sexual distinctions that have no place in the business arena.

Of course, if a woman tells you directly that she wishes to be addressed as "Mrs." or "Miss," it is best to comply. However, when using "Mrs." in a business context, use the woman's first name rather than her husband's. For example, "Mrs. Sally Kelly."

Career-conscious people entering the business world must be aware of more rules of behavior than they could expect to encounter in most social situations. It's important to be aware of the sort of behavior that is expected in the world of work in order to be able to move within that world with confidence and ease.

The Least You Need to Know

➤ The most important thing about introductions is that you make them.

➤ When making introductions, mention the name of the most important person first.

➤ Customers/clients outrank even the CEO of your company, especially when they come to visit.

➤ If you don't know the correct pronunciation of someone's name, ask! If you forgot the person's name, politely ask him for it, and go right ahead with the introduction.

➤ A handshake is the one acceptable physical contact for men and women.

Chapter 7

The Arena—Etiquette in the Workplace

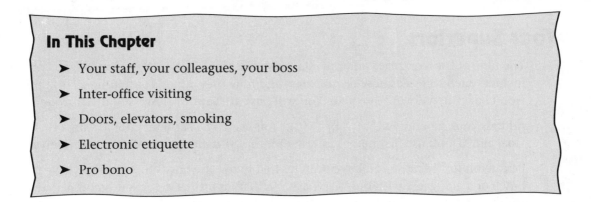

In This Chapter

➤ Your staff, your colleagues, your boss

➤ Inter-office visiting

➤ Doors, elevators, smoking

➤ Electronic etiquette

➤ Pro bono

Nobody wants to spend eight hours a day with someone who just doesn't know how to behave.

Proper etiquette in the workplace is more than just good manners. It generates efficiency, helps to eliminate distractions, and creates a pleasant environment in which people can work to their full potential. Since you spend so much time at work with so many others, it is crucial that you exercise good "people skills," and it is glaringly apparent if you lack these skills.

Your Co-Workers

You must know how to establish cordial and respectful relationships with your support staff. Not only do you work closely with them every day, but they are also the foundation of your effectiveness. "Boss" and "bossy" are not synonymous.

Decide up front how secretaries or assistants will address you—"Tom" or "Mr. Smith." Always acknowledge their presence, and keep greetings cordial. If you are introducing a secretary to a client or an associate, make the introduction according to the way those involved will later address one another. If you expect your secretary to address your client as "Mr. Foster," introduce him as "Mr. Foster," and use your secretary's surname as well, even if you normally use your secretary's first name.

If you are sharing a secretary, consult with your associate so that you will not be piling on too great a workload. Never ask someone else's secretary to do work for you without first clearing it with the secretary's supervisor. As a rule of thumb, never ask a secretary to perform a task you'd be unwilling to do yourself.

Watch those labels. Never call anyone above the age of puberty a boy or a girl. The words "honey," "dear," and "hunk" have no place in the vocabulary of the workplace.

Your Superiors

The tone of the workplace and the relationships therein are set by top management. This includes such things as how people dress and how they address each other. This probably won't be written down anywhere. You will have to learn by observing those around you.

Address your superiors as "Mr." or "Mrs.," followed by a surname, not as "sir" or "madam." Don't use first names unless and until you are specifically invited to do so.

Be careful. Just because you have been invited to use the boss's first name or have had lunch or a golf game with her, don't assume that an intimate or even "good pal" relationship exists between you. Remember that relationships in the American business world are based on rank, and rank should always be observed and acknowledged.

Visitors

When you receive a visitor in your office, remember that you are the host, and act accordingly. The visitor should be greeted cordially, which means that you or your secretary should go out to the reception area to meet him. The greeter should shake hands, make whatever introductions are necessary, and escort the visitor to the office.

If you stay in your office to receive the visitor, be sure to come out from behind your desk to greet him, or better still, meet him at the door, usher him in, and guide him to where you would like him to sit.

Visiting

Your role, when visiting someone else's office, is that of a guest, whether it is within your company or without. Don't walk in and settle down as if you were entering your own office. Here are some guidelines:

Tip
Never stay behind your desk when visitors arrive, unless you are planning to fire somebody.

➤ Don't be late. If you are, apologize, and explain.

➤ When you tell the receptionist your name and mission, also present your card.

➤ Ask where you can hang your coat, if you have one.

➤ In the office, wait to be told where to sit. If there are a number of chairs, ask which one you should use.

➤ Don't remain standing if your host is seated.

➤ Don't lay papers or documents on the desk or the floor.

➤ Put your briefcase or handbag on the floor beside you.

➤ Don't fiddle with or touch anything on the desk.

➤ Leave promptly when your business is completed.

➤ Send a thank you note for the meeting within 24 hours. Try to make the thank you note not look like a generic, one-size-fits-all product. Here's an example of a good note:

Dear Robert:

Your ideas on marketing new products in an untested region are very insightful and a great help to me.

Thank you for making time for our meeting and for sharing your wisdom with me.

Sincerely,

Harold Price

Doors

For such simple things, doors can cause a lot of confusion. Let's simplify matters.

➤ If you reach a door first, regardless of gender, you should open it, go through it, and hold it to ensure that it doesn't hit the person following. Men no longer hold doors for women just because they are women.

➤ If you are in the company of a senior executive, it is a good idea to allow him or her to reach the door and go through it first.

➤ If someone's arms are laden, hold the door for them, regardless of gender or status.

These rules are set aside when you are hosting others, in which case, you open the door for your guests and motion for them to precede you. For a revolving door, you go first and wait for the others to come through after you.

In any case, always thank a person who holds a door for you.

Elevators

Yes, even an elevator calls for a certain amount of etiquette:

➤ Do not dodge or delay so that somebody can be the first to get on or off.

➤ If you are nearest the door, you get on the elevator first, then hold the door until everyone else has entered.

➤ If you are near the control panel, ask the others what floor they need and select those buttons for them. You can also hold the "open" button to keep the doors open until everyone has had a chance to get on or off.

➤ If you are nearest the door, step out to let the people behind you get off, and then reboard.

➤ If you are among the first to enter and first to exit, stand to the side near the door rather than in the back. This way, you won't have to push through others to get off.

➤ Men should keep their hats on in a crowded elevator.

There is nothing to say about escalators except that whoever gets there first gets on first and gets off first. Don't crowd the top of the stairs waiting for someone.

Smoking

It must seem to smokers as if the only place where it's not illegal or improper to smoke is the dark side of the moon. Smoking, once seen as a sign of sophistication, is now seen by many as offensive and even dangerous to non-smokers and smokers alike. While it's not polite to rebuke smokers in public, it's acceptable to ask them to stop smoking or to smoke elsewhere.

The rule for smokers is, don't smoke if you don't see an ashtray. Don't say, "Do you mind if I smoke?" The other person may say he doesn't mind and still be secretly resentful. It is okay to smoke in your office if the company permits, but it will leave a smell that others may find disagreeable.

If hosting a lunch, it's polite to ask for a table in the smoking section if your guest is a smoker, whether you smoke or not—provided you aren't allergic to smoke. If you smoke, never light up during the meal. Wait until after everyone has finished eating and coffee is served.

Electronic Etiquette

Although there was once a time when this area of etiquette was unheard of, with all the advancement in today's technology, electronic etiquette guidelines have never been more necessary.

Telephone Etiquette

Everybody knows how to use the telephone, but so many, many people do not know how to use it to their best advantage.

Tip
Smile when you speak on the telephone because a smile can be heard. Use the old mirror-by-the-telephone trick. Place a small mirror next to the telephone so that you will be aware of your expression as you speak. It works.

When you speak to someone on the telephone, vocal quality counts for 70 percent of the initial impression you make, and the words spoken count for 30 percent. The person on the other end of the line bases his opinions of you not only on what you say but how you say it and the tone of your voice.

Speak unto others as you would have them speak unto you. It's up to you, the speaker, to make sure that the listener gets the message loud (but not too loud) and clear. The person on the other end shouldn't have to work hard to hear you and understand what you are saying.

When using the telephone, use your mouth for speaking only. Eschew chewing, eating, or drinking.

Answering

Answer the telephone no later than the second ring if you can. Identify yourself with both your name and company or department.

➤ Say "Hello" rather than "Hi."

➤ Say, "May I tell her who's calling?" not, "Who's calling?"

It is up to you to determine how your telephone will be answered, not only by you but by members of your staff. You have to let them know what you expect. You can try calling your own office to check up on this.

Also, don't let a phone call preempt an in-person visit. For example, if it's two o'clock, the person with the two o'clock appointment has priority over the person you are speaking with on the telephone.

Placing Calls

Place your own calls whenever possible. If the person you are calling has to wait for you to come on the line, he is apt to think you consider your time more important than his. This could cause the conversation to begin with a standoffish atmosphere, when you haven't even said anything yet.

Let people know right away "who's calling." Every business telephone call should begin with the caller introducing himself, identifying his company, and saying who the call is intended for. This enhances your chances of being put through promptly to the person you are trying to reach, and you will sound confident and self-contained.

Try to call when you know it's convenient for the other person. If you call a business just before closing time, you will be rushed and given half-hearted attention at best.

If you get another call while on the telephone, remember that the first caller has priority. Tell the second caller you will get back to him, and resume your first conversation.

Trivial or long-winded calls are annoying intrusions in a busy work day. Make sure you have a good reason to call, and deal with your business in a prompt, organized way. Another consideration is that such calls convey the impression that your job is of so little importance that you have time to make chatty, unnecessary calls.

Did You Know?
It is estimated that 70 to 80 percent of today's business is done over the telephone.

If your call somehow gets disconnected in the middle of a conversation, you should call back immediately—whatever the circumstances.

Closing a Call

People remember the way telephone conversations end. At the end of your call, thank the person for the call, and do your best to try to end on a positive note. Never conclude by just saying, "See ya," "Bye bye," or, "Later." Say good-bye, and let the other person hang up before replacing the receiver.

If you have a chatty caller who is droning on too long, say something like, "I'll have to hang up now. My two o'clock appointment is here," or "Much as I'd like to chat, I'm on a deadline at the moment. Is there anything else I can help you with?"

After the call, do your homework. Everybody appreciates a follow-through. Keep your agreements. If you have promised to provide information or data, get that material to the other person promptly.

"Telephone Tag"

This everyday occurrence is annoying, frustrating, and irritating, but seemingly inescapable. You might make a couple of dozen calls a day at your desk and connect with only about a fifth of them on the first try. But there are ways to improve your chances and help to reduce that stack of "to call again" notes by the end of the day.

Let's face it. Part of a secretary's job is to give the boss a chance to get some work done. However, the secretary that acts as gatekeeper can become your ally if treated with consideration and respect.

If you don't know the secretary's name, ask the receptionist when you first place the call. If you are calling for Mr. Jones, and you reach his secretary without going through a receptionist, simply ask the secretary his or her name after you identify yourself, and be sure to use the name during all conversations with the secretary. It scores a lot of points. Using the name on subsequent calls has the added benefit of displaying confidence and courtesy, and it gives the impression you and Mr. Jones know each other well.

Having established a cordial relationship with the secretary over the telephone can be very helpful in getting information, such as when Mr. Jones is apt to be free, when is the best time to call him, and what time he returns from lunch.

When you get the "best time," make it clear to the secretary that you will be calling then: "Fine, I'll call back about 2 p.m. then to have a five-minute chat with Mr. Jones about the Frazier property in Oregon. I know he's been anxious to get some information out it."

If you are put on hold, be patient. If the secretary has been especially helpful, a thank you note probably would be in order.

If you are asking that Mr. Jones return your call, tell the secretary the best time to reach you. Be as specific as you can. If you are not there for the return call, you will have to begin the whole process again.

Voice Mail Etiquette

This is another business fact of life that is here to stay. It's a very good and useful tool for conveying information within your company. However, clients or others calling in from outside are apt to find it annoying. And, depending on the message, it can be almost as bad as dealing with a real and really disagreeable person.

> **Tip**
> Vocal quality is crucial. Make sure you know what you are going to say. Practice saying it. Speak clearly without being either loud or sharp. The message within the message should convey confidence.

The message on this medium should give the caller some choices—leave a message, call another extension, or switch back to the receptionist. Few things are more annoying than "menu" messages, with too many, mostly irrelevant options.

The message you leave should embody the journalist's five Ws—who, what, when, where, and why: "This is Mary Mitchell on Thursday, June 1. I'll be traveling all day today and will not be able to return calls until after 7 p.m., Philadelphia time. Please leave your name, telephone number, and a brief message."

When you are the caller: "This is Mary Mitchell, calling on Thursday, June 1, about the training seminar. I'm calling to confirm that 12 people are registered from your company."

Answering Machine

Before recording your voice on your machine:

➤ Write out your specific words and make several practice tries.

➤ Smile when you speak so that you sound enthusiastic and approachable.

➤ Forget about sound effects or other gimmicks; cute is unprofessional.

➤ Briefer is better:

"This is Marjorie Matthews speaking. At the sound of the tone please leave your name, your telephone number, and the best time to reach you. I'll return your call as soon as possible."

When you get someone else's machine:

➤ Be sure to leave a message even if you get a wrong number. Saying you misdailed will allay security concerns.

➤ Give your full name.

➤ Say why you are calling.

➤ Mention the best time for you to be reached.

➤ Leave your complete telephone number, pausing between the area code and local number.

The Fax

Rule #1 — Don't tie up the fax machine. The transmission should be expected, important, and specifically addressed.

Rule #2 — Start off with a cover sheet saying who it's from, the number of pages (cover sheet is included in page count), and who it goes to.

Pro Bono—Community Involvement

As your rank and status improves within your company, you may be asked to volunteer your expertise and energy as a member of the board of directors of a charity and/or a community organization.

This is a feather in your cap. Your company thinks highly enough of you to ask you to represent it in the larger community. It can also evolve into a situation fraught with pitfalls. It may be that your boss has friends or important business associates who are involved with the organization you are to join. In any case, you may be sure that the impression you make will be conveyed back to the executives of your company.

In other words, this can be an important career opportunity. Don't blow it.

The rules of etiquette are extremely important in these situations. Remember that you will be dealing with people who may be quite different than your work colleagues. Some of them may be artists or scholars. Some may be wealthy dilettantes who "dabble" in organizations that foster artistic or charitable causes. They may include political figures or persons who represent the segment of the community that the charity supports.

Here are some basic guidelines:

➤ There may be petty personality conflicts or political cliques within the board. Do everything you can within reason to make it clear that you will not take sides.

➤ Be cordial but somewhat reserved in your relations with the other board members, at least until you get a good handle on how the relationships work. When in doubt, more formal is better than less formal.

➤ As with company meetings, arrive on time, and don't dash back to your office before the meeting is over.

➤ Do your homework so that the meeting will not be delayed while you are being brought up to speed.

➤ Offer to help the head of the organization with contacts or access to special information.

➤ Notice when something is amiss—such as inadequate computer support—and seek to correct it.

➤ Always thank the volunteers who work in that organization, including the people who organize the benefits.

➤ Remember promises made at board meetings, and take on specific responsibilities by keeping good notes and following up with action.

➤ Be a cheerleader back at your home organization. Speak proudly about the work your charity is doing. Nobody expects you to be a half-hearted volunteer.

➤ Always buy at least two tickets to your charity's benefits, or more if it is possible to do so without financial strain. Top executives of corporations are expected to "buy a table" as a corporate donation.

When you are on the job, you are on display. Familiarity can't be allowed to breed carelessness; in fact, the necessity of spending a great deal of time with your co-workers demands even more attention to the details of courtesy and kind behavior.

The Least You Need to Know

➤ Treat your staff with fairness, your colleagues with friendliness, and your boss with honor.

➤ Holding doors and other ways of showing deference to women have long since vanished from the business arena.

➤ Develop good telephone skills. Speak clearly. Be courteous. Leave complete but concise messages. Return calls promptly.

➤ When visiting someone's office, be polite, be friendly, be brief, and be gone.

➤ Women should be gracious and secure enough to accept a door opened for them. They cannot, however, expect such gestures simply because they are women.

Chapter 8

Meetings: The Board Room and the Dining Room

In This Chapter

➤ Board room etiquette

➤ The agenda

➤ Business meals

➤ The business card

Don't be misled about meetings. You've probably heard that corporate America spends too much time in meetings, that they hamper rather than promote productivity, and that the world of the laptop and other communication marvels is making meetings passe.

You may believe all of that or some of it, but the fact remains that important things *do* happen at meetings, and perhaps the most important of these is that people learn about—and form judgments about—each other.

Strategies for a Successful Meeting

Many of us go into meetings not fully prepared and make the wrong impression by what we don't say and gestures we unknowingly make. Think of meetings as opportunities, as chances to impress your colleagues and superiors, and as a way to meet others.

With that in mind, here are some tips about how best to take advantage of these opportunities:

➤ Do your homework. Make sure you have read all of the materials provided in advance, including the agenda. Find out who will be attending. Discover the purpose of the meeting, and focus your preparations on that. Prepare any comments in advance so that you are not rambling and repeating yourself.

Did You Know?

Speaking of homework, you might want to familiarize yourself with *Roberts Rules of Order*, which you can find at any library. This universally recognized guide to procedure will only come into play at the most formal of meetings. However, you never know when you'll be at a meeting and someone will say…"How should we proceed with this?" And you'll hear yourself saying…"Well, *Roberts Rules of Order* suggests…"

Tip
Meeting etiquette is like stage lighting. You only notice it when it's bad.

Tip
Invest in a fine writing instrument. People really do remember those nuances.

➤ Arrive at the meeting on time or a little early. Nobody takes a late-comer seriously. Lateness is an affront to those who troubled to arrive on time. And, no, it doesn't convey the message that you are very busy, only that you are disorganized.

➤ Bring with you all the necessary materials for the meeting—agenda, papers, pens, notebook. Have them at hand so that you are not fishing around while others are waiting for you to find something that should be in front of you.

➤ Keep briefcases and purses on the floor, not on spare chairs or, worse still, on the conference table.

➤ Don't play. That means leave the paper clips alone. Don't stretch the rubber bands or doodle on your notepad.

➤ Keep your feet on the floor. If you must cross your legs, do so at the ankles. Otherwise, you look inattentive and altogether too casual. Make sure your shoes are polished and in good repair. Scuffed shoes imply a person who disregards details.

➤ Keep jackets and ties on unless the person calling the meeting strongly suggests otherwise and actually sheds these items.

➤ Don't cross your arms in front of you. It communicates hostility. You want your body posture to suggest open-mindedness and approachability.

➤ Sit straight, and don't slouch. You will look alert and attentive.

➤ Maintain a high energy and involvement level, no matter how much your mind wants to roam. Meetings are a place for team players.

➤ Enter the meeting room decisively, looking your best. Unless you are certain about how the seating arrangements work, ask where you should sit. Shake hands with your colleagues, introducing yourself to those you don't know and calling those you do know by name. Do this standing. If you are seated and a new introduction is made, stand up.

> **Tip**
> Smile at your colleagues. It is, after all, the ultimate gesture understood by all people, and it does relieve stress.

Speak Up

Think before you speak, and keep it as brief and to the point as possible. Avoid confrontational language and public criticism. Establishing battle lines helps no one. Say, "I disagree because it seems to me that…," instead of, "You're wrong. If you took time to read the report, you would know…"

Don't interrupt someone who is speaking. No matter how much you hate what the other person is saying, wait for him to make his point before interjecting your opinion.

In addition, remember that it's better to make recommendations and suggestions than to give orders or take inflexible positions.

Other points to bear in mind:

➤ Use positive language. Don't introduce your points apologetically. "This might be a bad idea, but…"

➤ Use the editorial "we" when discussing the work and position of your department, company, and so on. Do not take personal credit for things when they are going well if you are not willing to take personal responsibility for them when they are going poorly.

> **Faux Pas**
> Don't ask for food or drink at a meeting unless they are being offered. If there are refreshments, get rid of your coffee cup, plate, and napkin as soon as it is convenient. Your place at the conference table should be clean.

➤ Refer to others in the meeting using honorifics, even though you may be on a first-name basis at other times. Say, "Mr. Daniels just made the point that..." It's much better than "Tom here thinks..."

The Chair

If you are chairing the meeting, pick a time that's convenient for everyone. First thing Monday, and Friday afternoon should be avoided if possible. People are often occupied and/or distracted at these times. Give plenty of notice. Two weeks is an ideal minimum.

OOH.

Did You Know?
The tradition of giving the most important people seats next to the chairman goes back centuries to when the king's worst enemy was seated on his left and his closest ally on his right. This assured that the king had control of his enemy's sword hand, the right, while the king's ally had control of the king's sword hand. This is the genesis of the phrase, "right-hand man."

Decide on the seating. Remember that the two seats on either side of the chairman are considered the most significant seats.

Create an atmosphere in which frank, open discussion is not only safe, but encouraged. If things get heated, it's your job to keep order and mediate any conflicts. Keep the spirit of the meeting positive. Don't criticize or chastise. Avoid undermining authority by hotly disagreeing with someone who outranks you, particularly your boss.

Consider the schedules and jobs of the participants. Make sure all paperwork is distributed well in advance. Provide breaks accordingly so that people can make telephone calls and use the restrooms.

At the end of the meeting, give credit to those who deserve it. Also, write a précis of the meeting within 48 hours, distribute it to the participants, and set the date for the next meeting.

Details

In some cases, it is appropriate to use formal name cards. They should be two-sided so persons on the other side of the table can read them. Name tags should bear the first and last names, without Mr., Ms., or Mrs. Use Dr. if appropriate.

Make sure there are plenty of pads, paper, pencils, post-its, paper clips, rubber bands, and tape. Also, find out in advance if a lectern, microphone, blackboard or whiteboard, flip chart, audio-visual aids, or photocopier will be needed.

If you are going to provide snacks, remember to avoid too much caffeine, sugar, and greasy snacks like chips and danish pastries. They can make people sluggish and/or on edge. Always provide a decaffeinated, low-fat, healthy alternative. Make sure water glasses, pitchers, or bottles of water are readily on hand.

The Agenda

The agenda should include all items to be discussed along with the amount of time to be devoted to each. It should be written so that the most important items are handled first, in case the meeting runs short. Make sure everyone has a copy of the agenda well in advance of the meeting.

Here is a sample agenda:

TO: Marketing and public relations staff

FROM: Chairman's name

PURPOSE: Meeting, Wednesday, February 28, 2 – 4 p.m.

(If the meeting is to take place at mealtime, such as 8 – 10 a.m., or during lunch or dinner, make note of that here with a phrase like, "Sandwiches and beverages will be provided.")

PLACE: Conference room, 10th floor

AGENDA:

1. Review quarterly goals and action plan (30 minutes)

   - Summary by public relations director on achievements

   - Report by publicity assistant on upcoming media coverage

2. Discussion of upcoming media opportunities (15 minutes)

3. Establish priorities for next six months (10 minutes)

4. Open discussion (20 minutes)

5. Conclusion, summary and action plan assignments (20 minutes)

Business Meals

No, it is not just a meeting with food. It's a test, really. It spotlights your social skills, your ability to plan and organize, and your level of sophistication.

Take these occasions very, very seriously, and prepare for them carefully.

Assume that you will be the host of a business lunch or dinner. Seeing the situation from the point of view of the host will make you a more knowledgeable and confident guest.

The host must decide, up front, that the best way to accomplish his agenda is to control the process from beginning to end. It's his job to eliminate distractions, in order to keep the focus on the purpose of the meal.

Here are some guidelines to keep in mind:

➤ *Don't experiment.* Save that for when you are feeling adventurous. Instead, frequent a couple of good restaurants and become known as a "regular." Become familiar with the menu. Get to know the maitre d' or manager.

Tip
The sommelier, or wine steward, is tipped (about 15 percent of the wine bill) if he provides some particular service to your table.

➤ *Hey, big spender.* Except for celebrations, extravagance shows bad manners and bad strategy in the business arena. Pick a quality restaurant known for its reliable service. Don't show off by consistently ordering the most expensive choices in food and wine. Your guests might feel they have to reciprocate, and they are likely to conclude that you are reckless with money—and therefore apt to be reckless in other areas.

Dress Rehearsal

Visit the restaurant a day or two before the meeting. Have a good look at the room. Is it too large? Too noisy? Look for a table in a good position, and reserve it if possible. Familiarize yourself with the menu and the house specialties.

Introduce yourself to the maitre d' or manager. Set up a corporate account or allow them to take a credit card imprint. Let them know that you may be ordering wine, depending upon the preference of your guests. Let them know what your price range is, and ask for recommendations. Tip the maitre d' when you leave, usually $10 or $20, depending upon the level of the restaurant.

Make the reservation in your name and your company's name. This is part of the emphatic message that this is a business meal. Make it quite clear that this is an important meeting, that you are willing to pay for service, and that you—and possibly your associates—will be returning if all goes well.

Invitations

Here is how a typical conversation might go when you are calling to invite someone to a business meal:

"Hello, Nick, this is Mary Mitchell. I'm calling to invite you to lunch to talk about our upcoming program. Is that something you'd like to do?"

"Sure. Sounds good."

"How about Thursday or Friday?"

"Friday would be better."

"Fine. How does Benjamin's or The Wharf sound to you?"

"Great."

"Which do you prefer?"

"The Wharf sounds good."

"Would twelve or twelve-thirty be more convenient?"

"Twelve-thirty."

"Fine. I'll make the reservation. Do you prefer smoking or non-smoking?"

"Non-smoking please."

"Great. I'll see you on Friday at twelve-thirty at The Wharf."

If there is to be more than one guest, and Nick is the most important one, introduce the information about the other guests after the "Sure. Sounds good." and before settling details about time and place: "I'd like also to invite Megan Newman and Nancy Love, who will be working with us on the program. Okay?"

Then, when you call Megan: "Nick and I are having lunch Friday at The Wharf. I was hoping you and Nancy could join us."

Timing

Once you have established the date of your business meal, clear your calendar. Rushing to get there on time or rushing at any point in the process can ruin your efforts to establish just the right atmosphere.

And, while allowing plenty of your time, pace the meal with respect for the schedules of your guests.

If it is a breakfast meeting, confirm the afternoon before and give your guest your home telephone number in case of an emergency. For a lunch or dinner meeting, call to confirm in the morning of that day.

If, for any reason, the meeting is cancelled, call the restaurant right away.

Arrival

Get to the restaurant about 15 minutes early, and check your coat. If you did not tip the maitre d' at the "dress rehearsal," do so now. Wait for your guest near the door. If you

Tip
When waiting for someone in a restaurant, stand where you can see the door without impeding traffic.

must take your seat because there is no place to wait, leave your napkin on the table, and don't eat or drink anything until your guest arrives. In other words, the table should remain pristine. Stand up when your guest arrives, and remain standing until he is seated.

If there is more than one guest, wait near the door, if possible, for five or ten minutes, then tell the maitre d' you are expecting someone, and ask to be seated.

Seating

Give the preferred seat to your guest. Usually that's the one first pulled out by the maitre d', but if a chair isn't pulled out, quickly decide which is the best seat (best view, most comfortable, etc.), and gesture to your guest to occupy it.

Aghast in the Past
"Never hitch up your sleeves, as some men have the habit of doing, as though you were going to make mud pies."

—Alfred Ayres, *The Mentor*, 1894

Sit at right angles to your guest, if possible. If there are two guests, try to avoid sitting between them, or you will feel as if you're watching a tennis match, looking from one to the other in the course of conversation.

The host always stands when someone new joins the table and remains standing until the other person or persons is seated. If someone at the table excuses himself, it is not necessary for the host to stand.

Napkins

Your napkin will be on your plate or to the left of it. As soon as you are seated, pick it up, and place it on your lap unfolded or half-open if it's a large dinner napkin. Don't tuck the napkin in your shirt or belt. It's okay to bring the napkin up to your chest with sips of soup or sauce. If you leave the table for any reason, place the napkin on your chair, and push the chair under the table. Watch the upholstery. You don't want your gravy-stained napkin to soil the upholstered seat of a chair.

Drinks

The server will now ask if you want anything from the bar. Decline if your guest does. Order a drink if your guest does. It doesn't have to be an alcoholic drink, and no explanations are necessary. You can remove any tinge of judgment about alcohol by using the convenient "today" tactic: "I'm not having wine today, but please do have some if you like."

Ordering

If you don't have drinks, spend five or ten minutes talking before asking for menus. If you have drinks, ask your guest if he would like another. If the answer is no, ask for menus then. If the answer is yes, ask for menus when the second round of drinks arrives.

Now it's time to order. Your "dress rehearsal" exploration of the menu pays off now. Give your guests clues about your intentions by mentioning specialties and encouraging them to order appetizers. Have the server take the guests' orders first, and be sure to keep pace with your guests by ordering the same number of courses, whether you want them or not.

As a guest, you should feel free to ask, "What do you recommend here?" if the host has not given clues.

Tip
If your guest has ordered the poached salmon hollandaise, don't order a cheeseburger.

Be decisive! Neither the host nor guest should spend a long time pouring over the menu. Steer clear of user-unfriendly items such as spaghetti, salads, large sandwiches, or anything that will be messy or difficult to eat.

Control and Damage Control

It is the responsibility of the host to pay attention to the service and the food. Make sure your guests are served properly and have whatever condiments they might need.

If it looks like something is wrong, ask your guest. If it is, call the maitre d', and have the item replaced. If things are going badly, keep your cool. Do not engage in a confrontation with the server or the maitre d'. Tell your guest: "I'm so sorry. They seem to be having a bad day." Then deal with the manager later.

Finishing Touches

Encourage your guests to have dessert when the server returns to the table from clearing the entrees. If they do, you do. If they don't, you don't—no matter how much you have been looking forward to that chocolate torte.

Ask your guests if they would like coffee or tea. When it is served, ask for the check. This is the right time to review your meal-time discussion, to make sure you understand whatever agreements have been reached and what follow-up steps have been decided on.

Paying Up

Settle the bill quietly with a credit card or a large bill if paying cash. Don't fiddle around with small bills or change.

It's fine to review the bill for accuracy. You should have a fair idea of what the total should be before it arrives. In any case, don't study the thing like the Dead Sea Scrolls. If you think there is a discrepancy, deal with it after your guests have left.

Please…no calculators at the table.

Nothing damages the effect of a smooth business meal as much as haggling over who should pay. Unfortunately, this is more apt to happen if the host is a woman and the guest is a man. If the subject arises, depersonalize it: "I invited you, and besides, XYZ company would like to take you to lunch."

Another tactic a woman may use if she expects this kind of difficulty is to arrange before-hand for a credit card imprint and for the addition of 18 to 20 percent for tip. In this way, there is no need for the presentation of a check at the table.

Before you leave the table, collect the check room tickets from your guests so that you can tip the attendant—at the rate of one dollar per garment—on the way out.

Taking Leave

Escort your guest to the door. Shake hands, and thank them for taking the time for the meeting. Remind them about the next meeting, or if one has not yet been scheduled, say you will call them within a week. (And make sure that you do call within that time frame.)

The guest should thank the host, praise the restaurant, and within two days, send a hand-written note. If your penmanship truly resembles Chinese algebra, you may type the note, but a hand-written note is infinitely more desirable. Under no circumstance should you fax or e-mail your thanks.

Business Cards

Since the kinds of meetings discussed in this chapter are often occasions for handing around business cards, this is a good place to discuss them.

Your business card is an important and personal part of your communications within the corporate culture, and it's important that you know how and when to use it.

There are three main uses for business cards:

1. They provide vital information about you—your name, your company, your title, and how you can be reached.

2. They can be clipped to a document, a photograph, a magazine, or anything you're sending to someone who might find the information useful, letting the recipient know that you're the sender, and providing your contact information.

3. They can be used as enclosures in gifts or with flowers.

How and when to present your card:

➤ Present your card with the type side up. When someone hands you a card, look at the person to connect card with face.

➤ Don't appear anxious to thrust your card on a senior executive. Wait until asked.

➤ Be selective. If you are with a large group of people, don't hand your card out to everyone. It's pushy, and it creates the impression that you're trying to sell something.

➤ Some people give their business card to anyone they meet. Not a good idea. On the one hand, it's irritating. On the other, you may regret supplying a stranger with your name and business address.

➤ Be unobtrusive about giving someone your card at a social function. Think of it as a private exchange between two individuals.

➤ If your cards are soiled, damaged, or out of date, get rid of them, and get yourself a new set. It's better to give no card than to give one that looks bad.

➤ You never know when someone is going to ask for your business card, so carry some of them with you at social as well as business functions. If you don't have a card, apologize, and write out the information on a piece of paper.

➤ Whether you are dining at Joe's Chili Joint or a black tie dinner, business cards should not surface during a meal. If asked, pass one as discreetly as possible. In fact, if the event has been billed as a social rather than business-related affair, you should be discreet about talking business at all.

Whether you are meeting with your colleagues, your bosses, or your employees, or whether the meeting takes place in the board room or the dining room, it takes preparation and a healthy helping of respect for all present and a knowledge of the basics of meeting etiquette.

The Least You Need to Know

➤ Do your homework before a meeting, and show up with everything you will need.

➤ If you haven't been assigned a seat, ask where you should sit.

➤ Show up on time or early. Stick to the agenda. If it's a meal, keep pace with the others.

➤ Think body language. A slouch says you don't care.

➤ Keep your jacket on during meetings. Anything else looks unprofessional.

➤ Keep your business cards in pristine condition, and always be discreet when exchanging them. Keep your cards with you at all times—you never know when an opportunity will present itself.

Part 3
Correspondence

Living in the era of e-mail does not exempt us from the rules and responsibilities that relate to correspondence—business or personal, formal or casual. The "pen," even if it takes the form of a computer printout, is still mighty, and people will still make judgments about you based on your correspondence.

How your correspondence looks is sometimes as important as what it says. The stationery should fit the occasion. Correspondence should be structured. Different people are addressed differently. There are rules and conventions that affect letters and notes which say thank you, offer condolences, convey congratulations, and so on.

In this part of the book, we will not only talk about the rules relating to correspondence, but will also provide some tips on focusing your message and making your correspondence easier to write and more pleasant for others to read.

Chapter 9

Letters and Notes

In This Chapter

➤ The power of the pen

➤ The structure of a letter

➤ Kinds of letters and how to write them

➤ Writing notes

There is nothing more pleasant than receiving a beautiful letter.

—Amy Vanderbilt

Not one of the communications marvels that enrich and bedevil our modern society can replace a letter. It is more than a communication. It is a gift. A letter can have special powers. It can be more intimate and touching than even a conversation. It can be more personal than any telephone call. This chapter will discuss the proper form and content of letters sent for specific business or social purposes. We'll also address the easiest ways to open and close a note. Whether you're writing a letter or a note, you'll learn how to conquer writer's block.

Personal Letters

Simplicity and clarity lend grace to what we call plain language. The thoughts and ideas that touch another person most profoundly should not be hidden by or entangled in convoluted phrases and unfamiliar words.

The best letters reflect the personality of the writer. In a way, it is a gift of that personality to the reader. This idea is reflected in a letter cited for its virtues in *Etiquette Letter Writer*, published by J. P. Lippincott and Co., Philadelphia, 1875.

> To her I very much respect—Mrs. Margaret Clark—Lovely, and oh! that I could write loving, Mrs. Margaret Clark; I pray you let affection excuse presumption.
>
> Having been so happy as to enjoy the sight of your sweet countenance and comely body sometimes, when I had occasion to buy treacle or liquorish [sic] powder at the apothecary's shop.
>
> I am so enamored with you, that I can no more keep close my flaming desire to become your servant. And I am the more bold now to write to your sweet self, because I am now my own man and may match where I please; for my father is taken away, and now I am come into my living.
>
> If you think well of this notion I shall wait upon you as soon as my new clothes is made and hay harvest is in. Your loving servant till death.
>
> Mr. Gabriel Bullock

The virtues of this letter include:

➤ Mr. Bullock's intentions and his reason for writing are made plain. There is nothing ambiguous about his feeling for the comely Mrs. Clark.

➤ He makes his situation clear. He is obviously a man of substance presenting an honorable proposal.

➤ He does not discuss the weather, his health problems, or nasty local gossip.

Keep these qualities in mind the next time you write a personal letter to someone.

Open and Shut—The Letter Format

Some people have trouble getting a letter started but, once started, can continue comfortably. It's a good idea to mentally go over the main things you want to say before starting. You can begin with a bit of good news: "You will be glad to hear that…" You can describe what you have been doing that day or depict the room in which you are writing. You can also refer to the most recent correspondence or the last time you met the person to whom you are writing.

Don't open a letter by apologizing for not writing sooner. You can say something like: "You may have thought I'd forgotten all about you, but really, you have been in my thoughts often lately. It's just that there's been a lot going on. For instance…"

Letters, by their nature, convey news. Therefore, in the body of the letter, talk about what has been happening to you and to those you both know. Talk about shared interests. Keep the tone conversational, and let it flow.

Tip
Sure, you want to convey your feelings fervently in a love letter. Still, it doesn't hurt to remember that love letters are usually kept, and may be read by others many years later.

Tip
"You" is a much better word than "I" for beginning a letter.

End formal letters with a "Sincerely," and progress toward familiarity with "yours truly, regards, best wishes, affectionately, love," and so on. The most informal and affectionate letters may end with "Miss you," or "Write soon," or "More later."

Letter Dos and Don'ts

Over the years, certain customs dealing with how the elements of a letter should be organized on the page have evolved and have been pretty much universally accepted. Knowing how the "skeleton" of a letter should look allows you to concentrate on the essential message you wish to convey. Accordingly, here are some general rules for writing business or social letters:

➤ If your address is not printed at the top of the page, write it in the upper right corner. (Don't bother if the person you're writing to knows perfectly well where you live.)

➤ The date goes under the address at the upper right or at the bottom left corner. Write out the month in more formal letters or if you think the letter might be preserved for posterity.

➤ The salutation goes flush left.

➤ Leave a space, indent, and begin the body of the letter.

➤ The complimentary close goes to the right, and it can take many forms:

> ➤ "Love" is a wonderful thing and is fine if you are writing to a family member or close friend. You can also use "Fondly" and "Affectionately."
>
> ➤ If you don't know the person very well, try "As ever" or "As always" or "All best wishes." A stalwart standby is "Sincerely," and you can soften it by putting "Very" or "Yours" in front of it.
>
> ➤ "Cordially" is considered to be out of date, but I like it and still use it because it is correct and, I think, warm.
>
> ➤ "Gratefully" is great for letters of thanks.
>
> ➤ "Respectfully" and "Respectfully yours" are reserved for the clergy.

123 Margo St.
Hartford, CT 93433

Nov. 8, 1996

Dear Mr. Petersen:

    Thank you so much for your letter of September 9. It certainly brought good news. We have had no difficulty organizing the workers according to your instructions, and I am certain you will be pleased with operations when you arrive for your inspection tour in January.

Sincerely,

Horace Grant

➤ Letter sheets are folded vertically with the fold on the left, somewhat like a handwritten brochure. Start writing on page one, and go to page three if the letter runs to a second page. Go with the usual sequence (1,2,3,4) if the letter requires all four pages. Number the pages as you write.

The sequence of pages in a letter sheet.

➤ "Dear Madam" and "Dear Sirs" are outdated if you are writing to a store, for example. It is better to use "To Whom It May Concern" if you don't know the name of the person to whom you are writing.

➤ If you fold a letter twice, fold the bottom third first, then the top third. The letter should be inserted into the envelope so that when it is removed and unfolded, it is ready to be read—right side up and facing the reader. It doesn't matter which way you put a letter that is folded only once into an envelope.

Tip
Bag the Bic pens and any other ballpoint pens. Ballpoint does not suggest performance. Fountain pens make letters look so much better. Colored inks are okay for casual notes and letters to friends, but use black ink for a condolence letter or when replying to a formal invitation.

Leave letters unsealed if they are to be hand-delivered, unless they are of a highly personal nature.

Faux Pas

If you are not going to include a handwritten message, don't send printed Christmas cards at all. A handwritten message—even something as brief as "Holiday Greetings"—may go above or below the printed material.

Post cards are useful for sending out notices of meetings or confirming appointments. They can be used as thank you notes for casual parties, but never for dinner, gifts, or being a house guest.

Insert a fold-over note into the envelope in this way.

Grammar

A letter on the best stationery, properly organized and beautifully presented, can be utterly ruined by one grammatical error. These errors can also have a nasty effect upon your reputation. Grammatical traps like to lurk in lengthy sentences. Brief, direct sentences are generally safer and have the added merit of being easier on the reader.

Here's a reference list of some of the most common grammatical errors.

➤ "Between you and I." When "you and I" follows a preposition—such as "between" or "to" or "for"—it becomes "you and me."

➤ Avoid the phrase "I, myself." In fact, use "myself" only for emphasis.

➤ "Fewer" refers to items, things you can count. "Less" refers to quantities such as water, effort, and time. (Yes, those supermarket signs that read "12 items or less" are ungrammatical.) Similarly, "farther" refers to actual distance, as in "a mile farther," while "further" indicates an extension, as in "further discussion."

➤ Don't use "irregardless" when you mean "regardless."

➤ Avoid "feel badly." It means you aren't very good at feeling things, in a tactile sense.

➤ "Capitol" is the building. "Capital" is everything else.

➤ The speaker implies, the listener infers.

➤ Make sure that nouns and verbs agree. "A group of employees is (not are) arriving."

Letters and Children

It is never too early for children to begin writing letters. Even before children can write, they can be told that you are writing to Aunt Margaret to thank her for the doll house. Remember that a thank you letter from a first-grader does not have to be spelled correctly or look just right. Just don't let your child get away with pre-printed thank-you cards.

Sample Letters

Whether you are writing a thank you letter or an apology letter (or even a Dear John letter), here are a few dos and don'ts, tips, and samples to help you along the way.

Thank You Letters

These notes can be boring—boring to write, boring to read: "Thank you for the present. It was nice of you to think of me."

To avoid this sort of letter, you can follow my foolproof, three-step formula:

1. Be sure to thank the person for the specific gift and mention the gift by name.

2. Acknowledge the effort and energy the giver put into selecting, purchasing, or making the gift.

3. Let the giver know how you have used or will use the gift.

Tip
Letters usually should be handwritten. However, most formal letters, particularly business letters may be typed. In addition, if your handwriting is truly cursed beyond redemption, typing is an alternative preferable to illegibility.

Tip
Drawings and other original artwork make correspondence more fun for the children and for the recipient.

Tip
If you thanked the giver at the time the gift was presented to you, it may not be necessary to write a thank you. For example, when your sister who lives a block away gives you a gift in person, you need not send a note (although it's nice to do so). When your Aunt Tillie, visiting from across the country, presents you with a hand-knit sweater, you should acknowledge all her efforts with some extra effort of your own.

Dear Helen:

Tom and I and the two girls want to thank you very much for the handsome "Deluxe Edition" Monopoly game you gave the family. I happen to know that you can't get this beautifully produced version of the game at most stores, and you must have had to do some shopping around to find it. The four of us spent last night playing the game. (Tammy won.) Your gift has made this familiar game very special for us.

Fondly,

Margaret

Faux Pas

Printed thank you notes from a gift shop are not acceptable as tokens of gratitude. Gratitude does not come pre-packaged. And, no, a telephone call is not good enough.

When thanking someone for a gift of money, don't mention the amount in your letter of thanks. A reference to "your generous gift" will suffice.

When you refuse a gift, a letter, or at least a note, is required. It should say that you don't feel you can accept the gift (perhaps in the case of a woman receiving expensive jewelry from a male acquaintance), but wish to give thanks for "your thoughtfulness."

Condolence Letters

A letter of condolence should do three things:

1. Acknowledge what a terrible loss the death is for the bereaved and that you sympathize with their suffering to some degree

2. Convey a sincere desire to help in some way during this time of grief

3. Praise the accomplishments, character, and devotion of the deceased

Remember this is a letter that may be read by a number of people, and may be saved as part of the family archives. Therefore, while it will be personal, the style should be at least somewhat formal.

Dear Mrs. Thompson:

   Please accept my deepest sympathy on the terrible loss of your fine husband, George, even though I know no words of mine can ease your grief.

   I met George on my first day of work at MicroTech, and I will never forget his kindness to me, a confused newcomer. He helped me to get settled and to understand how things worked there—all out of the goodness of his heart. George had that rare combination of kindness, good humor, and competence.

   I think you know that we live just a few blocks away, and if there is anything I or my family can do to help during the days ahead, we would consider it a privilege if you would call upon us.

Yours,

Tom

In a condolence letter, avoid stressing how much you feel bereaved. The purpose of the letter is to comfort others, not to have them feel sorry for you.

Writing after you have heard some bad news about a friend or acquaintance is a different matter. In this letter, you want to convey not only support, but a bit of optimism.

Dear Margaret:

We just heard that Tom was among those laid off at MicroTech. I know it must be a shock for you and your family. Joe and I will be home all weekend in case you and Tom want to stop by for a drink or dinner or just to chat.

Warmly,

Helen

Congratulation Letters

This is one of the easiest and happiest of letters. It is also the sort of letter that may be kept in the family for years.

Dear Mark:

Congratulations on receiving the fellowship and study grant from Princeton. It is not only a tribute to your brilliance and hard work, but it will give you the opportunity to explore some of the avenues of investigation we have been talking about so wistfully. All of us here at the lab share the joy of this moment with you. We will miss you during the term of your studies and look forward to welcoming you back.

With best wishes,

Jerry

Apology Letters

If you have offended someone and are sorry about it, the best thing to do is apologize in person and follow it up with a letter. In any case, the letter must say clearly and humbly that you are sorry. If there is some way in which you can make amends, promise to do so.

Dear Mrs. Fitzhugh:

Please accept my sincere apology for having failed to attend your dinner party after assuring you that I would be there. I know how this can upset the plans of a hostess and am deeply sorry for any distress I may have caused.

My guilt is even greater because I do not have the excuse of a family emergency or other crisis. I simply got the date wrong, and forgot to check to make sure.

Once again, I most humbly apologize and hope that you will forgive my carelessness.

Sincerely,

Elizabeth

Dear John

The overriding objective in this case is to end a romantic relationship with as little pain to the other person as possible.

➤ You have to start with a straightforward statement giving the reason for the letter.

➤ Apologize, and offer an explanation that does not blame the other person, something—if possible—that is beyond the control of either of you.

➤ If there is blame involved, blame yourself.

➤ Don't lie.

➤ Don't leave the door open—not even by a crack.

Dear Robert:

After a lot of thought and soul searching, I have come to the realization that it is time to bring our relationship to an end.

Our personalities, interests, and backgrounds are so different that conflicts and unhappiness are inevitable for both of us. I am firmly convinced that I will never be the sort of woman who would fit into your world. I am sure that you will come to realize that as well. I recognize that the reason for this is a lack of flexibility on my part, but I can't seem to help it.

I think we should make a clean break and not try to contact each other again. I wish you nothing but success and happiness.

Sincerely,

Mary

Congress, Etc.

Letters to people in power do have an effect. Ask any politician. These letters should be:

➤ Concise. Put the heart of your message at the very beginning of the letter.

➤ Don't carp or bluster. State your position and the reasons for it with as little emotion as possible.

➤ Say whom you represent. You may be speaking for a group or organization, or you may be writing as a father, businessman, or just concerned citizen.

Dear Senator Fulton:

I am writing to oppose the proposal to drain the wetlands in the Westphalia section of your district. As you know, wetlands are a critical part of the ecosystem in that area. Draining would not only damage the environment there, but would bring in the sort of development that would put great strain on the area.

I am writing as a resident of Westphalia, as well as someone concerned about the dangerous erosion of the environment through over-development.

I hope you will vote no on SB 188 when it comes before your committee.

Yours truly,

Elizabeth Gordon

You can be even more terse when writing to the White House. The President almost certainly will not see your letter. However, staff people keep a careful tab on how many people are writing with opinions on each issue, and these tabulations are passed along to the President.

Dear Mr. President:

    I strongly oppose the idea of sending American troops to Bolivia. In fact, I oppose military intervention in the affairs of any nation in the Americas.

                                      Sincerely,

                                  Robert Anderson

Complaints

One situation in which a face-to-face conversation is preferable to a letter is when you have a complaint about the behavior of a neighbor or friend. Keep things as pleasant and non-confrontational as possible.

However, a letter to a retailer, business, or government agency is sometimes necessary. These letters should be as unemotional as possible, while stating the facts emphatically.

To Whom It May Concern:

On May 1, 1996, I purchased a Populux 5000 dish-washer from your firm, and it was installed at my home a week later. I have had trouble with it ever since.

First, there was a leak under my sink. Your repairman came four days after I reported the leak and left without fixing it, saying he did not have a certain part with him. When he did not return within three days, I called to complain. Two days after that, he returned.

He worked for more than two hours in my kitchen. When he left, the leak was fixed, but the dishwasher did not work at all. I called again, and another repair-man came three days after the call. He said the problem was with the wiring in my kitchen and that I should call an electrician. I did. The electrician said the wiring is fine and charged me $45.

I have now had this dishwasher for one month and have yet to wash a single dish in it. Since your people apparently are unable to repair this machine, you should replace it or refund my purchase price.

Please contact me as soon as possible concerning this matter.

Sincerely,

Paula Smith

Keep a copy of the letter, and follow it up within a week with a telephone call.

Notes

Sometimes you have a great thought for a certain person or situation that you want to share. Of course, you can always place a phone call, but you know what usually happens.

You have an idea of what you want to say, not the exact words, but an idea. You may hesitate. The other person says something. The mood shifts. The moment is gone.

On paper, you can say exactly what you want to say, and you can take your time in finding the words, the very words that give you that certain sense of pleasure and that you know will please the object of your thoughts, affection, concern.

A note can work the magic. It doesn't have to be long ("Wish I was there...with you."). It doesn't have to be poetic ("I wish you chicken soup."). It doesn't have to be particularly clever ("It was great to see you last week. Happily, you haven't changed a bit.").

While drafting your note, think about:

➤ The person who will receive the note. Is it an intimate friend, someone you feel affection for, a person you know and like and would like to know better, someone you know only slightly? A personal reference to that individual or to your relationship separates your note from the anonymous platitudes on printed greeting cards.

➤ The occasion. A birthday is not the same as a confirmation or bar mitzvah. Are you sharing someone's joy, offering condolences, helping to mark a milestone in life?

➤ The "root" message. Once you are sure of this, you can find pleasing or proper ways of delivering it. Some "root" messages are:

I love you

I miss you

Thank you

Sorry you're sick

Congratulations

When writing a note on an "informal," don't write anything on the front if it has a monogram in the center of the page. Short notes go inside under the fold. If the note is longer, lay the paper out flat, start the note at the top of the page, and continue onto the bottom half of the back page. Sometimes it is impossible to write on the back of the monogram or engraving because of the indentation.

This is a formally engraved informal note, that is, a woman using her husband's name—the classic "informal."

Mrs. Timothy Randolph Bennett

Start writing here, on to the bottom half of the back of this sheet.

Openings

There are some easy ways to get started. Think of them as perennials.

➤ "What a…" This can be followed by…great trip, nifty surprise, grand occasion, excellent gift. Another similar beginning is "That was…"

➤ "I was thinking (or remembering)…"

➤ "I can't tell you how much…"

You can probably come up with a few perennials of your own. When you find a good one, write it down for future use. But remember that perennials wear easily and should be used sparingly.

Tip
Two good sources of quotations are *The Oxford Dictionary of Quotations* and *Bartlett's Familiar Quotations*.

Quotes

No wise man ever wished to be younger.

—Jonathan Swift

Sometimes just the right quote sends just the right message all by itself. Every library has books of quotations. A paperback book of quotes of your own might seem like a good investment even if it comes to your rescue only once.

You can even use a tired old saw such as "You inherit your family but you choose your friends." But you have to follow it up with something like, "With you in my family, I feel as if I am an heir to a fortune." Or, "I am so glad you chose me to be a friend."

Closings

A closing to your note should reflect the nature of your relationship with the recipient. A flat "yours truly" will disappoint and perhaps offend a close friend. Leave the "L word" alone unless the recipient is a *very* close friend.

Here are some closings listed in a more or less declining order of intimacy.

> All my love
>
> Best love
>
> Much love
>
> Love
>
> Fondly
>
> Affectionately
>
> Warmly
>
> Best regards
>
> Regards
>
> Just sign the thing

The following is an example of the type of letter which would receive "Love" as a closing.

Dear Sandy:

    You know me so well! I'm dashing through my living room in another headlong rush to another boring meeting, and I see your flowers and remember your admonition, "Take time to smell the flowers." So, I am taking time—time to write this note and time to smell the flowers. They smell wonderful. They smell like friendship.

                            Love,

                            Mary

Unblocking

"I never know what to say."

Even people who use this excuse for not writing a letter or note know that it is lame. What they mean is, "I don't know how to approach this thing—how to get started."

Every writer knows that the best way to beat writer's block is to write. Get the words, even the wrong words, flowing, and the right words will come along. So, when you decide to write a note, begin with scrap paper. Write a draft or two before you get out the good notepaper.

Even in our age of technological marvels, written correspondence retains a certain power and charm that can't be replaced by cellular phones, fax machines, and e-mail. A carefully prepared, thoughtfully written letter on nice stationery is a treasure—something to be put away and saved, to be enjoyed over and over. It's a gift that enriches both the sender and the receiver.

The Least You Need to Know

➤ When writing a letter, remember that the address goes at the upper right of the page with the date under it. The salutation is flush left, and the closing and signature are to the right.

➤ Always write a draft beforehand. This also helps when you can't think of what to say.

➤ Don't type your letters, unless your handwriting is truly atrocious.

➤ Make sure notes do their job. Focus. Brevity is the best policy, but don't be curt.

➤ Keep in mind that letters are a reflection of your personality, and some letters are saved for years to be looked back upon.

Stationery

Just as we judge others more by what we see than by the words they speak, we also make judgments based on the way people's letters *look*. A single-sentence letter can speak volumes about the person sending it, and that can be an advantage or a disadvantage.

People are far less restricted and rigid about their correspondence today, especially when it comes to correspondence mediums. Computer programs for word processing and graphics provide more resources for expressing personal style and creativity than anyone ever dreamed of in the past. Hence, the strict formulae for correspondence have been stretched to reflect the times.

It is still valuable to know and to understand the process for taking pen to paper, and what's what when it comes to stationery. Your personal choice of fuchsia paper with hot pink type might be great for a missive to your former roommate. It would be the kiss of death, however, if used to apply for a job with a conservative law firm.

As with any issue involving personal presence, grooming is more important than a fashion statement. If the engraved letterhead isn't even close to your sense of self or concept of reality, then clean paper, crisply folded with its written components done perfectly, will speak better in your favor than costly stationery, carelessly used.

Paper

Paper is judged by its texture and weight, both reflections of the material from which it is made. The best stationery is made from new, unlaundered, and undyed cotton rags. Cheaper papers are made from vegetable fibers, sometimes combined with wood pulp. The higher the rag content, the better the paper. Rag content is usually noted on the package.

Watermarks reveal the quality of stationery. A watermark is the manufacturer's identification, which can be seen when the paper is held up to the light. A genuine watermark looks slightly blurred. There are imitation watermarks, but they look artificial in their sharpness.

Printing

The kind of printing you use is another important factor in the overall quality of your stationery. Engraving is the highest quality printing. The words and symbols to be printed are cut (preferably by hand) onto a metal plate and then transferred to the paper. You can tell real engraving by its slightly raised, embossed quality, and by turning the paper over to see if the reverse of the printing is slightly indented. The indentation is the result of the force of the engraving plate as it is applied to the paper.

For obvious reasons, engraving is the most costly means of printing. While there are, mercifully, many other options, none makes the quality statement that engraving does. (A client once told me that he retained my company's services because, all other factors being equal, our engraved stationery projected depth and quality.)

Raised lettering, or thermography, imitates the look of engraving but cannot approach the quality. You can identify thermography by how easily the printing flakes off when you scratch it with your fingernail. It is the pretender to engraving, and personally, I think you should decide either to engrave or not. Stationery, like people, ought not to pretend it is something it isn't.

Most printing as we know it is done by a process called offset lithography. It is the least expensive method and, with good design, can achieve a high quality image.

Personal Stationery

Your personal stationery is as important and as noticed as an accessory like your wrist-watch. Most of us should own three kinds—formal writing paper, which can be engraved or plain, personal business stationery, and personal notepaper. Household informal stationery is an additional option.

Formal writing paper is used for things like condolence letters and responding to formal invitations. Do not substitute informal writing paper when formal writing paper is called for.

Personal business stationery is used for matters relating to your career or job and for letting the store know that your drapes have not arrived or are the wrong color.

Use personal notepaper for writing informal invitations and replies, friendly correspondence, thank you letters—basically for all informal social correspondence. Stationery stores call this kind of item "informals." They are generally folded and about 5 by 7 inches in size. The most widely used colors for notepaper are white and off-white. Pale pink or other pastel colors are called folded notes, and they are slightly less formal than "informals."

If you print household informal stationery, you might choose to include your telephone number for convenience' sake. A fairly impersonal type of stationery, this is used for notes to vendors, the post office, electric company, and so on.

You don't have to have your own custom-printed or engraved stationery. Any good stationery store, department store, or jeweler who provides engraving services will also carry plain stationery. Personalizing it is a nice and useful luxury, however.

Make sure your stationery meets the U.S. Postal regulations—that is, envelopes must be at least 3 1/2 by 5 inches. The Postal Service still allows envelopes with the return address printed on the back, which is a formal social custom. As a general rule, however, printing the return address on the front of the envelope is much more practical if the letter has to be returned to the sender. It is good manners to heed the Postal Service request that the return address be on the front of the envelope for everything but the most formal invitations.

Women and Stationery

There was a time when every well-bred woman used only fold-over notes, rather than flat stationery. Today, women are free to select stationery that complements their handwriting, style, and taste. For example, I know several women who choose large letter-sized paper for casual notes because it accommodates their large-script flair. However, unless you have a wardrobe of personal stationery, it's a good idea to avoid wild ink colors, in favor of more multi-useful, conservative ones such as black or gray.

With personalized stationery, a woman has the option of using her social title. Thus, a married woman might use "Mrs. Daniel Fleischmann" or the more contemporary "Ms. Mary Fleischmann." It is unnecessary and perhaps a bit pretentious for single women to give themselves the title of "Miss," although it is not incorrect. The name itself does just fine.

It's probably more practical to print notepaper with your address only, if you use different names or titles, for example, your maiden name in business and your married name socially.

Men and Stationery

For men's stationery, the name appears without a title unless he happens to be a medical doctor, in which case it is fine to use Dr. before the name. Use M.D. only professionally. A man would also use a title if he is a clergyman or member of the military so that others will know how to address him correctly.

Children and Stationery

Children are often "bribed" into writing thank you notes with the prize of personal stationery. There is a wealth of children's stationery available today that reflects a child's personality. They range from colorful sports motifs to delicate dolls and animals. Keep in mind that it makes sense to use lined paper for young children.

Monograms

Monograms continue to be popular. They should appear either centered at the top of the page, centered on the front of the folded note, or in the upper left corner.

A single-initialed piece of stationery leaves too many questions in the readers' minds. Stationery stores sell pre-printed notes with single initials, but these seem to me to be useless and silly.

If you choose to monogram your stationery, it is best to use three initials, unless they happen to spell something graceless. Alice Stanton Smith, for example, would be better off using just two initials.

Faux Pas
It is pretentious to engrave a young person's stationery until he or she is 18 or in college.

The most common styles for monograms are either three initials set in consecutive order or the initial of the last name in a larger size in the middle of the other two. A single woman or a married woman who retains her maiden name uses the initials of her first, middle, and last names. A married woman who uses her husband's name uses the initials of her first name, her maiden name and her husband's last name.

Always write out the names of your city and state in full with no abbreviations. Numerals for street numbers are fine. It is generally unwieldy and pretentious to spell out numbers greater than ten.

Printed or engraved envelopes generally carry the address in the upper left, and it is perfectly fine to use your printing or engraving plate with your name from your stationery for this, rather than have a new one made. If you print or engrave the envelopes, leave the name off the return address. It rarely adds extra cost to leave off a line of type from a plate, as opposed to making a new plate, which is expensive.

Engraved monogram styles.

Stationery Styles

Here are some descriptions of traditional stationery styles. All listed measurements are approximate.

Letter Sheet

Size: 5 1/4 by 7 1/4 inches high.

This is a formal stationery style and can be used for any correspondence, including a condolence letter. It can be used for extending and replying to informal invitations or for replying to formal invitations. (It is perhaps not a good idea to use it to extend an invitation if it is engraved informally with the address only.)

This stationery should be of white or off-white stock. The sheet comes folded vertically with the crease on the left. You can engrave it with a crest, monogram, name only, or address only—although it doesn't have to be engraved at all.

> **Tip**
>
> Any good stationer—Tiffany & Co. and J.E. Caldwell & Co., for example—can guide you through deciding what kind of stationery you need and how to use it. Most major cities have respected stationers relied upon by established families. When in doubt, shop in these places. The advice usually is free.

Informals

Size: 5 by 3 1/2 inches wide.

In spite of its name, this is a pretty formal piece of stationery. It is not used by men unless it is engraved with a couple's name on the front. It can also be engraved with a woman's full name.

Informals may be used for writing notes, gift enclosures, extending and replying to informal invitations, and replying to formal invitations.

Message Cards

Size: 5 by 3 1/2 inches high.

This is a single white card with a very smooth (satin) finish. It can have a woman's full name or a couple's name engraved at the top center of the card. The street address can be in the upper right hand corner. You can use these for thank you notes or other kinds of notes and for extending or replying to an informal invitation.

Correspondence Cards

Size: 6 1/2 by 4 1/4 inches high.

This is a most useful investment for both men and women, especially those in the corporate arena. It is a single card, about six by four inches in size. It can be colored and sometimes have a colored border. The card can also be plain or engraved with a monogram, the name alone, or the name with address. The card is used for any kind of short note, sending or replying to invitations, thank-yous, etc. Men find these particularly useful and often have only this one stationery item for personal use.

This is probably the single most used item of stationery in a business person's arsenal.

Caroline Newlin Gray

A woman's and a man's correspondence cards.

J•P•M

Half Sheets

Size: 5 3/4 by 7 3/4 inches high to 6 1/4 by 8 1/2.

This is a single sheet in any color. Use it for writing letters. If you are engraving it, the monogram or crest, or name and address, is centered at the top. You will need plain second sheets if you write long letters. These can be used interchangeably with the letter sheets for most correspondence, although the letter sheet is more formal and traditional. Pale colors are fine, although you should not use anything other than white or off-white to send a condolence letter or to extend or reply to a formal invitation.

A half sheet.

WILLIAM WARREN REDFIELD

Folded Notes

Size: 5 1/4 by 3 1/2 inches high.

These look just like the informals, but may be in pastel colors. The front page is blank or engraved with a centered monogram or with the monogram in the upper left corner. They are great for general correspondence, especially thank you notes.

A folded note.

Monarch Sheets

Size: 7 1/4 by 10 1/2 inches high.

These are used by both men and women for general correspondence and informal business letters.

KENNETH BRADLEY HAZARD

Sample man's monarch sheet.

115

Sample business monarch sheet, engraved.

Uncommon Courtesies®

215-574-1666

facsimile 215-574-1667

Post Office Box 40008
Philadelphia
Pennsylvania 19106

The
MITCHELL
Organization

Calling Cards

The tradition of "calling on" friends and acquaintances as a formal social ritual is pretty much gone today. It enjoyed its heyday before World War I. In those days, the woman of the household did the visiting. If the person being called upon was out, she left her husband's calling card and her own on a silver tray in the foyer of the home. Husbands went along only when the visit was to offer condolences, visit the sick, or congratulate a birth, a major birthday, career triumph, and so on.

The use of calling cards declined as women became major contributors to the workforce and had less time to go visiting. Economic factors also contributed. Calling cards are expensive. They must be engraved, which is a luxury. Also, the Postal Service will no longer deliver this size envelope, which severely limits their usefulness as an invitation.

Tip
Calling cards are also called visiting cards or social cards, to distinguish them from business cards.

Eventually, they began to be used primarily as gift enclosures, although most people these days use informal notes for that because they provide more writing space. However, if budget permits, there is nothing more elegant than receiving a gift with a calling card enclosed.

Always engrave calling cards in black ink with a simple typeface. White or off-white are the correct colors. The cards are engraved with either your name or your name and address. Generally, no abbreviations are used. If the address is printed on the card, it goes in the lower right hand corner. It is perfectly fine to write your address and telephone number on the card. Do so in ink, but not with a ballpoint pen, which insults the elegance of the card.

If you write a message on the card ("Have a wonderful fiftieth."), it should be simply written on the face of the card. This also applies when using the calling card as a gift enclosure. If the card is a gift enclosure, draw a single line through your name, and write your name ("Affectionately, Mary"). Make sure you write the receiver's name and address on the front of the envelope if it's a gift so that it doesn't get separated by mistake before delivery. Do not seal the envelope.

There are different sizes for men and women. Generally, a woman's card is more square than a man's. A man's card is longer than a woman's.

Correct approximate sizes:

Men, regardless of marital status: 3 3/8 by 1 1/2 inches high or 3 1/2 by 2.

Single women: 2 7/8 by 2 inches high.

Married women: 3 1/8 by 2 1/4 inches high.

Married couple: 3 3/8 by 2 1/2 inches high.

Men

The following are some important details concerning men's calling cards:

➤ The man's name is printed in full, except for "Mr." Spell out The Reverend, Doctor, Captain, and so on. If length is a problem, a man may decide to omit his middle name or abbreviate his title.

➤ A lawyer's card would read, John Silcox, Esquire, or Mr. John Silcox.

➤ A doctor's calling card would read, Doctor John Silcox, and his professional card would read, John Silcox, M.D.

➤ A comma always precedes "Jr." or "Sr." No comma is used before II, III, and so on.

➤ Don't use the letters of your academic degrees on your calling card, no matter how proud you are of them. Letters of an honorary degree are *never* used.

Women

Here are some important details concerning women's calling cards:

➤ A married woman's name appears exactly as her husband's, except for the honorific. Example: Mrs. John Montgomery Silcox or Mrs. John Silcox.

➤ A female doctor who uses her maiden name would use Doctor Lillian Mitchell. If she uses her husband's name, it would be either Doctor Lillian Gates, Doctor Lillian Mitchell Gates, or Mrs. Theodore Gates.

➤ Divorced women use either Mrs. Marie Webb, Mrs. Marie Mitchell Webb, or Marie Mitchell Webb. Divorced women with children keep their ex-husband's name to be consistent with their children's.

➤ A divorced woman without children can resume her maiden name. In that case, her card would read Marie Mitchell. No honorifics here. She is no longer a Mrs. Miss is only for women who have never been married, and Ms. is not used on a calling card because the term has not been in use long enough to be considered traditional by old-line engravers, particularly since the term itself came into existence as a designation for a woman in business.

➤ Widows do not change their calling card when they continue to use their husband's name.

➤ Single women may use their full names, with or without the "Miss."

Couples

When a couple uses a joint calling card, the home address is optional. The card is written, "Mr. and Mrs." with the husband's full name. Abbreviations are used only when necessitated by constrictions of length. In this case, options include leaving out a middle name, using an initial, or abbreviating a title such as Rev. for The Reverend.

If both are doctors, you can use: The Doctors Peterson, Doctors Judith Peterson and Michael Peterson, or Dr. Judith Holmes and Dr. Michael Peterson. In the last instance, Dr. was used because of length. If only the husband is a doctor, it's Doctor and Mrs. Michael

Peterson. If the wife only is a doctor, it's Doctor Judith Peterson (or Holmes) and Mr. Michael Peterson.

MR. JAMES JOSEPH WEISS

A man's calling card.

Mrs. Joanne M. Rivera

A woman's calling card.

Mr. and Mrs. James Joseph Weiss

A married couple's calling card.

A Coat of Arms

It all started with knights wearing special colors and insignia into battle and in tournaments so that they would be recognized and would get full credit for their heroic deeds. These devices were called coats of arms because they were embroidered on sleeveless jackets worn over their armor. Heralds organized the tournaments and kept records of the various colors and insignia of the participants. Thus, the term "Heraldry."

Direct male descendants who bear the family name inherit the family coat of arms. In the case of no sons, daughters inherit the coat of arms. They become heiresses or co-heiresses with their sisters until they marry. When a woman whose family has inherited a coat of arms marries a man who has none, she does not use her coat of arms after her marriage.

By the 15th century, so many social climbers had assumed a coat of arms for their families—even though many of them were not entitled—that the College of Arms was legally chartered in 1484 to regulate heraldry, and it continues to do so today.

In America, the New England Historic Genealogical Society in Boston will rule on a family's claim to "bear arms." However, the society does not grant the right to "bear arms." This is inherited individually. You can't buy it, no matter how pretty it is.

Following are several uses of the crest and the coat of arms. The crest is a part of the full coat of arms.

➤ The crest can be engraved or embossed on wedding invitations and announcements if the father's family has the coat of arms and if his name appears on the invitation.

➤ The crest can be embossed or engraved on place cards and menu cards for a formal dinner.

➤ The full coat of arms or just the crest and motto can be engraved on large pieces of silver and embossed or engraved on stationery.

➤ The coat of arms can be painted (blazoned) and framed and hung on the wall for decoration.

➤ A woman may use her father's or husband's coat of arms in a diamond-shaped lozenge, the feminine version of the shield. She may use a crest on personal possessions, such as writing paper, linens, and dressing table accessories. Again, when a woman whose family has coat of arms marries a man who has none, she does not use the coat of arms after her marriage.

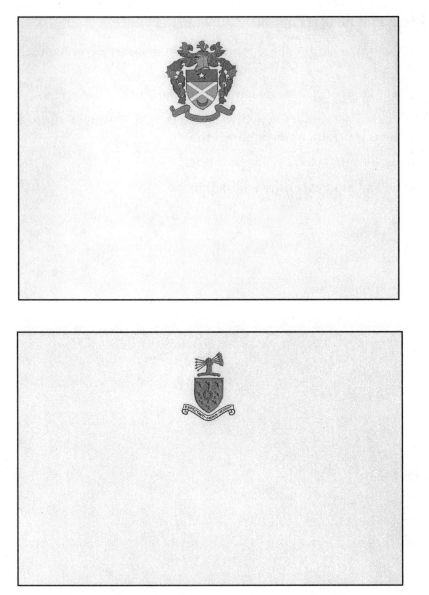

Sample stationery with family crests.

As you consider the style, color, and types of stationery to equip yourself with, it is wise to remember the factors that transcend all of these details. The stationery you choose is part of the message you will be sending and should reflect your personality.

The Least You Need to Know

➤ Paper quality is judged by the weight of the paper. The better quality paper has the higher rag content.

➤ Most people need three kinds of stationery: formal, personal business stationery, and personal notepaper.

➤ Informal writing paper is generally white or off-white.

➤ Calling cards are often used these days as gift enclosures.

➤ Engraving is the finest and most expensive type of printing.

Invitations and Addressing

We are all sensitive about how we are addressed and how people refer to us in writing. And, while many of us might be entrenched in the technological age, we are living in a multi-cultural, multi-generational global village. Within this "village," there are many who retain a reverence for the written word and a concern for addressing people correctly.

Even though we live in an age of e-mail and faxes, there will always be formal occasions that require formal correspondence and invitations that must be addressed properly.

Invitations

People are almost always pleased to receive an invitation, and there is a special pleasure in receiving an invitation properly composed and presented.

Replying

Examples of formal invitations are provided later in this chapter. First, let's have a look at some suggestions that will help you through the entire invitation scene.

Tip

Directions should be printed on a similar stock as the invitation and also in its style. If you enclose a map, keep it as uncluttered and clear as possible. Sometimes, too much information only causes confusion.

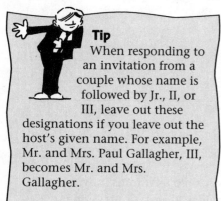

Tip

When responding to an invitation from a couple whose name is followed by Jr., II, or III, leave out these designations if you leave out the host's given name. For example, Mr. and Mrs. Paul Gallagher, III, becomes Mr. and Mrs. Gallagher.

My mother would rather be bitten by a rattlesnake than include a reply card in an invitation, but that's another generation. These days, the RSVP card is a fixture in most social situations. It evolved because so many people stopped replying formally and in writing to invitations.

The practical host must decide whether or not to use the reply cards, and either decision is acceptable. However, experience shows that it is far less stressful to use them than to mount a telephone campaign before the event to find out how many people are coming.

Reply cards follow the same style as the invitation and are made of the same stock. If you do not enclose a reply card with your invitation and you need to know who's coming, be sure to mark the invitation RSVP and provide an address or a telephone number.

When responding to a formal invitation that does not contain a reply card, follow the same general form as the invitation. Write by hand and in the third person. Use conservative stationery or engraved personal stationery. You can use a personal letter sheet, a half sheet, or an informal. Couples responding should use a Mr. and Mrs. informal.

Regrets

Briefly state the reason for the refusal in your reply. Two standard reasons to refuse an invitation are, "…due to a previous engagement," and "…because of absence from town."

Don't give "illness" as the reason, because that is a signal to the hosts to make some response concerning the illness (alleged or otherwise).

If you know the host, call to explain your regrets. Otherwise, an explanation is not necessary, and "...regrets she is unable to accept..." will suffice.

Informal Invitations

These are appropriately written on personal notepaper or on an informal or correspondence card. Though "informal," they are usually written in the third person but are less structured in form than a truly formal invitation.

There are a number of types of informal invitations. You can send a "fill-in." You can write on informal notepaper or on a folded note with a monogram. On a note with a monogram, start writing on the front if the monogram is placed to one side, or start inside, under the fold if the monogram is in the middle.

When replying, if there is a telephone number listed on the invitation, call to state your reply. If there is no number but an address, respond on your own stationery—either plain, informals, or correspondence cards.

If the invitation says "Regrets Only," it's still a good idea to call the hosts to let them know you are planning to attend. This phrase means only regrets need to respond; that is, if you can attend the function, you need not respond.

An informal fill-in invitation from more than one person.

Lisa and Steven Price
invite you
to *cocktails*
on *Wednesday, May 3rd*
6-8 (or six to eight) o'clock

430 Prince Street

R.s.v.p.
555-4203

An informal fill-in invitation from one person.

> *requests the pleasure of the company of*
>
> *at*
>
> *on*
>
> *at   o'clock*

Formal Invitations

The following are examples of formal invitations—whether they are handwritten or engraved.

Dinner

> *Mr. and Mrs. Harold Smith*
>
> *request the pleasure of your company*
>
> *at dinner*
>
> *on Wednesday the third of May at 8 p.m.*
>
> *1234 Beverly Drive, Toledo, Ohio.*
>
> *RSVP   Black Tie*

If the dinner is honoring a specific person, the phrase is, "...at 8 p.m. to meet Harold Stasson." Some dinner invitations may use the phrase "dinner and dancing."

Formal dance

> *Mr. and Mrs. Harold Smith*
>
> *request the pleasure of*
>
> *Mr. and Mrs. Jones' company*
>
> *at a small dance*
>
> *on Saturday, the first of May at ten o'clock*
>
> *at the Ashmead Beach Club.*
>
> *RSVP*   *Black Tie*
>
> *1234 Beverly Drive*
>
> *Toledo, Ohio 54321*

If a single person is to bring an escort, add "and guest."

An official luncheon

> Mr. and Mrs. Harold Smith
>
> request the pleasure of your company
>
> at a luncheon in honor of
>
> the Honorable Edward Rendell,
>
> the Mayor of the City of Philadelphia,
>
> Sunday, May 2, at 1 o'clock
>
> at the Four Seasons Hotel
>
> Logan Square, Philadelphia.
>
> RSVP
>
> Office of the City Representative
>
> City Hall
>
> Philadelphia, Pennsylvania

RSVP invitations require an immediate reply.

Accepting a formal invitation

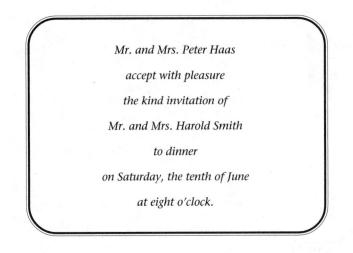

> Mr. and Mrs. Peter Haas
>
> accept with pleasure
>
> the kind invitation of
>
> Mr. and Mrs. Harold Smith
>
> to dinner
>
> on Saturday, the tenth of June
>
> at eight o'clock.

These days, it is acceptable to reply by telephone. However, meeting your host on the street or at the office and saying you will attend does not constitute a formal acceptance. You must still write or call.

If one-half of a couple is accepting, write

> Peter Haas
>
> accepts with pleasure
>
> the kind invitation of
>
> Mr. and Mrs. Harold Smith
>
> for Saturday, the tenth of June
>
> at eight o'clock.
>
> Mrs. Peter Haas regrets
>
> that she will be unable to accept
>
> because of absence from the city.

Regrets

> *Mr. Paul Gallagher*
>
> *sincerely regrets*
>
> *that because of a previous engagement*
>
> *he will be unable to accept*
>
> *Mr. and Mrs. Smith's*
>
> *kind invitation for the tenth of June.*

Addressing People

Before dealing with addressing envelopes, let's talk about addressing people. The name game can be confusing—who's a Ms., how to hyphenate, Misses and Messrs., and so forth.

Remember that this information about forms of address and titles is merely what has been the custom and what has been accepted by most people. These titles and forms of address, however, are no more "correct" than any you may decide upon for yourself.

You can use this information as a starting point, but you will ultimately make up your own mind about what titles and forms of address are most appropriate for you and for those you are corresponding with.

Women

"Ms." is the correct form of address in the business arena, and it is widely accepted in the social arenas as well. Its use, however, is sometimes confused. A divorced woman who goes by her married name would use Ms. because "Miss" is reserved for a woman who has never married. Thus, when Mary Mitchell marries Dan Fleischmann, she becomes Ms. Mary Mitchell (which is fine if she is single, as well) or Mrs. Daniel Fleischmann. She does not use Mrs. Mary Fleischmann.

Other rules for addressing women include:

➤ Married: A married woman who keeps her maiden name may be known professionally as, for example, Mary Mitchell and socially as Mrs. Daniel Fleischmann. When a married woman chooses to hyphenate her name, a practice that appears to be waning in popularity, the maiden name comes before the hyphen and the married name after.

➤ Widows: A woman using her husband's name does not change her name when her husband dies.

➤ Divorced: When a woman chooses not to drop her married name entirely, she uses her given name in place of her former husband's given name. If she is known professionally by her former husband's name, she can continue to use it, even if she remarries. When a woman resumes her maiden name, she becomes Ms. Mary Mitchell, dropping her former "Mrs." and never using "Miss," which denotes a woman who has never been married.

➤ Separated women: A woman who is legally separated continues to use her husband's name—given and surname—until she is divorced. It is fine, however, for a separated woman to use her given name if she chooses.

➤ Single mothers: Using "Ms." makes more sense than using "Miss," (although it is technically correct) or "Mrs.," which designates someone who is legally married. "Ms." can refer to either married or single women.

Men

A man is Jr. if his name is identical to his father's. If you spell out the junior, use a small j. If a woman marries a junior, her married name includes the Jr. If a junior gives his son the same name, the son becomes III or 3d. A comma is used between the name and the Jr. or Sr. but not between the name and a Roman numeral.

When a junior's father dies, he drops the junior. If the surviving son's mother lives in the same city, she may add Sr. to her name to avoid confusion with her daughter-in-law.

A man named after a family member other than his father—say, an uncle or grandfather—uses II or 2d, which is dropped when the family member dies. Men with III or IV usually keep it until death.

Signing

A married woman should sign legal documents and checks with her given name plus her married name—Mary Fleischmann. If she has a common name such as Jane Smith, she might want to distinguish her signature by using her maiden name as well. A single Jane Smith might want to use a middle initial.

When writing to a person you know very well, sign using your first name only. Never give yourself a title when signing your name. Thus, if writing to someone not on a first-name basis, write "Mrs. Daniel Fleischmann" in parentheses under the "Mary Fleischmann" signature. If the stationery has "Mrs. Daniel Fleischmann " printed at the top, simply sign "Mary Fleischmann" at the bottom.

A single woman may write in parentheses (Miss) or (Ms.) to the left of her name. A professional woman who uses her husband's name socially and professionally wants to make it clear that she is married. She signs business letters with (Mrs. John) Alana Kelty. In social correspondence, she proceeds as described in the previous paragraph.

Ambiguous Names

If your name can be either male or female, help the recipient to know your gender. It makes sense to include a title on your printed or engraved stationery, even though the rules dictate otherwise. Help the reader by including (Ms., Miss, Mrs., or Mr.) to the left of your signature. You can also write your full name, including title and address, at the top right of the notepaper or on the left corner of the envelope.

Joint Signatures

Only one person can write a letter, so only one person can sign one. If one half of a couple is writing to a mutual friend, relative, or acquaintance, he can say at the end: "Helen joins me in wishing you the best in your new job."

It is perfectly fine, however, for one half of a couple to sign both names on a postcard, greeting card, and so forth.

Addressing Envelopes

Here are some dos and don'ts on addressing envelopes:

➤ Type or write by hand all social envelopes. It's okay to hand-address an envelope when the letter is typed. Neatness counts, however.

➤ Keep the lines aligned on the left, or indent each line slightly more than the previous one. City, state, and ZIP are on a single line.

➤ It is no longer necessary to write out the names of states in full. And the practice of writing numbers out in full in the most formal situations has virtually disappeared. People use numerals rather than risk trying the patience of the postal service.

➤ Middle names are not always written out on formal envelopes. For example, if Michael Jack Schmidt uses Michael J. Schmidt, follow his lead.

➤ It is acceptable to write return addresses on the envelope flap, but it is more convenient all around, particularly for the postal service, if the return address is on the front of the envelope.

Here's how to address an envelope to a married couple when the wife uses her maiden name:

> Ms. Margaret Ferguson
>
> and Mr. Horace Fitzhugh

Yes, the woman's name goes first. Writing out the "and" indicates they are married. The exception is when the husband has a professional title, in which case his name goes first:

> The Reverend Horace Fitzhugh
>
> and Ms. Margaret Ferguson

Now, if Margaret only uses her maiden name professionally, the address would be "Mr. and Mrs. Horace Fitzhugh" or "The Reverend and Mrs. Horace Fitzhugh."

If Horace is deceased, do not address the envelope to Mrs. Margaret Fitzhugh because that would indicate she is divorced. Widows keep their husband's first and last names. If Margaret's son is a Jr., she may add Sr. to her name to avoid confusion.

If Margaret is divorced, address it to Mrs. Margaret Fitzhugh, unless she has resumed her maiden name.

Tip
When writing, "Mr.," "Ms.," and "Dr." are the only titles that are abbreviated. All others are spelled out.

Then it's Ms. (not Miss) Margaret Ferguson. A separated woman may continue to use her husband's name until they are divorced. Don't address letters to a single mother with "Miss." It is inaccurate and may cause embarrassment.

Doctors

When both halves of a couple are medical doctors, the envelope can be addressed:

> The Doctors Peterson

or

> Doctor (Dr.) Judith Peterson
> and Doctor (Dr.) Michael Peterson

or

> Doctors Judith and Michael Peterson

If Judith goes by her maiden name, it's:

> Dr. Judith Holmes and Dr. Michael Peterson

If only the husband is a doctor:

> Dr. and Mrs. Michael Peterson

or

> Dr. Michael Peterson and Ms. Judith Holmes

The name with the title goes first. So, if Judith is the doctor:

> Dr. Judith Holmes and Mr. Michael Peterson

Unmarried Couples

Address the envelope to a couple living together but not married with each name on a separate line, flush left, alphabetically, with no "and" in between to indicate marriage. This is also the way to address envelopes to gay couples living together.

Children and Teens

Girls are "Miss" from birth until 21, when they may wish to be become "Ms." However, girls' envelopes are generally addressed by name only until they become teenagers, when "Miss" is used more often.

Boys are correctly (but not necessarily) addressed as "Master" until age eight, when that is dropped in favor of the given name and no title. He becomes "Mr." at age 18. There is a comma between the name and Jr. or Sr. but not between the name and II or III.

Messrs.

Abbreviated from the French for Misters (Messieurs), Messrs. applies only to brothers, not other male family members like uncles or fathers. If the envelope is going to all of the brothers in the family, it is addressed to The Messrs. Smith. If it is going to two of the three brothers in the family, for example, it is addressed to The Messrs. Lawrence and David Smith. The same rule applies to Misses.

Esquire

Originally, Esquire was the title applied to a knight's eldest son or to the younger male members of a noble house whose hereditary title was borne only by the eldest male heir.

The title is seldom used today and only if the person being addressed is a lawyer, male or female. It follows the person's name and is usually abbreviated as Esq. It can also be written out in full in the address. Do not use a prefix (Mr., Mrs., and so forth) when Esq. is being used after the name. When writing to a lawyer and spouse, drop the Esq., and address it simply to Mr. and Mrs. John Smith.

Officially Addressing

Below are the proper forms for addressing various officials. The honorifics, Mrs. or Ms., may be substituted for Mr. where appropriate. If the official is a woman, give the husband's full name, "Elizabeth Smith and Mr. Harold Smith." If the wife of the official uses her maiden name, use that instead of "Mrs. Smith."

Personage	Official Address	Social Address
The President of the United States	The President The White House 1600 Pennsylvania Ave. Washington, D.C. 20500	The President and Mrs. Smith The White House 1600 Pennsylvania Ave. Washington, D.C. 20500
Former President of the United States	The Honorable Gilbert Scott Office address	The Honorable Gilbert Scott and Mrs. Scott Home address
Vice President of the United States	The Vice President Executive Office Building Washington, D.C., 20501	The Vice President and Mrs. Smith The Vice President's House Washington, D.C. 20501
The Chief Justice of the Supreme Court	The Chief Justice The Supreme Court One First Street, N.E. Washington, D.C. 20543	The Chief Justice and Mrs. Smith Home Address
Associate Justice	Mr. Justice Smith The Supreme Court One First Street, N.E. Washington, D.C. 20543	Mr. Justice Smith and Mrs. Smith Home Address
Cabinet Member	The Honorable Joseph Smith Secretary of the Interior Department of the Interior Washington, D.C. 20240	The Honorable Secretary of the Interior and Mrs. Smith Home Address
U.S. Senator	The Honorable Mary Smith U.S. Senate Senate Office Building Washington, D.C. 20510	The Honorable Mary Smith and Mr. Harold Smith Home Address

Personage	Official Address	Social Address
U.S. Representative	The Honorable Harold Smith House of Representatives Washington, D.C. 20515	The Honorable Harold Smith and Mrs. Smith Home Address
American Ambassador*	The Honorable Harold Smith The American Ambassador American Embassy 2 Avenue Gabriel 75382 Paris, France	The Honorable The Ambassador of the United States of America and Mrs. Smith 2 Avenue Gabriel 75382 Paris, France
Foreign Ambassador	His Excellency Ricardo Smith The Ambassador of Brazil Embassy of Brazil 3006 Massachusetts Avenue Washington, D.C. 20008	His Excellency The Ambassador of Brazil and Mrs. Smith Home Address
Governor	The Honorable Harold Smith Governor of Connecticut State Capitol Hartford, CT 06115	The Governor and Mrs. Smith Home Address
Mayor	The Honorable Edward Rendell Mayor of Philadelphia City Hall Philadelphia, PA 19101	The Honorable Edward Rendell and Mrs. Rendell Home address

* When addressing or referring to the American Ambassador to a Latin American country, call him the Ambassador of the United States of America. Latins consider South and Central America to be "America" too.

Judges are addressed as "The Honorable."

The Pope of the Roman Catholic Church is addressed as "His Holiness, the Pope" or "His Holiness, Pope John Paul II, Vatican City, 00187 Rome, Italy."

Cardinals are addressed as "His Eminence, John Cardinal Krol, Archbishop of Philadelphia."

Bishops and archbishops are addressed as "The Most Reverend Thomas Jones, Bishop of Dallas."

Monsignors are addressed as "The Right Reverend." Priests are addressed as "The Reverend Father." Nuns are addressed as "Sister Mary Catharine," and Brothers as "Brother Thomas Mann."

Protestant clergy are addressed as "The Reverend Thomas Jones," with the letters "D.D." after the name if they have a Doctor of Divinity degree.

Episcopal bishops are addressed as "The Right Reverend." The words "The Venerable" precede the name of Archdeacons.

A Jewish rabbi is addressed as "Rabbi Thomas Jones," with degree initials following the name. Cantor is addressed as "Cantor Thomas Jones."

The Patriarch of the Eastern Orthodox religion is addressed as "His Holiness, the Ecumenical Patriarch of Constantinople, Istanbul, Turkey." In this religion Archbishops are "The Most Reverend," Bishops are "The Right Reverend," and Priests are "The Very Reverend."

The rules and customs for addressing people and for extending and acknowledging invitations are not new. They have evolved over many generations and have come into existence for very good reasons. All of us care about how we are addressed, and part of having good manners is caring enough to address others properly.

The Least You Need to Know

➤ If you do not enclose a reply card with your invitation and you need to know who's coming, be sure to mark the invitation RSVP and provide an address or a telephone number.

➤ Reply to invitations promptly. If you are sending regrets, briefly state the reason, but do not cite illness because the host would feel obligated to inquire about your condition, taking up her valuable time before the function.

➤ Replies should have the same form and structure as the invitation.

➤ If a title is in the address, it should also be in the salutation, as in "Dear Dr. Smith." Never give yourself a title when signing correspondence, such as "Miss Abigail Dunwoody."

Part 4
Home Etiquette

Teaching children about etiquette is an important way of getting them ready for the world. Free expression and unbridled responses may be cute around the house, but will be received with considerably less tolerance elsewhere.

Children learn the first and most important lessons in etiquette at home. Not only must they learn these lessons from scratch, they face questions about courtesy and behavior that adults do not. For one thing, the rules are different for dealing with adults and dealing with peers. They need guidelines for dealing with parties, school, playmates, and later, dances, dating, and dressing.

Also in this section, we will look at the problems of home entertaining, particularly staging the successful dinner party.

Chapter 12

Manners Begin At Home—The Fundamental First Steps

In This Chapter

➤ The basics

➤ Adults—ugh!

➤ Handling sticky situations

➤ Table manners

➤ How to answer the most frequently asked questions

➤ Children and correspondence

Why do I have to learn this etiquette stuff?

Because I say so.

This time-honored bit of logical persuasion, like its colleague, "siddown and shut up," may end an argument, but does not create a wonderful learning environment. "When I was your age..." is not much better. (These tactics also weaken your position when you tell youngsters that the best way to make their point is to not yell or interrupt or make faces, but to listen to what the other person has to say before stating your ideas or point of view.)

The unspoken but mutually agreed upon code of conduct that is the glue of a civil society is so much a part of our daily adult experience that we may have forgotten the fact that we had to learn it, that children have to learn it, and that we have to teach them.

No matter how cute their capers around the house might seem when they are very young, there will come a time—sooner than you may expect—when others will judge children harshly and, possibly, criticize them sternly for the sort of behavior parents may be inclined to overlook or dismiss as high spirits or "growing pains."

Thus, etiquette training begins at a very early age. We are teaching as we interact with children around the dinner table or in the playground. While we teach the rules, we also teach the reasons behind the rules—we are teaching respect for others.

When you begin to teach children about the idea of manners and the rules of etiquette, you can expect to be challenged. The challenge will almost certainly take the form of questions, and you had better be armed with some answers.

The Most Basic Rules and Why

One of the most asked questions about etiquette is: "Why do we have these rules, and what wise guy made them up?"

You can respond to this question by telling a story:

About 11,000 years ago, humans made a big change in the way they lived. They found they did not have to continually roam through the forest hunting animals and gathering nuts and berries to eat. Instead, they learned about planting seeds and domesticating animals. They discovered that they could live in one place, and survival was not such a desperate daily struggle. There was more food, more leisure time, more security.

Tip
Here are some easy ways to let people know that you have good manners:

➤ Say "please," "thank you," "you're welcome," and "excuse me."

➤ Look people in the eye when you speak to them.

➤ When you are introduced, stand up and say, "Nice to meet you," or "Hello," or "How do you do?"

Soon after, they began to develop ways of getting along with each other with as little fighting, anger and confusion as possible. They even began to eat together at the communal table, and you can imagine what this would have been like without rules.

During the 11,000 years between then and now, the rules changed and evolved as ways of living changed. But the reasons for these rules are as valid now as they were at the beginning.

Young people like things summarized. So, you can tell them that, after all of these uncounted generations during which the rules of behavior have evolved, there are a couple of basic guidelines that have held up through the centuries, a dual bedrock of good manners:

➤ Be kind.

➤ Treat people with respect.

The second most asked question is: "What's in it for me?"

You can answer this question by telling your child one reason we learn the rules of etiquette: knowing them gives us confidence. If you know how to behave wherever you are, you will be more at ease, and you will be able to put those around you at ease. People will get the message that you are one together person.

Another reason to know the rules of etiquette is that people will treat you with respect if you treat them with respect.

Speaking of Respect...

Remember that you are not dealing with a lower life form here. Children possess a basic, uncluttered wisdom. We cheat them by failing to share our losses and insecurities, our joys and triumphs. When you discover a commonality with your child, try saying something like, "I know. I feel the same way when…"

Children's questions may be blunt and basic, but often, they want to know the same things as adults. For example, a child may say: "Suppose I don't know anybody at the party. Who do I sit with? What do I talk about?"

Whereas, adults may say: "Do you have any hints on how to work a room?"

Keep this point in mind the next time your child asks you a question.

Alien Nations—Relations With Adults

Kids and adults sometimes think of each other as alien species. This is tougher on kids than adults because adults are bigger and know more. Both, however, tend to be a little uncomfortable with each other when they meet for the first time. Adults may deal with this by saying dumb things like "Last time I saw you, you were wearing diapers." Children sometimes deal with it by sulking or being silent or trying to be invisible.

This awkwardness is generally called shyness, and almost all children are afflicted with it to some degree. You can help by passing along some of the tips below. However, your child or any young person will be on their way to overcoming the curse of shyness if you can get these two basic ideals across to them:

1. Everybody, regardless of age, is shy to some degree around new people or in unfamiliar surroundings.

2. Stop worrying about yourself, and focus on the other people.

Here are my own helpful tips and tricks for young people:

➤ *Meeting Someone New.* When young people meet someone new, they should:

Stand up.

Shake hands. In the Western world, this is an almost universal gesture of goodwill.

Smile.

Look the other person in the eye, and say hello. Use Mr., Miss, or Mrs. When in doubt, use Ms. (pronounced "mizz").

➤ *Breaking the Ice.* Teach your child to use the following to easily open up a conversation with someone:

Do you live in the neighborhood?

Do you have children?

How did you meet my parents?

➤ *Conversation Tidbits.* Young people need to know some of the conversational tricks we all use without thinking. Let them know some of the basics:

People like to talk about themselves.

People don't mind questions, as long as the questions are not too personal ("How much money do you make?") or downright rude ("Why do you wear that ugly dress?").

There are lots of personal questions that are okay to ask: "Do you have any children?" "Do you live around here?" "Did I see you out running in the park the other day?"

Tip
If your child asks what is the worst "bad manners" thing a person can do, the answer is "to hurt someone's feelings."

➤ *Other Tricks.* Teach your youngster to become aware of the details that can spark a conversation. Remember that the idea behind all of this is not necessarily just to get your child to talk but to also get the other person talking.

If you notice skis or roller blades lying around, for example, ask about these sports. If you just finished reading a book, ask the other person if he too has read it. Talk about the latest flick you've seen or one you'd both like to see.

Listen carefully to the other person, and don't interrupt while she's speaking, unless something important has come up that she should know. Then say, "excuse me."

The truth is that when people say so-and-so is a good conversationalist, they really mean the person is a good listener.

Handling Sticky Situations

Remember how much you hated it when Aunt Myrtle kissed you? It doesn't hurt to let your child know that you hated it too, but that you put up with it. Tell your youngster that the best strategy in handling this situation is simply trying to avoid it by sticking out your hand to shake. If that doesn't work, turn your head a little at the last moment so that the kiss becomes a brush on the cheek. This is also a way of communicating the fact that you don't like being kissed. But, no matter what, relatives are going to kiss kids, and it is uncool to refuse or to squirm around like an angry eel.

Also, it's okay for your child to tell you that Aunt Myrtle's gift is silly or ugly, but Aunt Myrtle must never know. Your response is that not everyone shares the same tastes and that the important thing is that Aunt Myrtle likes you and respects you enough to give you a gift. Explain to your child that he should, at the least, say "thank you" and "it was really nice of you to think of me." If pressed, the child can say, "Of course I like it. You gave it to me."

On the subject of gifts, keep in mind that youngsters are often discriminated against in stores. Teach them to speak up for themselves in the right way. If they can see that they are being passed over in favor of adults, it is okay for them to politely say, "Excuse me, I think I'm next in line." If they are being ignored when there are no other customers, they can say: "Could you please help me?" Teach your child to ask for assistance, rather than trying to get someone's attention by coughing, for example.

If your child asks you if it is okay to ask an adult to stop smoking, say, "It depends." One *can't* ask someone to stop smoking in someone's home or in other private places where smoking is permitted. Tip-off: if there are ashtrays around, it means that smoking is expected and permitted. One *can* ask someone not to smoke in public places where smoking is prohibited, but must do it correctly.

Here again, coughing is not an adequate way to let people know that smoke bothers you. Tell your child to say, "Would you please stop smoking?" but don't make a challenge or an accusation out of it. A good strategy is to tell the child to imagine they are saying something like, "It's raining outside." and say, "Would you please stop smoking?" with the same facial and vocal expression.

First Names and Introductions

First names is an area that most kids goof up. Tell young people that it is rude, even for adults, to call people by their first name when they don't know them. Upon meeting, a youngster calls an adult "Mr.," "Mrs.," or "Ms." until the adult asks to be called by his or her first name. Sometimes this happens right away, sometimes it takes a while, and sometimes it never happens.

When your child decides to introduce you to one of her friends or finally decides that it's okay for you to meet her teacher, tell her the cardinal rule about introducing people: the star of the show gets top billing. In other words, mention the most important person first: "Mom, this is my friend, Marjorie Matthews."

Use honorifics—"Dr.," "Captain," "Mr.," "Mrs.," "Ms.," and so forth: "Doctor Cooper, I'd like to introduce you to my father, Mr. Carter."

When introducing a teacher to a parent, the teacher's name is used first: "Mrs. Bornson, I'd like you to meet my mother, Mrs. Eastwood."

Tip
The *most* important thing about introductions is to actually make them. Even if you get the protocol all wrong, it's a whole lot better than just standing there.

It helps to provide a little information about the people you are introducing so that they will have something to talk about: "Mom, this is my friend Frank Hales. We're in the glee club together."

In introducing dignitaries—congressmen, clergy, elected or appointed officials, etc.—they are mentioned first, to show respect for the offices these people hold. It does not mean that, as people, they are better or more important than anyone else.

Table Manners

When your child has that first job interview over lunch or has dinner for the first time with the parents of a romantic interest, both of you will be glad that good table manners were a matter of routine at your house.

That doesn't mean that every meal has to be a lesson or that eating has to be a chore interrupted by frequent admonitions. Children learn best through immersion and osmosis. In other words, if you have good table manners, it goes a long way toward assuring that your children will also.

The good news is that we are not talking about astrophysics here. Good dining etiquette requires only a simple awareness of the basics. Here's a list of the most common mistakes that your child should be made aware of:

1. *Cutlery*: The worst mistake is *not* using the wrong implement, but using it incorrectly—holding the fork in your fist like a cello or holding the knife like a dagger. In addition, once you use a piece of cutlery, it never goes back on the table. It is placed fully on the plate and not "tipped" like the oars of a rowboat with the handles resting on the table and the tips on the rim of the plate. The knife blade faces in, touching the inside of the plate; only the handle touches the rim of the plate. Never wave cutlery around to make a point.

2. *Napkins*: Never tuck. Place the napkin on your lap. Don't flap it to open it. If you leave the table, leave the napkin on your chair, making sure the soiled part doesn't mar the upholstery, and push the chair under the table.

3. *Posture*: Food doesn't go down as well and you don't look attractive when you slump. Sit up straight. You will actually be more comfortable. Keep your elbows off the table. If you don't know what to do with your hands, put them in your lap.

4. *Chewing*: Chew with your mouth closed, and don't talk with food in your mouth. Also, don't eat too fast. It's bad manners and bad for digestion. Try to adjust your eating pace with others' at the table: begin and finish about the same time as everyone else.

5. *The Table*: Keep keys, purses, gloves, and hats off the table. Nothing goes on the table unless it is part of the meal. Think of the germs they might spread and how unattractive it looks.

6. *Breaking Bread*: Do not butter the whole roll or the whole piece of bread and cut it with a knife. Break bread or a roll into bite-sized pieces, and butter each piece before eating it.

Did You Know?

The custom of breaking bread is a throwback to times when uneaten food was distributed to the poor. A person never broke off more from the communal loaf than he or she wanted to eat.

Frequently Asked Questions

Whenever I talk with children about table manners, they are full of questions. Some are delightful, some are difficult, and all are unfailingly interesting. Here are some of the most common questions:

➤ What do I say if I burp?

Say "Excuse me" to no one in particular and go on eating. Don't make a big deal out of it.

➤ Why do I have to act differently when people come to dinner?

From the beginning of time, guests in one's home have been given a place of honor and other special treatment. We are on our best behavior so guests feel comfortable, special, and welcome.

➤ What do you do if somebody at the table is a sloppy eater?

The real question here is, when is it our place to tell somebody he is being rude? You can tactfully tell a good friend, out of the earshot of others, especially if you make light of it, but you can never tell a stranger. If you happen to be seated next to a slob, chalk it up to experience, and set a good example yourself.

➤ Which place setting pieces are yours?

Your bread plate is always on your left, and your drink is always on your right. A good way to remember this rule is to remember that the word drink starts with the letters "DR"—for "drinks right."

➤ What about finger foods?

When it comes to fingers, use your head.

Certainly, you eat things like ribs and tacos and corn on the cob—no matter what company you are in—with your fingers. For most foods, you will use cutlery. There are however, situations in which doubts may arise.

In the Middle East and parts of Africa, for example, people still eat properly with their hands. The food of those cultures is designed to be eaten that way. So, the best rule is: "When in Rome, do as the Romans do." Adjust to the standards and customs of the culture you are in. It might even be acceptable to eat with your feet, but only if you are dining with a family of baboons.

➤ Should I help to clean up?

Offer. Whether you are at a dinner party or a picnic, the offer is the important thing. Sometimes the host will not want you to help. If so, don't insist.

➤ What if I don't like what is being served?

If eating at someone else's house or with guests in your house, do not reject food outright.

Eat some of everything that is served. If you don't like a certain food, eat some, and move the rest around on your plate as if you were eating it. This is a skill that will serve you well through the years.

➤ What if you can't finish your food?

In restaurants, where you can't control the portions, there's no problem. Either leave the food, or ask for a doggie bag. At someone's home, never take more than you know you can eat, and make sure there is plenty left for the others. If someone is serving you, you can always say, "Just a little, please."

➤ Should I bring a gift when I'm invited to dinner?

Yes. Something simple and small. Plants are nice because they remind people of the giver as they grow. Lovely paper napkins, small books, candy, and fine nuts are also good ideas. If you bring brownies or cookies, give them in a sealed tin, and say something like, "I thought you might like these for the weekend." Cut flowers sound like a good idea, but they require the host to take time out to find a vase and arrange them.

Did You Know?
When forks first appeared in Italy about 900 years ago, they were not widely accepted. People at that time still preferred to use their fingers and a knife. Forks became widely popular only about 200 years ago, but not all cultures embraced the new-fangled invention.

Tip

Here are a few helpful hints to pass on to your youngster:

➤ Conversation makes a meal more enjoyable. Join in.

➤ Don't begin to eat until everyone is seated and has been served.

➤ If you drop something during a meal at home, pick it up. At a friend's house, leave it until the meal is over, then pick it up. At a restaurant, ask the server to replace it if you wish.

➤ If you have to blow your nose, scratch, etc., excuse yourself and leave the table.

➤ The trick to eating spaghetti is to swirl a *little* on your fork into a bite-sized portion with no dangling ends to drip or flick sauce.

Children and Correspondence

Children who write notes and letters give a great deal of pleasure and have a better chance of experiencing the pleasure of receiving correspondence in return. More importantly, they grow up imbued with the knowledge of the power and pleasures of personal correspondence.

It is never too early to begin giving your children a respect for the written word and the ceremonies surrounding it. Even before children are old enough to write, they will be aware that this is something people do. "I'm writing to Aunt Nora to thank her…"

Thank You Letters

This is probably the first kind of correspondence your child will send. Make the experience as comfortable as possible. There is no need for a thank you note from a seven-year-old to be spelled and punctuated perfectly. It is all right for a note from a child to look like a note from a child. Praise any effort a child makes to correspond.

But the basic rules apply even to the very young. The note needs a salutation. Mention the specific gift or favor. Sign with "love" or other appropriate sentiment.

Later on, thank you notes can include an acknowledgment of the effort behind the gift: "You must have spent the whole day baking these cookies." You can also let the giver know how the gift will be used: "These cookies will be a big hit at my sleepover party tomorrow."

And yes, a child must send thank you notes for Christmas gifts unless the giver is present—and is properly thanked—when the gift is opened.

Don't teach your children to use pre-printed thank you notes. They are a cop-out.

Apology Letters

Let's pretend that your child knocked a baseball through a neighbor's window. Even if the child apologized on the scene, a note of apology is called for. It should:

➤ Be prompt

➤ Acknowledge fault and apologize

➤ Offer to make amends

It should also be written in ink and signed, "Sincerely." The envelope should have the sender's name and address in the upper left, and the addressee's name should be preceded by an honorific, such as Mr., Mrs., Ms., Dr. (These, by the way, are the only honorifics that are abbreviated.) The letter will look something like this:

Dear Mr. Smith:

Please accept my apology for breaking your window the other day. It was careless of me, and I feel bad about it. I know all the trouble it has caused you. If you would like, I will repair the window myself. If you have made other arrangements, please send me the bill so that I can pay for the damage.

Sincerely,

Tommy Jones

Condolence Letters

A parent of your child's close friend has died. Even if your child has attended the funeral, sent flowers, visited, or telephoned, a condolence letter is a must. A "sympathy card" will not do. Remember that condolence letters are comforting and diverting for those who have suffered a loss. Sometimes they become part of the family history to be passed down through the generations.

The letter should be written in ink with a fountain pen if possible. Try to use black ink. If the child's handwriting is hard to read, it is all right to have the letter typed and signed in ink.

This should not be a formal, formula letter, but written from the heart. Your child can begin by acknowledging his friend's loss and saying that he feels sad about it. The condolence letter is the place to recall the special characteristics of the deceased, visits to your home, lessons learned from that person, good times shared. Such reminiscences celebrate the life of the deceased rather than being morbid and depressing about the loss.

Above all, don't spend all your time saying how upset you are. The person who receives it might think *you* wish to be getting the condolence letter.

Love Letters

Watch out. You never know who will end up reading love letters. Keep them newsy on the surface. Your feelings will come through in the style and tone of your letter.

A good rule of thumb is that the best love letters are written in the sand.

RSVPs

Translation: Respond if you please. And, please, respond promptly.

A telephone number on the invitation absolves you from writing. So does "regrets only." However, if you were planning a party, wouldn't you like to get a note saying your guest is pleased to be invited and looks forward to coming?

If you can't attend, let the host know the reason you can't be there. If you accept, do your best to honor your commitment.

They don't teach it in school, and "charm school" is something rarely heard of these days. So, basically, it's up to parents to first, convince their children that courtesy is crucial, and second, teach them the rules of courtesy—also called etiquette. If parents don't do it, children can only learn by offending people, and suffering the consequences. We learn by watching the example of others.

The Least You Need to Know

➤ If you want children to be respectful, you must treat them respectfully.

➤ The two basic rules of proper behavior are: Treat people with respect, and be kind.

➤ When first meeting someone new, stand up, smile, shake hands, and say, "Hello," or "How do you do?"

➤ When introducing people, speak the name of the oldest or most important person first.

➤ Children will reject what you tell them if it contradicts what they see you do.

Peer Pressure and Promise

Chapter 13

In This Chapter

➤ School daze: cheating, bullies, teachers

➤ Spats

➤ (Oh no!) Parties

➤ Dating and the new rules

By all standards, children ask more questions about getting along with other children than about any other aspect of human interaction. No matter how straightforward and even trivial the questions may seem to you, remember that, to the youngster, these are worrisome, complicated and urgently important matters.

There are a lot of things children absolutely need to know when dealing with other people their own age, and it's a lot less painful to learn these things from adults than through experience. They need to know that there are rules—etiquette if you will—that will help them to know how to behave in difficult situations:

➤ Parties: What do you wear? What do you say? What do you do?

➤ Dates: Who asks? Who pays? What do you wear? What do you say? What do you do?

Youngsters also have to know that all friends have disagreements, even fights, and that doesn't mean they have to stop being friends. They have to know about how to respond to bullies and kids who cheat in school.

It's a complicated world. Children need all the information they can get.

ABCs of School Etiquette

School comes along at the worst possible time. On top of the normal childhood fears, awkwardness, and other growing pains, children are for the first time meeting authority figures who are not parents and peers who are not siblings.

It's a time when a child should be armed with a code of behavior, an attitude about manners and respect for others. In a word, etiquette.

Unfortunately, etiquette is not included in the curriculum of most schools.

Consider how life would improve for most students if that missing code of conduct were provided early in elementary school in an orderly and systematic fashion, by someone other than parents and via textbook to give the code weight and authority. We have to make up as best we can for this lack.

Tip

If somebody drops her books and papers in the corridor, it is not geeky to stop and help, especially when everybody is hustling to get to the next class. Also, if you are going through a door, and the person behind you is burdened down with books and things, hold the door to let him get through.

Bullies

This is one of the problems kids face at school. Make it clear that they do not have to put up with physical abuse. If this happens, they must tell their parents or teachers, and something must be done about it. (You might want to consider one of those martial arts training programs that are so popular with children. The good ones emphasize self-defense as opposed to aggressive behavior, and they tend to develop self-confidence.)

Let your child know why bullies act the way they do. The main points you want to make are:

➤ Bullies use threats and force to try to control people by making them afraid. It is the only way they have of gaining acceptance or status.

➤ Bullies have no real friends.

➤ No matter what they say or do, their behavior is a reflection of *their* problems, not yours.

➤ Don't try to please or placate the bully or his clique. This is not the kind of group you want to be accepted by. There are certainly others at school who feel the same way, and these are the people you want for friends.

While we're on the subject of bullies, also let your child know that he does not have to share his lunch if he doesn't want to. He should simply say no, and if someone tries to get it from him by threats or force, he should tell both you and his teacher.

Lastly, it is not abusive but instead considered part of the school tradition for lower classmen to be treated somewhat "second class" by upperclassmen, for example, fifth graders being confined to a certain part of the cafeteria. Your child should accept it as cheerfully as possible and wait until she becomes a sixth grader.

Cheating

Your child tells you that somebody in class is copying answers from his test papers, and he doesn't like it. Should he tell the teacher?

The answer is, probably not.

Cheating is wrong, and he should not be a part of it. But shielding his paper should do the trick and may even send a message to the teacher without him saying a word. If that doesn't work, he should get the miscreant alone and say something like: "Look, quit trying to crib from my test papers. You know what you're doing is wrong. Others have noticed it, too."

In the unlikely event that all of this fails, the teacher should be notified.

New School

If your child is about to enter a new school, you can be sure that there will be a certain amount of anxiety about how to behave in the new surroundings. Here are some helpful tips you can pass along:

➤ Pay attention to your classmates instead of feeling uneasy because you don't know them. This way, you will discover which of them shares your interests about school subjects, sports, etc.

➤ Don't be afraid to strike up a conversation: "Hi. I'm Julie Thomas, and I just started at this school. I noticed that you really seem to like math class. So do I. What other things do you like to do?

➤ Get involved. Extra-curricular activities, like sports and clubs, are an excellent way to get involved with the new school. Don't be afraid to volunteer. Many, many stars got to the top by starting out as volunteers.

Relations With Teachers

If her teacher pronounces your child's name wrong, tell her not to make a face. She should *never* correct the teacher in front of the class. She should ask to see the teacher before or after class and say how "our family" pronounces the name.

If your child gets blamed for something unfairly, it doesn't help to argue the issue in front of the class. It embarrasses everybody and only makes matters worse. Instead, discuss the situation with the teacher in private. This could and should result in a public apology in class.

A birthday, Christmas, or end-of-year gift to your child's teacher must not be extravagant, and should be something that everyone in the class can contribute to. It is important that no one in the class be embarrassed about not being able to afford to contribute. Super gifts are plants or CDs or nice chocolates. An even better idea is for the class to make something for the teacher, perhaps a poster with a signed class picture. Wrap it, and don't forget to get a card that everyone can sign.

The (Oh, No!) Party

Do you remember when you were invited to your first party? If you do, you probably remember the turmoil that went with the invite: "What should I wear?" "Suppose I don't know anybody?" "What will I talk about?"

In regard to attire, your child can call the host and ask what he or she will be wearing. Or your child can call the parents of the host and check it out. But the attire problem is not the entire problem.

Whether your youngster wants to admit it or not, this is all about our old friend—shyness. When you talk to your child about it, you might want to call it nervousness. In addressing this subject, I often give a little talk about the Olympics. It goes like this:

> If you have ever watched the Olympics, you have seen athletes push themselves beyond what they thought were their physical limits. If you ask the athletes how they do this, and how they overcome the nervousness they must feel before the competition, they will say, "Preparation." They get ready not only physically, but mentally. They go over what they must do again and again, anticipating difficult patches and challenges, and deciding how they will deal with them. By the time the event begins, they are ready, excited, and confident.

Tell your child to deal with her nervousness about the party in the same way. Or in other words, dope it out in advance.

Also, ask your child what he expects to happen. Will there be dancing? Games? How large a crowd will there be? Tell him to write down the answers.

Now, tell your child to make a second list, a private one, and list the good things about herself. Maybe she really likes her hair or eyes? Maybe he has a great sense of humor that nobody knows about? Maybe she knows a lot about soccer or a certain kind of music?

Next, tell your youngster to make a list of things he can talk about at the party. Magazines, newspapers, the radio, or television are all good sources for ideas. Now tell your child to imagine herself at the party, laughing and talking with others. Imagine seeing somebody who looks nervous and shy, and walking over to that person to start a conversation. One thing your child might say is, "I noticed that you don't seem to know a lot of people here either. My name is…"

Dances

It is perfectly all right for girls to ask boys to dance. If the world waited for boys to do everything, only half would get done. There was a time when custom dictated that boys do the asking, but those days are past, to the benefit of both boys and girls. (Girls also ask boys for dates these days.)

Spats

If your child happens to be human, there will be fights with friends.

Let them know that everybody, even someone as wonderful as yourself, gets into arguments, and they generally feel rotten about it afterwards. Not only are these fights not the end of the world, they are not necessarily the end of a friendship.

And part of feeling rotten is knowing that you said or did something during the fight that you regret. Let your young warrior know that there is absolutely nothing wrong with saying to the co-combatant: "Look, I'm sorry I called you a no-neck dweeb. I didn't mean it." Often, this results in a similar statement from the other person, and fences get mended. The point is that disagreements do not mean disrespect.

But, when making apologies, they have to be careful not to rehash the fight as if it were a movie they saw together. That's how fences get unmended very quickly.

Fights cause problems for non-combatants, as well. Suppose your youngster tells you that two "best friends" have had a fight, and each of them is telling your child about it.

The trick here is to listen without taking sides. The situation also presents an opportunity to act as peacemaker by telling each of the friends separately that the other one is "really bummed out about the fight you two had."

Clueless

There will be times when a youngster (or an adult, for that matter) will be in a group that is discussing something he knows nothing about. Kids sometimes respond by sighing theatrically, rolling their eyes, or yawning. Let them know that this is not only rude, but uncool. The thing to do is to be quiet and listen. See if you can get a handle on what's happening. Ask questions. People love to demonstrate superior knowledge and will be glad to answer. If somebody asks your opinion, just say you don't know enough about the subject to have an opinion.

> **Tip**
>
> Young people have a lot of doubts about how to behave during their first experience as a houseguest. Here are some tips:
>
> ➤ Be yourself. You were invited because they enjoy your company.
>
> ➤ Bring a gift. Nothing big: chocolates, a plant.
>
> ➤ Leave the room you are staying in and the bathroom you use neater than you found them.
>
> ➤ Join in family activities, even if you hate volleyball and find Monopoly tedious.

Behavior Between The Sexes

Proper conduct between the sexes can be puzzling and troublesome even for those of us who have had years of practice. Imagine how difficult it must be for children and teenagers. No area of etiquette is changing faster. What was once considered "polite" might now be considered insulting. What was once common sense might now be irrelevant.

The old rules of chivalry dictated how men and women treated each other for centuries. They called for deference by virtue of gender, age, and social caste. These rules have been supplanted to a great degree by what may be called "corporate etiquette." In the past 30 or 40 years, women and minorities have exerted enormous influence on corporate culture, which is based on deference according to corporate "rank," much like any military system.

As parents of both sexes and from all society groups entered the corporate culture, they absorbed this military-like system of etiquette. Naturally, their children learned far more of these corporate attitudes and manners than of those based on chivalry. Thus, the rules of chivalry have faded, and corporate etiquette has emerged as the dominant force governing modern interpersonal relationships in most parts of America.

Did You Know?
The custom of men walking on the outside (or street side) of women companions began as a way of protecting the ladies' finery from splattering by horses and carriages.

The impact of all of this on relations between the sexes has been dramatic and confusing, particularly for young people. Remnants of the old rules of chivalry remain to haunt and sometimes confuse budding relationships. Young people often look to parents for some road maps through this antic landscape.

When young people ask about rules in the area of relations between the sexes, they are really asking about clues to the mystery. It seems to them that there are two distinct species inhabiting the earth. The opposite sex acts, speaks, and dresses differently, is interested in different things, and relates to his or her same-sex friends differently.

However, there are very clear rules that will help young people deal with the usual and, for them, terribly, terribly important questions and situations that arise between the sexes.

Dates

Whether it is the guy or girl asking someone for a date, the rules are the same: Familiarity. The invitation should not be entirely unexpected. There should be some positive, friendly feelings for each other. Get to know the person on a casual level before proposing a date. If the person declines, listen for verbal clues that will tell you whether you should ask for another date at another time. If you are the one saying no, and you really would go if you could, say you are sorry about the conflict and hope the person will ask you again.

Suppose you are not allowed to date. Tell the truth, and don't be embarrassed. We all have to live by rules we don't like at one time or another. Say: "Thank you for asking, but my parents don't allow me to date yet." Don't make a big deal out of it. Don't act as if your parents are from the wax museum. You might even suggest other ways you can get together—school activities, sports, cultural events, parties.

If you really don't want to go on a date with someone, ever, say something like: "Thanks very much, I have other plans. It was really nice of you to think of me."

You don't have to talk about these other plans. They could involve taking a nap or washing your hair.

When asking someone on a date, ask face-to-face or by telephone. Give plenty of advance notice, at least four days. If the invitation comes late, it could give the impression the person is being asked because somebody else couldn't make it. Also make sure that you're specific when posing the question, to avoid any confusion or misinterpretation.

For example, "Would you like to go to the new Jackie Chan movie with me on Friday night?" is much clearer than, "Wanna go to the movies sometime?" Make it plain that you are asking for a date for a certain place, time, and event. You might also clarify whether you would like to provide transportation or just meet the person there. "Would you like to go to the new Star Trek movie with me on Saturday afternoon? I can meet you outside the theater at 4 p.m."

Decide what kind of date it will be. Remember that the idea is for both of you to have a good time. A staunch football fan might not enjoy an evening at the ballet. First dates should be easy and casual for both people. Don't make it into a big deal that causes nervousness. Keep the cost down so that reciprocating won't be difficult.

Remember that it's up to you to take care of the details. Get to the theater early, and buy the tickets. Usually the person who does the asking does the paying. Don't expect your date to split expenses unless you have worked that out in advance. If you are going to share expenses, which is okay and often done, it's important to be clear about it: "I was hoping we could catch the discount early show and then go to the Pizza Kitchen. It shouldn't cost more than $10 each."

Whatever the arrangement, never go on a date without money. It's wise to make sure you have enough to get home on your own, at the very least.

Finally, if your date is going to pick you up at home, brief your parents in advance. Greet your date at the door. Lead him to your parents, and say, "Mom, Dad, this is David Smith. We got to know each other because we're in the same history class." Allow a few minutes for conversation before you leave. This will put your parents at ease and make you look self-confident. These few minutes could pay off later on. Your parents will feel better about the company you're keeping and be more inclined to condone the relationship.

The Big Question

The questions about dating, parties, and meeting people may eventually give way to the more serious question: "Is this the real thing?"

Of course, you can't give this question a yes or no answer. What you can do when this question arises is talk about the elements that make relationships between people of any age work.

➤ *Honesty*

Can you be truthful with this person? Can you be "yourself?" Do you really like heavy metal music, or are you just listening to it because your partner does? Are you going places and doing things and saying things just to please the other person or because you want to?

➤ *Support*

Do you support and praise each other? Support doesn't mean you have to agree all the time. Players on the same sports team don't always agree on the next move, but once the decision is made, they honor and back it 100 percent.

➤ *Friendship*

Are you the other person's best friend? Do you show that you are listening and trying to understand his or her feelings? Never dismiss the feelings of a friend as silly or unimportant.

➤ *Faithfulness*

Do you stick by each other when disappointments arise? Do you try to see disappointments through the other person's eyes?

➤ *Respect for others*

Do both of you respect important people in each other's life? Maybe you would rather be bitten by a snake than visit your friend's parents, but you go anyway, you are polite, and you don't complain about the visit later, no matter how awful it was.

➤ *Fun*

Do you have fun together? Laugh a lot? Shared laughter is a sign of an easy relationship.

➤ *Giving space*

Are you able to accept the fact that the other person has his or her own life? Everybody needs time on their own. Possessiveness is unnecessary in a healthy relationship.

It's tough enough, what with all the changes going on in their bodies and their heads, with new situations, new people, complex problems, and murky waters. Why make it tougher by telling young people there are no rules, or that rules are meant to be broken? It is a comfort and a steadying beacon for young people to be told that there certainly are rules and guidelines for interpersonal behavior—even if they don't always pay attention to them.

The Least You Need to Know

➤ Many of the old gender-based rules concerning dating, paying, and so on, are passe.

➤ Everybody suffers from some degree of shyness, and everybody can get past it to an acceptable extent.

➤ At school, you don't have to put up with cheats or bullies. The best way to deal with bullies is simply to not play their game.

➤ Relationships that are not based on mutual respect will not work.

Chapter 14

The Ins and Outs of Home Entertaining

In This Chapter

➤ Reasons *not* to entertain

➤ Getting started

➤ The guest list

➤ Invitations

➤ Hired help and caterers

➤ Wine

What a pleasure it is to be invited to someone's home. Parties are the best kind of sharing. They boost your spirits, stimulate your imagination, and make you smile.

These are only a few of the many excellent reasons people *go* to parties. Let's have a look at some of the reasons people dread the very idea of *giving* parties.

Too many people cheat themselves out of the pleasure of bringing people together for good conversation and good food by telling themselves they can't entertain. Fear grips their heart. They will be judged. They will be found wanting. It will be a mess. They can't possibly be ready. It is all too much, too much, too...

"My House Is a Disaster Area!" and Other Party Phobias

You can't possibly give a party until you have added a wing, knocked out a wall, repainted everything and landscaped the yard.

Come on. You know the truth. You are your own best witness. The truth is that when *you* leave a really good party, you leave with the overall impression of having been warmly welcomed by gracious people and of having had a fine, comfortable time. You do not leave a really good party thinking about cracking paint or whether the china matched.

The truth is that everything must be neat and clean. All else can be forgiven. Here are a few more excuses for not giving a party.

"I Don't Have the Stuff!"

Can life as we know it continue without a silver chafing dish?

Sure. There are friends and relatives who can supply some of the necessities, and you can improvise in ways that will actually make the party more fun. Remember the hostess who filled her bathtub with ice and kept wine and beer chilled there? Her inventiveness is now part of entertaining tradition. The possibilities are endless.

And isn't it sort of insulting to believe that your friends will think less of you because your spoons are not monogrammed or your furniture is not brand new or tastefully antique?

> **Tip**
>
> Soft lighting can be flattering and can provide a delicate dusting to what might otherwise be jarring imperfections. Everybody looks better by candlelight. Another trick is to replace your usual light bulbs with 25-watt bulbs or experiment with the soft pink variety. This can make cracking paint disappear, and it can make both people and places look less stressed.
>
> As legendary American humorist James Thurber said, "Seeing is deceiving, it's eating that's believing."

"I Can't Cook!"

No excuse. There are catering firms and even neighborhood restaurants that will supply complete meals already cooked. Or you can have friends bring food. As long as the food is fresh and flavorful and has some eye appeal, it doesn't matter who actually cooked it.

Or, you can discover that preparing food is not as tough as you thought. You will find the experience very satisfying and a boost to your self-esteem. You don't need an extensive repertoire to have some style. One of my friends knows how to make just two entrees. She calls them Fish Forman, after herself, and Chicken Mary Monica, after me. These form the centerpiece of her parties, and she fills in with prepared side dishes and desserts to create different moods and menus.

"I Can't Handle this Alone!"

Sure you can. But, in any case, you can always ask for help. Team up with a friend or two and jointly host the party. Or get one person to serve officially as your co-host. You can divide the labor—one of you watching the "back of the house," to make sure food and drinks flow generously, and the other watching the "front of the house," to keep the conversation flowing and getting the guests interested in one another.

And when assigning party duties, remember that men no longer can get away with the outdated notion that entertaining is for women only.

"People Will Be Bored to Death!"

You can rid yourself of the dread that your party will resemble a low-rent funeral, by being prepared. Make a list of topics to bring up if there's a black hole in the conversation. This probably won't happen, but you will feel better knowing that it never has to. Another tip is to practice your introductions and the tidbits of information you will supply about each person when you introduce them.

> "Jill is a writer, so you may end up in her next book if you're not careful."

> "Tom is a detective, and he has some wonderful stupid-crook stories."

"Something Awful Will Happen!"

Yes. Something is bound to go wrong. But guess what? Guests are forgiving. Glitches can actually enliven the party atmosphere, bring people together, and generate conversation. And apparent disasters morph into amusing anecdotes that become topics of conversations for future parties.

Nobody ever notices if the china doesn't match. And if they do, they don't care. There are bound to be last-minute cancellations and additions. Remember that the only way these things can have a negative impact on your party is if you let your guests know that you are upset.

> **Tip**
>
> When preparing to entertain, remind yourself repeatedly of the following truths:
>
> ➤ You don't have to be the next Julia Child with a house like Martha Stewart to give a successful party.
>
> ➤ Giving a successful party has nothing to do with how much furniture you have or how much money you are able to spend.
>
> ➤ You do not have to impress people with what you have, and you never have to apologize for what you do not have.

Getting Started

The best way to get over your worries about entertaining is to just go ahead and give a party. Think about starting small. Most people are so pleased to be invited to someone's home that the magnitude of the party doesn't matter. One of my most pleasant memories is of my neighbor's annual holiday dessert get-together. Several of the couples from the neighborhood gathered at her house for after-dinner desserts, all purchased from nearby pastry shops and served with so much warmth and grace that we all felt very special. The fire was roaring, the candles were lighted, the coffee and cordials were warming. She was a working mother with more chores than time, but these small, uncomplicated gatherings were always successful.

Guest Lists

A party is only as good as its guests, so consider the chemistry of the group you are putting together when you make out your guest list.

This is an entirely subjective exercise, and every host has a private formula. There are some general rules, however:

DO:

> ➤ Think of the party as an opportunity to bring together people who don't know each other but who will probably enjoy meeting one another.

➤ Think of the party as an opportunity to bring together old friends who never seem to have enough time to visit with one another.

➤ Invite people who will appreciate the invitation and will make an effort to contribute to the success of the party.

DON'T:

➤ Invite just one type of person. A room full of nothing but lawyers or nothing but doctors is almost antithetical to the very idea of a party.

➤ Throw in a person or a couple who don't really fit the group just because you owe them a dinner.

➤ Don't invite known adversaries on the theory that it will make the party livelier. It may make the party livelier than you had hoped.

Everybody has their own little tricks and preferences when it comes to making up a guest list. My personal formula, for example, always includes:

➤ A banker, because they know a little about a lot of industries and can talk about what's going on in the economy.

➤ A journalist, because they ask great questions.

➤ Somebody involved in politics, however tangentially.

➤ A restaurateur, because the entire world is interested in dining out and in food.

➤ Someone in marketing, because they usually have something interesting to say about trends and tastes and what people are buying.

WDYS?

The debate between the Republican real estate broker and the New Age existentialist is heating up, and you are worried that others will start taking sides.

What do you say?

Anything.

If you are giving a party, always be ready with a store of anecdotes or comments about something in the news that will change the subject. If this fails, propose a toast to something or somebody.

The best guests are those who know how to sing for their supper. They know that guests as well as hosts have a responsibility to contribute to the party. They will encourage and add to conversation. They are positive and cheerful. You can depend on them. An interesting person who loves to talk—even if it's about himself—will amuse a handful of people and get others talking as well.

Motives

The host's motivation for the party has a lot to do with the guest list. Motives are many:

➤ To "pay back" for invitations you have received.

➤ To reaffirm friendships.

➤ To show off a new home, painting, furniture, and so on.

➤ To honor someone.

➤ To say "thank you" to people who have helped with a particular project or problem.

➤ To get to know new neighbors or colleagues.

➤ To generate future party invitations for yourself.

I know a woman who travels widely and spends at least two weeks in each destination. She gives a cocktail party the first evening she arrives. The next day, she waits for invitations that will comprise the rest of her visit.

Friends

Don't be afraid to tell friends that you are giving a party that doesn't include them. I was pleased to learn, for example, that I was not invited to a cocktail party given by a scientist friend for his colleagues. There would have been, necessarily, a lot of shop talk exclusive to the group and baffling to me. If shop talk is inevitable, the general rule is to invite only those who can participate and/or enjoy it.

Men and Women

Fortunately, we're beyond the days when only an equal number of men and women were invited to parties. It's too much trouble to try to strike an even balance, and you don't want people to have the feeling that they are "assigned" to someone. Today's career-oriented people are happier flying solo than being stuck with trying to amuse some unamusing fellow guest. Of course, it is always best to have a reasonable balance, but it is a bad idea to try to match people up.

Unfortunately, many divorced women and widows still tend to get left off guest lists, even in what we like to think of as our enlightened times. It is not only kind, but fair to make an effort to include them. After all, they are no less interesting now than when they were married.

Negative Additions

What do you do about the unexpected guest or the last-minute addition?

If you can accommodate the extra person without undue disruption, do so gracefully and as cheerfully as possible.

However, there are situations in which you should refuse to accept the added guest. It may be that adding a seemingly discordant plate or flatware to your perfectly set table would just make you crazy. And you can't just fabricate a seventh Cornish hen when you have planned a party for six.

The refusal should be accomplished with as much grace and good humor as possible, otherwise it can create bad feelings. One reputedly excellent hostess used to call on me regularly to attend her seated dinner parties. One day, she called to invite me to dinner, and I told her that I had gotten married the month before. "That's terrible," she said. "What will I do? You can't bring your husband. It will ruin my seating arrangement."

Happily, I never heard from her again.

Faux Pas
It is a bad idea to attempt to bring together newly-separated or divorced persons with your other single friends, solely for the purpose of "fixing them up" with someone. This almost never works, and such obvious attempts at matchmaking are embarrassing to all concerned. Think interesting people rather than interesting couples, and let what happens happen.

Invitations

If you want an immediate response and your party is of a fairly manageable size, invite guests by telephone. It is true that voice mail and answering machines may make the contact less direct than you would like, but people tend to respond more promptly to telephone messages than to written correspondence. Remember to smile when you make that call. It is true that a smile can be heard over the telephone. (If you are wondering what your voice sounds like, record it, and listen.)

Remember that invitations of any kind should be welcoming and inviting. This doesn't necessarily mean engraved stationery, but it does mean that the invitation should convey a spirit of festivity. Even if you write a personal note, it should convey this spirit and make the person feel especially welcome.

171

Whether you are inviting people by telephone or by mail, be sure to communicate all of the vital elements of an invitation—who, what, when, where, why. It is also kind to clue people in about how to dress. If you are inviting someone you have just met or don't know well, it is also kind to give that person some idea about the others who will be present. Include a map and verbal directions.

Singles feel awkward going solo, so decide well in advance whether to invite them to bring a friend. If not, make sure they know there will be others in the same boat at the party. You don't have to be a matchmaker and shouldn't be tempted into those murky waters. Just prevent people from feeling like fifth wheels: "I am calling to invite you to dinner next Friday, the tenth, and if you'd like to bring a friend, by all means do, although we'd be delighted to have just you."

Or: "We'd like to invite you and a friend for dinner on the tenth."

Or: "We'd like to invite you to dinner on the tenth."

As a guest, never assume an invitation means to bring a guest.

Always respond to an invitation immediately after receiving one. It's fine to ask who else will be there, but not until after you have given your answer. Otherwise, your reply will seem conditional on who else will be present.

Hired Hands

It's a good idea to hire one person to help if you are entertaining more than six people for dinner. There are agencies that provide aspiring actors and students who are experienced at garnishing, serving, and cleanup. This frees you to prepare the menu and be with your guests.

Above all, do not feel guilty or self-conscious about hiring help. Guests do not expect super-human efforts on the part of their host. They expect their host to relax and enjoy the party along with them.

You may be able to hire a friend's college-age children. Some amateur cooks love to work parties and are flattered to be asked. Best of all is hiring your own children, as long as you pay them fairly. They know where things belong, and the experience helps them to become at ease at parties.

Faux Pas
When things go wrong with the hired help, you should never, ever criticize them in public.

If these less-expensive alternatives are not available, you will have to go the agency route. These workers are bonded and insured. If something is stolen and you can prove it, the insurance company will pay to replace it.

Agencies work in two ways: The host pays the agency, which pays the workers; or the host pays the workers, who give a commission to the agency. In either case, it is not necessary to tip bonded household workers, because their cost is so high to begin with. You also do not tip independent workers who are their own boss.

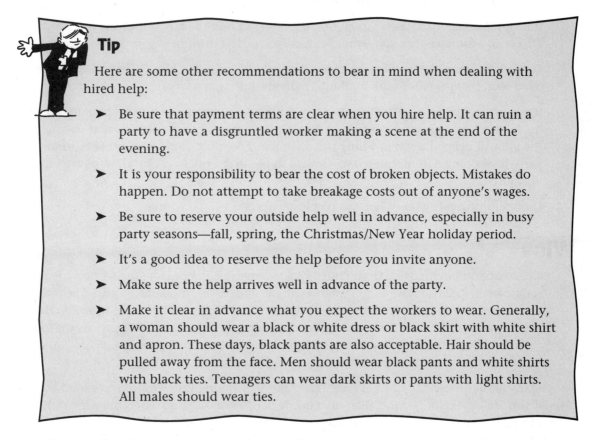

Tip

Here are some other recommendations to bear in mind when dealing with hired help:

➤ Be sure that payment terms are clear when you hire help. It can ruin a party to have a disgruntled worker making a scene at the end of the evening.

➤ It is your responsibility to bear the cost of broken objects. Mistakes do happen. Do not attempt to take breakage costs out of anyone's wages.

➤ Be sure to reserve your outside help well in advance, especially in busy party seasons—fall, spring, the Christmas/New Year holiday period.

➤ It's a good idea to reserve the help before you invite anyone.

➤ Make sure the help arrives well in advance of the party.

➤ Make it clear in advance what you expect the workers to wear. Generally, a woman should wear a black or white dress or black skirt with white shirt and apron. These days, black pants are also acceptable. Hair should be pulled away from the face. Men should wear black pants and white shirts with black ties. Teenagers can wear dark skirts or pants with light shirts. All males should wear ties.

Here are the chores you hire people to perform:

➤ Take coats

➤ Make drinks

➤ Serve appetizers and dinner

➤ Clear the table

➤ Clean up in the kitchen

The Caterer

A caterer can be a godsend for a large party. Costs vary widely, depending on how elaborate your menu needs are, the kind of help you need, and the time of your party. Night hours are more expensive, as are "prime time" occasions, such as New Year's Eve.

It is not unusual for a caterer to require a retainer of half the amount of the food costs. This is an assurance that you won't back out at the last minute.

Tip caterers' employees unless a service charge is added to the bill. Otherwise, give the head waiter 20 percent of the total bill to divide among the workers.

If you are not familiar with the caterer's work, make sure you see his equipment and taste his food before you sign a contract. And make sure the contract specifies that payment of the bill will depend upon fulfilling the contract. If possible, ask if you can peek in on a party he is doing. Often, catered parties are so big that a brief visit by an observer can pass unnoticed.

Communication is vital. Whatever you leave unclear will go wrong.

Wine

Get advice on buying wine from either a knowledgeable liquor store owner or a friendly restaurateur. Tell them what your menu will be, and ask for moderately-priced selections. One friend of mine simply went to a liquor store and purchased a case of its most costly red Burgundy. The proprietor was thrilled, of course, but the value of the wine was lost on virtually all of the guests. You don't need to be extravagant to be elegant. What you need is to be generous and make sure there is enough.

Many parties these days do not have "hard bars," meaning they do not serve hard liquor. If you are serving only wine, plan on a bottle per person. If you are serving wine only during the meal, plan on half a bottle per person.

Tip
Guests especially appreciate being invited to parties at times when parties are scarce—Valentine's Day, Thanksgiving, Mother's Day. Never hesitate to entertain at "odd" times—a breakfast party might be the best time to catch busy people.

Serve red wine at room temperature. To allow the wine to "breathe," open the bottle about 30 minutes before you serve it. This permits the air to develop the bouquet and improve the taste of the wine.

Chill white wines about two hours before serving them. If you must chill the wine more quickly, the best method is to immerse the bottles in a tub of water and ice cubes up to the neck. It does not help to put the wine in a freezer, and it could be dangerous.

When the meal begins, the host should stand and walk around the table to fill each wine glass. If it's an informal party, the host can simply fill the glasses of the persons closest to him and ask them to pass the other glasses down. It is the host's job to make sure the glasses are replenished. Guests should not help themselves to wine or ask for more. It is fine for a host to offer the wine bottle to a guest with an empty glass and say, "Please help yourself."

Wine glasses should only be filled halfway, so that the bouquet of the wine can be appreciated. Don't wrap your wine bottles in napkins when you serve.

Tip
Most hosts today use an all-purpose wine glass. If you don't, remember that the white wine goes in the smaller glass while the red wine goes in the large glass so that the wine will have more space to breathe and develop its bouquet.

Wine glasses should hold at least five ounces.

In the final analysis, inviting people into your home involves careful planning and considerable effort, but it repays both many times over. Having guests under your roof provides a special pleasure. And you flatter people by inviting them because you are bestowing a gift that only you have the power to give—the hospitality of your home.

The Least You Need to Know

➤ Beginner hosts should start small, and keep it simple.

➤ Invite a good mix of people, not just the same old crowd.

➤ You don't have to be a good cook—or cook at all—to give a party with food.

➤ Hire help if you need it, but make sure everyone understands the terms and conditions up front.

➤ Hosts should not spend all of their time in the kitchen.

➤ Elaborate menus and extravagantly expensive wines often go unappreciated.

The Dinner—
Freedom of Choice

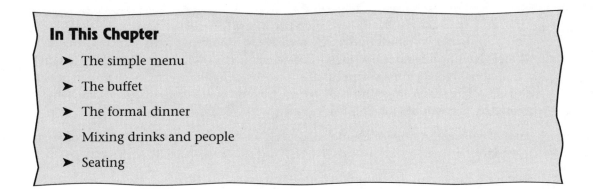

In This Chapter

➤ The simple menu

➤ The buffet

➤ The formal dinner

➤ Mixing drinks and people

➤ Seating

It's your party, you can fry if you want to. Or bake. Or stir fry. Or none of the above. The important thing is that the party should reflect *you*.

I have friends who run the gamut from "hands on, everybody helps" party givers to those whose parties are almost *too* perfectly staged and neatly executed. If you are a casual sort of person, don't attempt to give a fancy, formal, seated dinner. It will seem to everyone, including yourself, to be inauthentic.

Everyone who gives parties frets over the menu, and too many of them end up trying too hard. A cheerful, unstressed host does more for a party than a gourmet meal served with a side dish of anxiety.

The food at every type of gathering except the most formal dinner should be:

➤ Simple

➤ Identifiable

➤ Attractive

The Simple Menu

People are so busy and so health- and weight-conscious these days that most are perfectly pleased to consider the hors d'oeuvres the first course. These can be served during the cocktail hour, attractively arranged on platters placed around the room for people to sample. This is a perfect opportunity to take advantage of the great variety of prepared foods available today. Avoid user-unfriendly foods that are perilous to furniture and clothing. There should be nothing so complicated that it can't be picked up with the fingers, speared with a toothpick, or spread with a knife.

Your main course can be as simple as a casserole with a salad or baked ham. It is a good idea to avoid roasts, which depend on precise serving time and taste like shoe leather if left uneaten for too long.

Don't think that you must purchase expensive food for your party. Once, I attended a dinner given by a famous Philadelphia hostess for out-of-towners. She served scrapple—a traditional Philadelphia cornmeal dish—lentils, scrambled eggs, hash brown potatoes, and chocolate ice cream with raspberry sherbet and told her guests they were being treated to "a flavor of Philadelphia." The guests loved it.

And, of course, the story of Eleanor Roosevelt serving hot dogs to the Queen of England is legendary.

Balance is important. If your main course is light, a heavier dessert works well, and vice-versa. In any case, dessert is important. I have noticed that otherwise diet-conscious persons quickly develop calorie amnesia when dessert arrives at someone else's table. However, when a guest doesn't eat what you are serving, don't think you have to whip up something special just for him.

If you like exotic foods and plan to serve them, ask your guests when you invite them if they like, say, moussaka. A guest who is too polite to refuse something he doesn't like after you cook it, often will not hesitate to tell you candidly about his dislikes before-hand.

As a guest, it is up to you to let your host know if you have special dietary needs. If you are a vegetarian, have serious food allergies, are kosher, or have been advised by a doctor to avoid certain foods, make it known when you are invited. The host then can create a menu that will please everyone and still take your needs into consideration. Or, the host may prepare an additional side dish for you, augment the side dishes, or just advise you to bring your own food. Carol Channing is famous for bringing her own food to parties.

Cocktails

If you are invited to dinner, arrive within five minutes of the time on the invitation, no later.

The cocktail *hour* should be just that—one hour—preferably less, just long enough for the guests to arrive, have a drink, and become accustomed to the group. It is rude, unsafe, and unhealthy to let the alcohol flow on endlessly, and it ruins your taste for the meal.

If you are serving hard liquor, keep the choices simple. All you need are gin, vodka, bourbon, scotch, club soda or mineral water, soft drinks, fruit juice, and tonic. You can go the extra mile and provide garnishes, such as fruit, green olives, and pearl onions, but it's not necessary.

It's fine to set up a self-service bar. Remember that people are consuming less alcohol and caffeine these days, so stock some non-alcoholic drinks and caffeine-free colas.

Be a Mix Master

Arrange your furniture so small groups will gather to chat instead of forming one large ring around the center of the room. Never have all the appetizers and hors d'oeuvres on one table or tray in the center. This discourages conversation.

It's a good idea to keep lighting fairly bright at the beginning. It looks festive and guests like to see what's going on. Dim the lights as the evening progresses.

The host should be most visible and available at the start of a party as he greets his guests. Put your guests at ease by taking their coats and offering them each a drink. Even if you have hired help, it's important to greet all your guests personally unless the party is so huge that it is physically impossible to do so.

Take each guest around the room, and introduce him or her to everyone. Don't ever leave a guest unless he is well into a conversation. Shoving a drink into a guest's hand does not assure that he will immediately begin having a good time. Guests need attention.

Seating

It takes perseverance and a clear voice to get guests in to dinner. The host should announce with authority that dinner is ready, and then take a couple of guests by the arm and lead them into the dining room. Don't worry about interrupting someone's conversation. After all, it *is* a dinner party. Once you have started the procession, drop back to the rear, and round up the stragglers.

Leave drink glasses behind as you go into dinner. If the party is informal, and you are drinking wine, it is fine to carry your wine glass with you to the table, although you will probably find fresh glasses there.

At the Table

Never let seating happen by accident.

Every party of more than eight people should have place cards. (See "Place Cards" later in the chapter for details.)

For groups smaller than eight, the host should have a clear idea of seating and so instruct his guests.

Without assigned seats, guests often feel awkward making their way to the table, afraid to interrupt a conversation or afraid to branch out. This can result in an uncomfortable scene with people trying to decide where to sit, people sitting and then moving, and impromptu field marshals trying to take over to organize the seating according to their own prejudices. Place cards, on the other hand, make people feel special, protected, looked-after.

Guests should never, ever, rearrange place cards to suit themselves.

Tip

Here are some additional seating tips:

➤ Try to pair up a talker and a listener, and sprinkle an assortment of the two around the table.

➤ Do your best to seat guests near at least one familiar person.

➤ Don't seat spouses or couples together.

➤ Consider those across the table as well as those on either side as conversation partners.

➤ If your group has 4, 8, or 12 persons, the host, who serves the meal, is seated at the head of the table, and the guest of honor of the same sex sits opposite. The guest of honor of the opposite sex sits to the right of the host. This prevents two persons of the same sex sitting next to each other, although this has nowhere near the importance it once had if, in fact, it has any real importance at all.

The Meal—Beginnings and Endings

The host should be prepared to start the dinner-table conversation if it doesn't start by itself. Purists say that the only music appropriate for dinner is the arpeggio of sparkling conversation. I'm not sure I agree. Soft, upbeat background music can be very pleasant and brighten the mood.

Don't hold up dinner for one or two late guests. Let them join the party when they show up, at whatever point in the meal you happen to be. It is not the host's responsibility to turn into a short-order cook for someone who has missed a course or two.

Decide in advance what your response will be when a guest asks if he can help. If you think another person in your kitchen will be in the way, or be more of an annoyance than a help, be prepared to say: "Thanks so much for the offer. I've got my own foolproof system, so why don't you just stay where you are and enjoy the conversation." (Guests: If you help to clear dishes, clear each dish separately, one in each hand. Never scrape or stack.)

The host signals the end of the meal by putting his napkin on the table, to the left of the plate. At this point, the host leads the guests out of the dining room for more conversation. Otherwise, the guests might begin taking their leave. While you want to keep the party going for a time after dinner, there is nothing wrong with telling late-staying partiers that you are tired and must call it a night.

Guests who leave the party early should do so with as little fanfare as possible so that others don't start following suit, thereby bringing the festivities to a premature and awkward close. Do say good-night to your host, however. You can avoid being persuaded to remain by simply saying thank you and good-night. Send a thank you note to your host the next day. At the very least, call.

Tip
It is a gracious custom to serve coffee away from the table after dessert. However, if conversation is spirited, it is usually best not to interrupt the flow.

The Buffet Dinner

Many hosts these days prefer the informality of buffet dining, and there are plenty of good reasons:

➤ These meals are easier to prepare in advance.

➤ They require less help.

➤ They can accommodate more people, and stragglers seem less conspicuous.

➤ The buffet meal usually consists of only one course and dessert.

➤ It is easier for people to move around and meet new people, and there is less chance of getting stuck with a dud for the duration of the meal.

Buffet food must be easy to eat, especially if it is a standing-only party. Think about accommodating the clumsiest person you know, and you'll do fine. Make sure the food is cut into small pieces and rolls are buttered.

Do your best to make your buffet table a beautiful still life decorated with flowers. Place the table so that guests have an easy time getting to it, serving themselves, and getting away from it. Sometimes two buffet tables are best for a large crowd. Another workable idea is one long table with identical dishes on either end, plates and cutlery in the center.

Don't display desserts at the same time as main courses. If people put dessert on the plate with other food, things get mixed up and messy and the food ends up looking as though it has already been eaten. If possible, either clear the table, and reset it with dessert, or serve dessert from a separate table.

For a seated buffet, it is a nice touch to serve dessert and coffee rather than do it buffet-style.

Guests at a buffet must remember that they are in a private home and not at an all-you-can-eat cafeteria.

The Formal Dinner

We set our tables far more informally these days for any number of valid reasons— the lack of time being the main one. Who has time to fuss over linens, crystal, and china, much less polish the silver?

However…

If you are planning a formal dinner, it is time to make a special effort. These are occasions when attention to detail, when doing things right, are important.

Place Cards

When you are having more than eight persons for dinner, it is important to have place cards, even if you have a seating chart.

Place cards can be either folded "tents" or single cards meant to lie flat on the table. The tent-style cards have the advantage of standing up on the table so that the name can be written on both sides. In this way, others at the table can see who's sitting where.

The most elegant and costly place cards are made of thick white or off-white stock, with a narrow border of silver, gold, or another color. They measure about 2 by 3 1/2 inches, and you can purchase them from a good stationer or jeweler.

Never hesitate to make your own place cards from materials readily available in your home. If they serve the purpose, use them.

There are several correct locations for place cards on your table:

➤ On top of a napkin, set in the middle of the plate.

➤ On the table at the upper left of the place setting (above the forks).

➤ Leaning against the stem of a water or wine glass.

➤ On the table, just above the middle of the plate in the place setting.

Write the names in black ink. You may type them for a business meal. The important thing is to make sure the names are readily legible and large enough not to require bifocals. If possible, use calligraphy on them or have someone do it for you.

If all the guests know each other at an informal dinner, just write the first name of each on the place cards. If there are guests with the same first name, use the first *and* last names on their cards. If not all of the guests know each other, use both names on all of the cards: "Dan Fleischmann."

At a formal dinner party, such as a business dinner or official function, or any meal where there will be persons of rank, use only surnames on the cards: "Mr. Fleischmann." If there are two Mr. Fleischmanns, use the full name on their cards: "Mr. Daniel Fleischmann.

Use the full titles of military officers and persons who hold or have held political or high appointed office, whether or not they still hold that office or title.

Place cards for the mayor and governor read "The Mayor" and "The Governor." If they no longer hold those offices, the cards read "Mayor Rendell" and "Governor Ridge."

Once an ambassador, always an ambassador. And a military officer is called by his retired rank forever.

Menu Cards

Menu cards can make a dinner more of an event. They also provide useful information to those concerned about diet. For example, knowing that the entree is poached fish might give a dieter license to finish off the cream soup or look forward to enjoying the dessert with a clear conscience.

Menu cards may be typed, calligraphied, or written in black ink. Lean them against a glass, rest them flat on the table to the left of the forks, or lay them centered over the plate, above the dessert fork and spoon. Two guests may share one card, or each may have his own.

Write the date or the occasion at the top of the card. The courses follow in a vertical list. Wines may or may not be included.

Setting the Formal Table

Here's what you need:

1. *Table Decorations (Centerpiece)*: When it comes to the placement of table decorations, there are many interesting variations and options for you. Some examples of these decorations include flowers, fruits and vegetables, collections of figurines, and candles.

2. *Butter Plate and Knife*: These go to the upper left of your plate, above the forks. The butter knife is placed horizontally across the top of the plate, with the blade facing down. It is gracious to have a couple of butter pats already placed on the butter plate, although it's also fine to pass around the table a small plate containing butter pats with a butter knife for guests to help themselves.

   Don't own butter plates? Don't worry. Pass around a small dish containing butter pats or balls. You can also use a dish into which you have spooned soft butter or margarine from a plastic tub or a decorative container which disguises the plastic tub of butter or margarine by fitting around it perfectly. Pass around a butter knife or other small knife with the container so that guests can serve themselves. Guests should take from the container what they want, put it on the side of their plates, and pass the container on to the next person.

3. *Salad Plates*: Salad plates range in size from about 7 1/2 to 8 1/2 inches in diameter. (Salad plates can also be used for dessert or to hold soup cups and saucers or to serve small food items.) Many people don't have salad plates these days and simply put their salads onto dinner plates. Also, a separate salad fork is nice but not necessary. It is no great hardship to eat your salad with your dinner fork.

   If, however, you are serving a separate salad and cheese course between the entree and dessert, each guest will need a salad fork and a small knife as well. The sequence is this: the salad plates should be in front of all guests at the center of the place setting. Then, pass the salad bowl, followed by a cheese tray with a cheese knife. Next, pass crackers. You can choose to follow the crackers with softened butter and a butter knife, if guests have a coronary death wish.

4. *Napkins*: These are best folded and placed in the center of the plate. However, they can also go to the left of the forks, or they can be folded imaginatively in the

glassware. If you are an avid napkin folder, you can pick up some books on the subject and enjoy this opportunity to be creative.

> **Tip**
> There is no reason to use butter plates if your menu does not include something that warrants bread and butter or some food that may require buttering, such as corn on the cob or baked potatoes.

5. *Flatware*: Set the table so that people eat with utensils from the outside in. As a guest, when in doubt, this is always a pretty safe bet. Another idea is to single out the classiest-looking, most composed person at the table and do what that person does. If you are wrong, at least you will be in good company.

The dessert fork and spoon can go horizontally at the top of the plate, the bowl of the spoon facing left and the prongs of the fork facing right. It is not necessary to have both, but the fork often makes a useful "pusher" for the dessert. You can also serve dessert implements with the dessert.

6. *Glassware*: "Drink right, eat left." This means that glasses go on the right and bread and butter plates go on the left. Another way to think of it is that if you hold the fork in your left hand you'd drink with your right hand.

7. *Salt and Pepper Shakers*: Place a pair of salt and pepper shakers at each end of the table. If you have a large supply of them, it's nice to provide a pair for each guest or a pair between two guests. Sometimes people use *saltcellars*, which are tiny receptacles for loose salt. These have a tiny spoon either in them or on the table next to them.

8. *Candles*: Use candles only if it's an evening meal. Place them in the center of the table or elsewhere, as long as you make the arrangement visually appealing and keep candles out of guests' sightlines.

> **Tip**
> You face a tough decision when it comes to the question of whether to include an ashtray as part of your formal table setting. In the past, it was routinely included; however, it is not necessary these days.
>
> If you know your guests smoke and you decide to put ashtrays on the table, place a small ashtray and matches in front of each person who smokes. They should know enough to not even think about smoking until after everyone has finished dessert.

Many people also place candy dishes on the table, and it is a nice, sweet touch. Place one at each end. You can use a small dish or bowl or even a stemmed glass. A good idea is to include small, excellent chocolates.

Serving the Meal

Form follows function when you are serving the meal. Before you entertain, it is a good idea to review the principles yourself and most certainly with any people you have hired to help you.

➤ Serve guests from the left. The utensils should be positioned on the platter in a way that's convenient for the guest to reach them. Keep arms close to the body to avoid banging people. The idea is to make it as convenient as possible for the diner to access the food.

➤ Starting points. The woman on the host's right is served first. If the man on the hostess' right is the guest of honor, he is served first. After that, service goes around the table counterclockwise.

If a couple are guests of honor, then the wife sitting next to the male host is served first. The service goes counterclockwise and ends with the host.

➤ Food is served from the left side of the guest, and finished plates are removed from the right side. A good trick is to use your thumb or otherwise contrive to anchor utensils to the plate so they don't end up in people's laps. Never scrape or stack plates while removing.

➤ Wine is served and removed from the right side.

After Dinner Coffee

After dinner coffee comes in little demitasse cups and saucers with small coffee spoons. The cup, saucer, and spoon are to the right of the guest's place setting. Coffee is served from the right, as are other beverages. Next, pass a tray with cream, sugar, and a sugar substitute.

Tip
Remember that coffee and teacups do not belong in a setting because they are correctly served after the meal.

It is also fine for the host to bring a large tray containing the coffee service to the table, place it conveniently on the table, and then serve each guest, passing the cups to each.

If you have serving help, you might want to have coffee served away from the dining table, or you can bring the entire coffee service into the living room to pour. In this case, each guest would come up to the host to receive his coffee.

Cordials are served with coffee. This is also a good time to ask guests if they would care for a glass of water.

It's also a good time to relax and congratulate yourself on a job well done.

Preparing and serving a dinner for your guests can be as easy or as difficult as you wish. A good idea is to decide well in advance how much effort you are prepared to expend, make a plan, and stick to it. Whatever you decide, your guests will be appreciative.

The Least You Need to Know

➤ Build your menu around one dish. Give it variety, and add a dash of flair. Make sure all of the food is not of one color.

➤ Work out the seating in advance, and never let guests decide for themselves where they will sit. Use place cards for parties of eight or more.

➤ It's important for even a busy host to greet guests and to spend a little time with them after they arrive.

➤ Curtail the cocktail hour, and be persistent and insistent when it comes time for people to go to the dining room table. Start with brighter lights for cocktails, and dim them later.

➤ It's up to the host to make sure wine glasses are replenished. Guests neither refill their own glass nor ask for more.

➤ If serving a buffet meal, make sure the table is nicely decorated, easy to get to, and easy to get away from.

Part 5
Saying the Right Thing

In addition to the usual conflict and criticism that is part of life, most of us will, from time to time, encounter people from other cultures and people with disabilities. We have to be ready to react appropriately and with all the grace we can muster.

There are techniques for dealing with conflict situations and for receiving and delivering criticism. These situations can be approached in a way that will reduce the tension and defuse some of the potential fireworks.

Meeting and dealing with people from different cultures and those with disabilities too often cause confusion, apprehension, and tension. This is true even when people on both sides are doing their utmost to make the encounter pleasant and relaxed.

We also will deal with happier encounters, those involving giving and receiving compliments and gifts.

Chapter 16

Dealing with the Disabled

In This Chapter

➤ Ten enabling tips

➤ What Do I Say?

➤ Taboo terms

➤ Wheelchair and visual impairment etiquette

➤ Hearing loss and speech impairment etiquette

➤ Developmental disabilities

One who is sincerely interested in human communication and cooperation, in being genuinely helpful, will pay only so much attention to the disability as is necessary to give the other the help he needs and wants, will not call undue attention to it by extravagant gestures of sympathy and elaborate offers of undesired help, will give such help as is asked for or indicated in a matter-of-course way, neither evading nor emphasizing the fact of the disability, and will in general keep his companionship with the other on a basis that will keep communication and companionship...as nearly normal as possible.

—Eleanor Roosevelt

There are 43 million people in America with disabilities, making the disabled the largest and most diverse minority in our society. You will meet them in all walks of life, and now, with passage of the Americans with Disabilities Act, you will be meeting them more frequently in the workplace.

Many people feel uncomfortable in situations involving the disabled, partly because they remind us of our own vulnerability, but mainly because we are unsure about how to behave toward those with disabilities.

On the other hand, the disabled may also be suffering discomfort in the same situations because of restrictions imposed on them by physical structures and the uninformed or callous attitudes of the non-disabled.

Disabled persons are sensitive to the reactions of those around them and want to put *you* at ease every bit as much as you want to put *them* at ease. A few simple rules of etiquette and some common sense can go a long way toward making everyone more comfortable. First, remember the three R's—respect, relax, reason.

➤ *Respect.* Persons with disabilities deserve the same respect you would extend to anyone else.

➤ *Relax.* There is no reason that meeting, talking to, and dealing with a disabled person should generate undue tension. Relax and behave naturally.

➤ *Reason.* Reasonable common sense and common courtesy will allow you to avoid or resolve difficult situations involving the disabled.

Ten Enabling Tips

Here are ten practical tips that will help you avoid feeling socially disabled when dealing with the disabled:

1. If you offer assistance, wait until the offer is accepted. *Listen* for information about what form the assistance should take.

2. Speak directly to the disabled person, not through a third party. This is particularly important when addressing a hearing impaired person and someone else is "signing" for him.

3. Always offer to shake hands.

4. Identify yourself and others to a visually impaired person. Always let them know when you are leaving the room.

5. Treat adults like adults. Don't use a person's first name until they ask you to. Don't pat. Don't patronize.

6. Don't shout.

7. Don't touch, lean on, or move a wheelchair without permission. Treat the chair as part of the person occupying it.

8. Don't distract a working seeing-eye dog.

9. When conversing with a person with a speech impediment, listen carefully, and never pretend to understand. If in doubt, ask questions. Wait. Don't interrupt or inject comments during pauses. Don't try to fill in a word for someone with a stutter. Don't raise your voice. Louder is not better.

10. Don't fret about phrases. Speak as you would normally, and don't worry about using terms such as "running around" (to someone in a wheelchair) or "listen to that" or "see you later."

Did You Know?
Some disabled writers have referred to non-disabled persons in general as "TABS," for "temporarily able-bodied."

What Should We Talk About?

Persons who have disabilities may also have families, pets, jobs, hobbies, cultural interests, and sports that they participate in. Get to know about them and their interests the same way you would with anyone else, by making conversation. You may be surprised at the range of interests and activities. Focus on them, and not the disability.

This *does not* mean, however, that the subject of the disability is taboo. If it comes up naturally, talk about it:

> "The meeting is at four o'clock. Do you need me to come by for you, or will you get there on your own?"

> "I'll meet you in the auditorium. There's an accessible entrance to the left of the main entrance."

However, when talking to someone with a disability, avoid the term "handicapped." Use the word "disabled," and save "handicap" for golf outings.

In addition, say "the person with the disability" rather than "the disabled person." Say "the person who has epilepsy" rather than "the epileptic." It is not only more considerate, it is more accurate.

Did You Know?
The reason some people find the word "handicapped" objectionable is that it derives from the phrase "cap in hand," a reference to begging.

Taboo Words and Phrases

The National Easter Seal Society advises that certain words and phrases be eliminated entirely from your vocabulary when it comes to the disabled. They can be replaced with positive, non-judgmental terms:

Eliminate: "Victim," "cripple," "afflicted with" or "by," and "invalid"—which connotes "not valid."

These can be replaced by: "The person with a disability" or, more specifically, "the person with" or "the person who has."

Say: "Uses a wheelchair" instead of "wheelchair-bound" or "confined to a wheelchair." "Employed in the home" is better than "homebound employment," when referring to people who must work at home.

Never say: "Unfortunate," "pitiful," "poor," "dumb," (as in mute) "deformed," "blind as a bat." Terms such as these are stereotypical, judgmental, and downright vulgar.

Wheelchair Etiquette

Think of the wheelchair as an extension of the person who uses it. Here are some tips, many of which also apply to those who use crutches, canes, or walkers.

➤ In general, you should keep your hands off the wheelchair.

➤ Respect personal space. Particularly avoid patronizing pats. Consider what your own reaction would be to this sort of thing.

Tip
"Pity for another implies inferiority. Pity avoids contact. It explains the man who will not employ the blind man even if he is proven as fit as the next man for the job, but instead makes out a check to the nearest blind service institution—his form of magical gesture to exorcise guilt."

—Ludwig Jekels, *The Psychology of Sympathy*

➤ It's a good idea to place yourself at eye level when conversing for any length of time with a person in a wheelchair. It's impossible to deal with another as a peer if one of you is looking up and the other is looking down. Besides, it's easier on the neck for both parties and generally more comfortable.

➤ Don't move a wheelchair or crutches out of reach of the person who uses them unless you are asked to do so. And, if you do move them, remember to place them within the sight of their owner. This will avoid possible uneasiness or even panic.

➤ Don't just decide to help out. Ask first. Push a wheelchair only after asking the occupant if you may do so. A good time to offer help is when the person in the wheelchair is encountering steep inclines or ramps, or thick carpets.

➤ If you are planning a party or other social function, consider whether the location has access for wheelchairs. Think about such things as steep hills and obstacles when giving directions to the location. Remember that it may take the disabled person longer to reach the destination than others.

Visual Impairment Etiquette

In general, guide dogs are working animals, not pets. So don't pet them. In fact, don't call their name or distract them in any way. Allow the dogs to accompany their owners into all stores and buildings. These dogs are trained to pay no attention to strangers while working except as objects to be avoided. Attempting to pet them while they are in harness is like urging someone to abandon a good, carefully-formed habit. If the dog's harness is off, it's okay to ask his owner if you can pet him—but don't touch him without the owner's permission.

If you are in an environment familiar to a blind person, don't move things, or if you do, put them back exactly as you found them. Leave closed doors closed, and open doors open. Never leave doors ajar.

Go ahead and offer assistance if you think it might be helpful, but remember that sometimes a person who is blind prefers to get along unaided. If you see a blind person without a guide dog waiting at an intersection, offer to help him across. The fact that he has stopped at the intersection may signify that he is waiting for help.

However, if he says, "No, thank you," don't insist. If the person wants your help, offer your elbow. You will then be walking a step ahead, and the movements of your body will indicate when to change direction, when to stop and start. Hesitate but do not stop before stepping up or down. You can say "curb" or "step down."

Here are some other tips:

➤ Watch out for half-opened doors. They are a hazard to everyone, but especially to a person who is blind.

➤ Give directions with the person who is blind as the reference point, not yourself. Say: "*You* are facing Broad Street, and *you* will have to cross it and turn to *your* right to go east on Chestnut Street."

➤ When helping the person into a car or taxi, place her hand on the inside door handle, and let her go in alone.

➤ When entering an unfamiliar office or restaurant, offer your elbow, use specifics such as "right" or "left," and then place his hand on the back of the chair so that he can be seated without further assistance.

➤ Don't let self-consciousness or a misplaced sense of protectiveness make you hesitate to tell a blind person that he has egg on his shirt or that his tie is in his soup. Do so in a matter-of-fact tone of voice, and let him deal with the problem himself.

➤ For some reason, some people have a tendency to raise their voices when speaking to a blind person. If you catch yourself doing this, cut it out. It's annoying.

➤ When accompanying a person who is blind, do your best to describe the surroundings, especially terrain and spatial relationships.

Recently, I witnessed the following encounter in one of those large chain drug stores. A blind man entered and stopped inside the door. Seeing this, another customer walked over to him.

"May I assist you?"

"I want to have a prescription filled."

"The pharmacy section is in the rear of the store. I'd be glad to take you there."

"Great. Thanks."

"Take my elbow. We're going about six feet straight ahead. Now we're turning right. The floor inclines up, and there are some displays of soda in the middle of the aisle. About four steps more. Okay, shall I get the pharmacist for you?"

"No, thanks. I'm fine now that I'm here."

"Would you like me to wait and escort you out?"

"No, thanks. I can do it now. Thanks a lot."

Tip

In a restaurant, you can use an imaginary clock to describe the placement of the food on the dish in front of a visually impaired person: "The mashed potatoes are at four o'clock; the chicken breast is at two o'clock," and so on.

As you can see, the person who helped out in the above situation was able to combine common sense with simple courtesy in offering to help and in providing just the right amount of assistance that was required or desired.

Meeting a Blind Person for the First Time

If the person is alone when you enter the room, make your presence known right away by speaking. Identify yourself when greeting the person, and if others are with you, be sure to introduce them and to specify where they are: "On my left is Helen Carver, and on my right is Mary Thompson."

When offering a handshake, say something like, "Allow me to shake your hand." If the other person extends a hand, shake it or explain why you can't. "I'd like to shake your hand, but I'm afraid I may drop all these files."

Remember to talk to a person without sight as you would to a person who can see. In a group, use the people's names as a clue to whom you are speaking. Address those who can't see by name if they are expected to reply, and speak to them directly in a normal tone of voice. Excuse yourself when you are leaving. This is especially important when ending a conversation so the person isn't left talking to thin air.

When a person with visual impairment has to sign a document, provide a guiding device such as a ruler or a card. When handing money to a person who is blind, separate all the bills into denominations and specify if they are ones, fives, and so on. Coins will be identified by touch.

Hearing Loss Etiquette

Hearing impairment is a less dramatic disability than blindness, but it is much more common.

Hearing loss can be slight or complete or anywhere in between. Your response may be keyed to the degree of hearing loss. In any case, here are some tips that you will find helpful.

➤ Be sure that you have the person's attention before you start speaking. If necessary, wave a hand, give a tap on the shoulder or make some other signal. Gently.

➤ Some deaf people depend entirely on lip reading to discern what others are saying, and many with partial hearing loss depend upon it to one degree or another. Accordingly, face the person you are addressing, and make sure the light is on your face so that he can see your lips more clearly.

➤ Don't get frustrated if you have to repeat yourself. If necessary, write it down, or get someone to "sign" for you.

➤ Don't keep repeating the same phrases. Be flexible. Switch words, and rephrase the sentence. Some words "look" similar to a lip-reader. If, "I'll drive the car around front," doesn't seem to work, try "I'll bring the car to the front door." Keep your hands away from your face while speaking, and don't eat, chew, or smoke. You should be aware that a moustache may make it more difficult for you to be understood.

➤ Remember that the person with the hearing loss will rely to some degree on expressions, gestures, and body language.

➤ Never talk from another room. When people who are hearing impaired can't see you, they may not be aware that you are speaking.

➤ Turn off the television or radio, and reduce other background noises so that you can be heard more clearly.

➤ Don't shout. Don't use exaggerated lip movements. Speak slowly and clearly.

➤ Face the other person, preferably on the same eye level. Do not turn away until you have finished speaking.

➤ You can bend down to get a little closer to the ear of the listener, but don't speak directly into the ear, don't touch, and don't shout.

➤ Remember that fatigue, stress, illness, or fright affect those with hearing impairments as they affect us all. Be aware of external factors like jet lag or a common cold that can increase difficulty in communicating, and adjust your behavior accordingly.

➤ When a hearing impaired person is in a group, and the others are laughing at something he hasn't heard, explain the joke to him, or let him know that you will explain it later. Because of past cruelties, your friend may be over-sensitive, and may think that the others are laughing at him.

Speech Impairment

The most important thing to remember is to give your complete and unhurried attention to those who have difficulty speaking. That means giving them time to express themselves. Don't interrupt or complete their sentences for them, but give help when they indicate that they need it.

➤ Don't correct their pronunciation.

➤ Ask questions that require short answers or that can be answered with a nod or a gesture.

➤ Don't pretend to understand when you don't. Repeat what you thought you understood. The person's reactions will guide you.

Developmental Disability

Dealing with persons who have developmental disabilities may present you with the most difficulties and require the most patience. This is particularly true if you are dealing with such a person in the workplace.

The key is to treat them as normally as possible and to set the same standards for them as you would for others. If, for example, the person tries to become too affectionate, explain that such behavior is not appropriate. Make sure your tone is firm but not reprimanding.

➤ Be careful about touching the person. This may signal approval of such behavior, which is often used by a person with developmental disabilities to curry favor.

➤ Sometimes persons with developmental disabilities are very sensitive to body language and tone of voice. Make sure your silent messages are non-threatening. Be firm, but pleasant. Speak with a smile on your face and in your voice.

➤ Criticism and accusatory language have a demoralizing effect on everyone. Instead of saying, "You made a mistake," try, "How about doing it like this?"

➤ Recognize that repetition is important in teaching the developmentally disabled, and be prepared to be patient.

Tip
Don't be so quick to say, "You don't look handicapped" to someone getting out of a vehicle with a "wheelchair" license plate. There are many people with serious health conditions that are not immediately apparent to strangers.

The Lately Disabled

You may need an extra supply of tact and generosity if you have a friend or acquaintance who has become disabled later in life, possibly because of Meniere's Disease, Lupus, or Multiple Sclerosis. Often, you may only know of such disabilities if the person actually tells you.

One of the most common reactions among the lately disabled is a feeling of extreme self-consciousness in the company of able-bodied persons. They are acutely sensitive to "pity" from others.

The lately disabled may also suffer from a loss of self-esteem. They may have lost their jobs and are worried about money. Keep in mind that they are unable to do many of the things that once defined them in their own minds—things that were part of their sense of self-worth.

They may also be suffering from depression, grieving for the person they once were, and struggling toward a realization of the new person they now must be.

The lately disabled may also experience boredom and wish for structure. You can help by getting them involved in activities, particularly those activities that involve exercise. Provide structure by offering to make appointments or arrangements for certain definite times and sticking to the plan.

Therefore, be prepared for displays of bad temper and frustration. And don't take them personally.

People with disabilities are very much like people without disabilities except, perhaps, that their daily lives may require a bit more courage and character than the rest of us need. If you are uncomfortable in their presence, it is your fault, not theirs. This discomfort will disappear if, while acknowledging that they have a disability, you treat them with the same respect that you expect for yourself. They don't want your pity, and they deserve your admiration.

The Least You Need to Know

➤ Disabled persons are often as anxious to put you at ease as you are to put them at ease.

➤ Avoid terms such as "victim," "crippled," and "invalid." Instead of "handicapped," say "disabled."

➤ Do not pet or otherwise interfere with a working guide dog.

➤ Face the person with a hearing loss when you speak to him so that he can see your face. Never shout. It doesn't help and may cause damage.

➤ A wheelchair is an extension of a person's body. Don't touch it, even to help out, without asking permission.

Chapter 17

It's a Small World

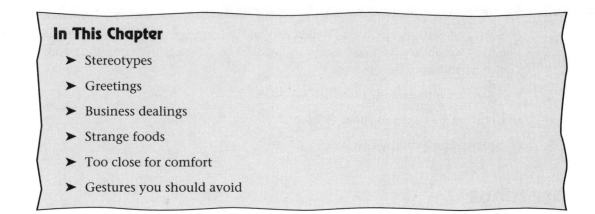

In This Chapter

➤ Stereotypes

➤ Greetings

➤ Business dealings

➤ Strange foods

➤ Too close for comfort

➤ Gestures you should avoid

Today, Americans are encountering persons from different cultural backgrounds more often and more intimately than ever. In 1980, the percentage of foreign people born in America (living in the U.S., but not citizens) was 14 million. In 1990, it was 20 million. More than 31 million people speak English as their second language.

The ease and speed of overseas travel, the ability to communicate instantly through satellite and computer, the interlocking and overlapping business interests in the Americas, Europe, Africa, and Asia mean that we are in touch with the world's diversity as never before.

It's exciting, fascinating and full of opportunity. It's also full of snares and dangers.

In this chapter, ways of avoiding some of the more common errors will be discussed. While this information will be helpful, it will be even more useful to simply keep in mind the basic foundation stones of etiquette—kindness and respect for others. This implies a willingness to set aside your ingrained ideas about "correct" behavior and to approach new situations with an open, inquiring mind.

If you are visiting another country or are hosting or otherwise spending time with persons from other cultures, don't hesitate to confess ignorance and ask for help. Your candor will be appreciated and your errors more cheerfully tolerated.

Stereotypes

A good way to begin to learn about others is to get rid of what you think you already know about them. Here are some common generalizations that need to be jettisoned:

➤ All Latin cultures hold the "siesta" inviolate.

➤ Visitors from abroad are eager to be taken to an "ethnic" restaurant serving what Americans consider to be the visitors' favorite foods.

➤ Signs and gestures and loud English will bridge language gaps. (Noise never helps, and as we will see, gestures send varying messages, depending upon the background and traditions of the observer.)

➤ Asians are remote and "inscrutable."

➤ Germans are cold and super-efficient.

➤ Japanese are basically shy.

Greetings

When greeting someone, an American's first instinct is to stick out his hand, look directly at the other person, and smile. In some situations this could mean making three mistakes all at once. Methods and styles of greeting vary greatly around the world, and it is important to know what is expected in differing circumstances. It is the moment of greeting in which crucial first impressions are made.

➤ When greeting Asians for the first time, it is a good general rule not to initiate the handshake. You may be forcing a physical contact that the other person finds uncomfortable. Many Asians, particularly the Japanese, have learned to accept the handshake when dealing with westerners. Since the bow is the customary greeting in Japan, a slight bow of the head when responding to a proffered handshake is appropriate. Westerners generally are not expected to be familiar with the complex Japanese bowing protocols.

➤ Most Latins are more accustomed to physical contact. Even people who know each other only slightly may embrace when greeting one another.

➤ Middle Easterners, particularly Muslims, avoid body contact with the opposite sex, but persons of the same sex commonly hug when greeting each other. When shaking hands, men should be careful not to pull their hand away too quickly.

➤ People from France, Spain, Italy, and Portugal greet friends by kissing on both cheeks.

➤ The smile is the near-universal gesture of friendliness, and, in America, its meaning is usually clear. The person smiling is happy, amused and/or sending out a friendly signal. In other cultures, the smile may be sending other signals. In some Latin cultures, for example, the smile may be used to say "Excuse me," or "Please."

If a person from another culture does not return your greeting smile, it doesn't indicate hostility or bad manners. In some Asian cultures, smiling is considered a gesture to be reserved for informal occasions, and smiling while being formally introduced would be considered disrespectful.

➤ In many cultures, avoiding eye contact is a sign of respect. This can lead to misunderstandings. For example, there have been many cases of non-Korean customers deciding that they are being treated with disrespect by Korean shopkeepers who avoid eye contact with them. The same sort of misunderstanding has occurred between American teachers and Asian students who do not look at the teacher while he is speaking.

Let's Do Business

When asked their impressions of American business people, foreigners often begin by saying Americans are very open and friendly. They find, however, that this friendliness tends to be shallow and short-lived. Americans come on strong at the beginning, but do not live up to the implied promise of an ongoing friendship or, at least, personal relationship.

Many business people from other cultures say they are put off by the abruptness with which Americans seem to want to get things done. We say, "Time is money." We "work hard and play hard" and eat lunch standing up or at the desk. Some people, particularly Asians and Middle Easterners, don't consider "Let's get right down to business" an admirable approach to getting things done in the business world.

Another problem is that Americans tend to jump into a first-name basis rather quickly, apparently laboring under the delusion that everybody enjoys being called by his first name by everybody else.

High-Context vs. Low-Context

An insight into how to avoid these and some other problems American business people encounter on the global scene can be gained by considering what anthropologist Edward T. Hall calls high-context and low-context cultures.

The United States, Germany, Switzerland, Canada, and the Scandinavian countries can be considered low-context cultures. This means business people tend to send unambiguous messages with a lot of specificity and clear descriptions. For them, time is a straight-line commodity when it comes to getting things done. You start at point A and you go right to point B.

High-context countries include China, Japan, Korea, Spain, Greece, Turkey, the Arab world, and Latin America. In high-context cultures, there is more emphasis on non-verbal communication, indirect verbal signals and implicit meanings. Rituals are more important. Time is not a straight-line concept. The road from point A to point B is highly textured. The road has curves and detours and scenery.

Low-context people tend to view high-context people as sneaky, secretive, or at best, mysterious, while high-context people tend to view low-context people as moving too fast on the one hand and being excessively talkative and redundant on the other.

So, when dealing with high-context business people, it is best to be patient and to recognize that a lot of things are happening at once. Let's take the example of a savvy American visiting the office of a Korean on business:

> His appointment is at noon, and even though he knows it is important to arrive on time, he expects to be kept waiting. He waits quietly. Reading or doing something else while waiting is not a good idea: it would indicate that the upcoming meeting is not his primary focus.

His host comes out to greet him. They shake hands, and the American gives a slight bow. There are others in the office where the meeting is to take place. The American greets them: more handshakes, slight bows. He sits, keeping his feet on the floor.

If refreshments are offered, he accepts after a mild and insincere refusal. He uses his right hand to drink.

All the while, his host is being gracious and hospitable, and he responds in the same spirit. Neither of them discusses business just yet. His host may hold several conversations at once, talk on the telephone, digress. But he will always return to the important issues, and inevitably, things will get done, and all parties will part cordially.

This experience may strike the American business man as inefficient, but it works for a considerable segment of the world.

Gifts

In some cultures, if you effusively admire a possession of another person, particularly your host, he may feel obliged to offer it to you as a gift. You, however, need not accept. In fact, you should firmly, but politely, refuse.

Here are some cautionary notes for gift giving when other cultures are involved:

➤ In some Asian cultures, including Japanese and Chinese, gifts are not opened in the presence of the donor.

➤ Avoid wrapping gifts for Japanese in either white or black paper. Japanese do not use bows or bright colors when wrapping gifts.

➤ White flowers symbolize mourning to the Chinese. Yellow flowers have similar negative connotations among some Latins and Middle Easterners. In Europe, red roses often signal romantic intent, and chrysanthemums are linked with death.

➤ In the Middle East, do not give gifts that are representations of partially-clad women or of pets, such as dogs, which are considered lowly creatures.

➤ Cash gifts for Chinese should be in even numbers and given with both hands.

➤ Gifts of knives to Latins can signal the "cutting" of a relationship.

➤ Don't give four of anything to a Japanese or Korean.

➤ Don't give a clock to a Chinese.

➤ A handkerchief suggests tears or parting in the Middle East, making it an inappropriate gift.

Is It Time to Eat?

Many foreigners find the customs and terminology that accompany eating in America odd, disconcerting, or baffling. Why do some American executives like to do business at breakfast? Lunch is sometimes little more than an afterthought here. We load our water glasses with ice. We drink denatured (decaffeinated) coffee. We eat strange things and at odd times. Consider the following:

➤ The main meal of the day in other countries is taken at midday. In America, the main meal comes at the end of the work day. We call the evening meal "dinner," a word that signifies the midday meal in other English-speaking countries.

➤ The evening meal in America is served, generally, within a hour either way of 7 p.m. Elsewhere is it generally later, and generally lighter. In Spain, supper commonly begins at 10 p.m.

➤ The English have "tea" in the afternoon, usually around 4 p.m. This meal consists of tea, small sandwiches and pastries. "High tea" is not a more elaborate version of "tea." It is, in fact, an informal replacement for supper, which is eaten later in the evening.

In addition, "brunch" is considered a curious American invention in places where it is known at all. A foreign visitor will probably find its timing disconcerting.

"Strange" Foods

Here are some commonplace American foods that foreigners find unusual or, in some cases, repulsive.

Marshmallows

Corn on the cob, which many Europeans consider fit only for animals

Pumpkin pie (also pecan pie)

Sweet potatoes

Crawfish

Grits

Hot dogs

In other countries, some Americans may have the same reaction to things like sea urchins in Korea, horse meat in Japan, toasted grasshoppers in Mexico, sea slugs in China, sheep's eyes in the Middle East, haggis (sheep's organs and entrails) in Scotland, or kidney pie in England.

Also, what many Americans think of as Mexican food and Chinese food would not be welcome in Mexico and China. (When Chinese Americans want to say someone is losing touch with his Chinese heritage, they may say he is "a chop suey man." This is a dish that Americans think is Chinese and Chinese think is American.)

Here are some general rules of etiquette to follow when you are confronted with unfamiliar food in a foreign land:

➤ If you don't know what it is, you might be better off not asking. Taste it. If you don't like it and are asked for your opinion, say something like "It has a very distinctive flavor."

➤ If you know what it is and don't want to try it, politely refuse. Or you can say something like, "I know this is quite a delicacy, but I've tried it before and found it doesn't sit well with me."

➤ If you sense that a refusal would offend your host or fellow diners, cut it up and move it around on your dish so that it looks as if you are eating.

Some cautionary notes:

➤ It is particularly important to respect the dietary rules of Muslims. They do not eat the flesh of any animal that scavenges, including pigs, goats, some birds, and sea scavengers, like lobster. Food may not be prepared using the products derived from these animals, such as oils. Muslims do not drink alcohol and avoid foods cooked with alcohol.

➤ Do not point with your chopsticks or suck on them. Do not stick chopsticks upright in your rice. This is thought to bring bad luck.

➤ In Europe, you may expect salads to be served before, rather than after, the main dish.

➤ Orthodox Jews do not eat pork or shellfish. Meat and fowl must be "kosher," which means they must be ritually slaughtered.

➤ In Europe and elsewhere, the main dish is served at the beginning of the meal, so don't think of it as an "appetizer." Also be careful at formal Chinese banquets. They consists of many more courses than Westerners expect. Eat sparingly in the early going.

Did You Know?
Many Americans would just as soon eat a rat's tail as a cooked snail. And some people who consider snails to be a delicacy are repelled by the very idea of those good old Yankee standbys, corn on the cob and pumpkin pie.

You're In My Space

While Asians stand farther away during conversations than Americans are used to, many Mediterraneans and Latins stand so close that Americans feel that their "space" is being violated. Inexperienced Americans usually react by taking a step back. This doesn't work because the other person will simply take a step forward. If you keep backing up, you may find yourself backed into a corner. On the other hand, if an Asian steps back during a conversation with you, control the urge to pursue him.

Faux Pas
What Americans call diapers are called "napkins" in England. This could lead to some hilarious and/or embarrassing misunderstandings.

When dealing with Asians, remember that touching can be a touchy subject. For example, you don't put your arm about the shoulders of a Japanese or take hold of his arm during a conversation. Don't be offended if Asian shopkeepers avoid contact by placing your change on the counter instead of in your hand. They are just being polite.

Gestures

When traveling abroad, some innocent or even friendly gestures can get you into trouble. These include making a circle of the thumb and index finger, pointing the index finger, and giving the thumbs-up sign.

Some other cautions:

➤ Avoid using the crooked index finger in a beckoning gesture. In many cultures, the beckoning gesture is done with the arm extended and the fingers making an inward sweeping motion.

➤ In some places, you may see people clap their hands or snap their fingers to get the attention of waiters or servants. In general, however, it is wise for the visitor to avoid doing either.

Did You Know?
In Columbia, people tap their elbow with their fingertips to say somebody is stingy. Americans point to their chest to indicate "me," while the Chinese point to their nose.

➤ The "V for victory" sign is insulting in England if the palm is turned inward. In fact, this is another gesture that should be avoided altogether.

➤ Propping up your foot so that the sole of your shoe is facing another is considered grossly insulting in most Asian countries and in parts of the Middle East.

➤ In some cultures it is considered rude to engage in conversation with your arms folded over your chest or with your arms akimbo (hands on hips).

It's difficult, and it may well be impossible, to avoid making etiquette errors when dealing with persons from other cultures, either at home or abroad. The world is a complex mosaic of customs and attitudes, and even the most well-traveled and well-read can unknowingly transgress against one or the other.

So, while it may not be possible to always be "correct," it is essential to always be courteous. A willingness to confess ignorance and ask for help, the ability to apologize gracefully, and a friendly, open attitude will get you through most difficulties.

Don't let anxiety about making social blunders cause your relations with those from other cultures to be mannered or stiff. Approach learning about new places and people with a spirit of adventure and a desire to learn, and you will generally find that people are more than willing to forgive innocent breaches of etiquette.

The Least You Need to Know

➤ In the U.S., when you meet someone, you look them right in the eye, smile, and stick out your hand for a shake. In some places that would be making three mistakes all at once.

➤ Latin Americans and Middle Easterners are accustomed to physical contact. Many Asians find it disconcerting and even offensive.

➤ Foreigners say Americans tend to plunge into the business at hand too abruptly, that they are superficially friendly, and that they move to a first-name basis too quickly—both socially and in business.

➤ Certain kinds of flowers have negative connotations in some cultures. White flowers signify mourning in China; yellow flowers have similar negative connotations among some Latins and Middle Easterners, and some Europeans connect chrysanthemums with death.

➤ Many familiar American gestures are considered offensive elsewhere—for example, the "OK" gesture, which involves making a circle of the thumb and forefinger. When in doubt, the safest thing to do is not make the gestures at all.

Chapter 18

Conflict, Compliments, and Criticism

In This Chapter

➤ Giving and receiving criticism

➤ Giving and receiving compliments

➤ Delivering bad news

➤ Tips on handling difficult situations

Into each life a little strain must fall. Handling disagreements, delivering and receiving criticism and compliments, and working through conflicts are all crucial skills. Since conflict is inevitable, it is wise to be armed with some ideas and techniques for minimizing the pain and keeping disagreements from scarring a relationship or escalating into nuclear warfare.

The "Critical I"

Julia is having lunch with cousin Carla. Julia has the egg salad on whole wheat. Carla has the smoked salmon. Even with the iced tea and tip, Julia figures her bill will come in under $10. Carla says, "Sixteen-fifty should cover your end."

There are a number of ways for Julia to respond.

> Wrong: "Carla, you're wrong. How on earth do you get $16.50?"

> Worse: "What are you trying to pull?"

> Better: "I'm getting a different total. Shall we check the math?"

By using the last example and starting out with the magical "I" word, Julia could take over the "ownership" of the comments and the situation. This is the "critical I" method. This way, Carla is less likely to feel she is under attack and needs to throw up a defense or launch a counter-offensive.

But, let's assume that, instead of the "I" approach, Julia says: "Carla, you're wrong. How on earth do you get $16.50?"

Carla takes it calmly. She knows that it's always a bad idea to try to laugh off criticism or become defensive. People usually only become defensive when they know they are wrong.

Carla's possible responses:

> Wrong: "Are you accusing me of trying to cheat you?"

> Better: "I don't understand what you mean." Or: "Let's have a look at this."

Julia, it turns out, forgot about that glass of expensive chardonnay. They had a little laugh about it and parted friends.

This little scenario is typical of the situations in which you find you must challenge or criticize someone. When it happens, think first of the "critical I."

> "I think you've been misinformed."

> "That doesn't sound quite right to me."

> "I'm having trouble understanding why you..."

Softening the Blow

When delivering criticism, keep these points in mind:

➤ Avoid the "but" bomb: "I thought the points you made in your report were excellent, *but*..."

The "but" bomb immediately sends up a flare and triggers a defensive reaction. The person hears "but" and begins constructing a reply instead of listening closely to your further comments. Try: "I thought your report was outstanding, and *next time*, I suggest you include..." "Next time" does not invalidate the first part of the sentence, as "but" does.

➤ Keep it impersonal. Never say that some act or person was "dumb" or "wrong." Talk about behavior, not personality.

➤ Keep it private. If you criticize in the presence of others, the person is not thinking about your message, but about being humiliated.

➤ Be specific.

➤ Soften the impact. This is done effectively by beginning with a compliment: "You are usually a very considerate person. That's why I was so surprised at your behavior at lunch today."

You can also deliver criticism in the form of advice. Instead of saying, "You'll never even reach the basket if you shoot the ball like that," say, "I've found that keeping the elbows in close gives the shot more power."

Tip
The most important factor in any communication is the receiver of the information, not the sender. Thus, what *you hear* is more important than what *I say*. "I'm not sure I was clear about that" is much better than "You don't understand."

The Receiving End

Whether you deserve it or not, you will be the subject of criticism. Be ready. If it is justified, accept it, and treat it as a problem that needs to be resolved. Acknowledge that there is a problem, and make it clear that you want to fix it.

If the criticism is unjustified or delivered harshly or publicly, you have every right to react. However, if you get angry and start shooting back, you will both end up saying things you will regret. In this situation, it is usually best to put off discussing the matter: "Let's talk about this when we're both a little calmer," or: "We ought to get together and work this out. What's a good time for you?"

If someone says something critical about you in the presence of others, you can try "freezing" him by stopping whatever you are doing or saying and looking him dead in the eye for a moment. Or you can say something like, "Very little good comes of criticizing others in public. Please tell me your objections (or problems) in private."

If you are not sure the criticism is justified or want time to think it over, you can say something like: "I'm glad you're letting me know what's on your mind. I'd like to think about it and get back to you."

If you *know* you've goofed, it's sometimes best to just say, "I apologize," and that's all. Sometimes, something more is required: "I never intended to (embarrass, upset, offend) you, but I can see that I did, and I'm sorry." But don't whine, don't grovel, and don't make excuses or try to shift the blame.

When All Else Fails—The Insult

It is not good manners to insult people. But, if you are going to do it, please do so with grace and style. Tradition, gossip, and literature present us with some excellent examples that may help you in such circumstances.

The following conversation is reputed to have taken place between Lady Astor and Winston Churchill:

> "If you were my husband, Winston, I should flavor your coffee with poison."

> "If you were my wife, I should drink it."

There is the story of a Louisiana legislator who, having been insulted by a colleague, rose to say:

> "I am reminded that the Emperor Caligula once sent his horse to represent him in the Roman Senate. Caligula was more fortunate than my learned colleague's constituents. At least he was represented by the whole horse."

Another incident involved Dorothy Parker. Someone stepped aside to allow her to pass, saying:

> "Age before beauty."

She swept past, saying:

> "Pearls before swine."

Andrew Lloyd Webber wondered aloud why people took an instant dislike to him. "It saves time," responded Alan Jay Lerner.

Compliments

A compliment is one of those two-way gifts. It benefits the giver and the receiver. Too often, people deprive themselves of the pleasure of giving a compliment because they hesitate and let the moment slip by. Or perhaps the other person is so consistently well-groomed that we don't bother to say, "You look great today." Or they are so consistently efficient that we fail to say, "Good job."

When giving a compliment, remember these points:

➤ Be sincere. Complimenting someone just because you think it's a good idea is a bad idea. A phony compliment is easy to spot and instantly destroys the credibility of the speaker. If the luncheon speaker was a total flop, don't compliment him on his speech. Talk about the effort he made to attend the function and his past achievements, if any.

➤ Be specific. "That was a marvelous casserole," is better than, "You're a terrific cook."

➤ Be unqualified. Don't make the mistake of damning with faint praise: "That was a good report, considering," or, "This casserole is pretty good."

➤ Don't compare. It often diminishes the compliment to compare it to some other achievement, unless you are comparing it to something heroic, and then it sounds insincere.

WDYS?

An acquaintance has changed substantially in appearance since you last met. It could be a weight loss, a major "make over," or cosmetic surgery. You want to say something complimentary about the change, but you don't want to refer explicitly to the reason for the changed appearance.

What do you say?

"You look absolutely marvelous!" with an exclamation point in your voice.

The other person may respond by saying something like:

"Yes, my dieting really paid off this time," or, "Everybody seems to agree that a little bit of cosmetic surgery makes a big difference."

Then you can engage in a conversation about the rigors of dieting or new laser techniques for removing wrinkles. If the other person merely says, "Thank you," talk about something else.

When receiving a compliment, just smile and say "Thank you." Never try to shrug off a compliment or disagree with the person who is trying to compliment you. If someone compliments you on your dress, and you say, "Oh, this old thing?" you are telling the other person he has poor taste or doesn't know what is fashionable.

If someone compliments you on a good job at the office, don't say, "It was nothing," or, "It should have been more complete (or finished earlier)." This is insulting to the other person, implying that his standards are not very high. "Thanks, I worked really hard on it," is much better.

Don't unilaterally upscale a compliment.

"The sales managers liked your presentation."

"Liked it? They loved it. I knocked their socks off."

If there are others who deserve a share of the credit, don't fail to mention that when you acknowledge the compliment.

Cosmetic Surgery

Thousands of people will undergo cosmetic surgery this year. Their reactions will fall somewhere between silent confusion and a straightforward willingness to discuss their decision to change their appearance.

More people than ever are electing cosmetic surgery, but today's motivations often are far different from the erstwhile stereotype of the suburban matron with too much time and money on her hands. In today's downsized job market, many people elect cosmetic surgery for reasons other than vanity.

And, with more and more people appearing publicly in various stages of pre-surgical and post-surgical conditions, the problem of what to say and what not to say arises for both the patient and the friends and acquaintances of the patient.

Although most people today are open about having cosmetic surgery, it can still be a touchy topic for conversation. To avoid hurt feelings, follow these suggestions:

➤ Never tell a person he or she is "crazy" to have cosmetic surgery.

➤ Wait until the person opens the subject before you ask if they have had cosmetic surgery.

➤ If you are curious, try saying, "You look wonderful today." If they reply that they have had surgery, ask only: "Are you pleased with the results?"

➤ Even if pressed, never criticize the results. If you must, you can say: "I see what you mean, but only when you point it out."

➤ Never volunteer the names of others who have had cosmetic surgery.

➤ Never gossip about the subject.

➤ Cosmetic or not, it's still surgery. Be solicitous about people's health and well-being.

➤ If you have had cosmetic surgery and look markedly different, make it easier for those around you by opening the door for comments.

Bad News

People get fired, go into bankruptcy, have accidents, get indicted, and experience the death of loved ones. If it happens to someone you know well, it is less than useless to act as if nothing has happened. It is up to you to acknowledge the misfortune at the earliest opportunity and to offer your sympathy. Don't wait for the other person to fumble around looking for an opening. And, if neither of you brings up the subject, it becomes the proverbial elephant in the living room—an undeniable presence that is being ignored.

Say: "I heard about the fire at your house last week. I'm so glad that you're all right," or say, "I was so sorry to hear about Jim being sentenced to prison. It must be terrible for you."

If you attending a funeral, express your condolences as directly and simply as possible: "I'm very sorry about your loss," or, simply, "I'm sorry." You may also want to remind the bereaved of some characteristic of the deceased: "Our office won't seem the same without Bridget's daily baseball team updates," or, "I'll miss seeing all her crazy t-shirts."

When someone begins to tell you bad news, be quiet, and listen. Your concern will be mirrored in your attentiveness. You can nod and say, "Uh, huh," and when you feel it is appropriate, say, "This must be draining for you. I'm so sorry."

Don't think for a moment that it is helpful or encouraging to tell the person in trouble about someone you know who is suffering even more. That kind of one-upmanship only makes people feel worse. Imagine that you are telling someone about suffering from a severe headache and they say, "You haven't had a headache until you've had one of my migraines."

Neither is this the time to express opinions about proper behavior or judgments about people's character. Nor is it the time to offer unsolicited advice.

Above all, don't use the opportunity to pry into the other person's life. At a time such as this, you two may reach a level of intimacy unprecedented in your relationship. A casual acquaintance might for a few minutes become uncharacteristically open and candid with you—and might regret it later on. Try to stay within the boundaries that previously characterized your relationship while still remaining sympathetic and attentive.

Firings, Lay-Offs, and Demotions

The work arena is fraught with difficult and disappointing situations. People get fired, laid off, passed over for promotion, transferred against their will, and chewed out unjustly by the boss. In these situations, nothing you can say will fix the problem, so it is important to "mirror" the person's distress. Let him know that he isn't alone, that he is, in fact, in good company. Reinforce his good qualities.

Don't say, "Things will work out for the best," or, even worse, "I told you something like this would happen." Don't say that what happened to somebody else is even worse than what happened to him.

Try expressions such as:

> "I'm so sorry you must go through this."

> "Is there anything I can do to help?"

> "This must be very, very tough for you."

Do not indicate in any way that the unfortunate turn of events was predictable or even partially the fault of the injured party. If a colleague was denied promotion for what you believe to be very good cause, don't launch into a lecture about the skills he needs to acquire or improve upon, or tell him that somebody else was more qualified for the position. If the injured party says, "Don't you think that this was a rotten trick?" and you know luck had nothing to do with it, just say, "You must be really disappointed," or some other phrase that lets him know you identify with his emotional state.

Conflicts

Since conflicts are unavoidable and inevitable, here are some short tips on how to handle everything from sexual harassment to embarrassing situations. Since conflicts usually occur without warning, we are often not ready for them. Let these ideas allow you to be better prepared.

Sexual Harassment

What to do? Go right to the senior officer in your company or department, report it, and demand justice? Put up with it until it becomes blatant? Cry? Hit somebody?

If the idea of a strategy appeals, it could begin with a response that attacks the ego of the offender: "I hope you don't think that was sexually attractive. In fact, it was comical. You're making a fool of yourself."

Or, stronger: "I didn't realize how pathetic you were. You're really a silly little man."

Or, begin with a warning: "I'm going to forget this happened. But if anything like this ever happens again, everybody here is going to know about it, and you're going to be in more trouble than you can imagine."

Be prepared to follow through on your warning if necessary.

Embarrassing Situations

You notice that someone's fly is open, that there's a giant run in somebody's stocking, that someone has spinach stuck between their front teeth, or has feloniously bad breath. What do you do?

You have to be direct but discreet. Get the person out of earshot of other people, and say, "Your fly is open," in the same tone of voice you would use to say, "It's raining outside."

If you don't know the person, find somebody in the group who does to give the message.

You are in a more serious situation if you have a friend who has a particular and persistent bad habit or something like chronic bad breath. If he's a real friend, you have to tell him about it, even if you know he won't like it. Use the "critical I" if you can.

"I've been told that I've had bad breath from time to time, but it seems to be a chronic problem with you. Maybe you have a dental problem you don't know about, or it might be just a matter of using mouthwash more often. That's what worked for me."

The story or analogy you convey doesn't necessarily have to be about the exact problem that your friend has. If you haven't had that exact problem before, choose a story that shows parallels to the other person's situation.

Tip
When you forget a name, you can try to bluff your way through, hoping the other person will drop a hint. Or you can focus on the solution instead of the problem: "Please tell me your name again. I seem to be in a dead zone at the moment."

Inappropriate Questions

"Are you two sleeping together?"

"How much money do you make?"

"How come you don't have any children?"

If someone comes up with a nasty or particularly inappropriate question, you can ignore them or tell them you consider the question to be rude. My favorite tactic is to say: "Why do you ask?"

Tip
If someone asks you how much your outfit cost or where you bought it, and you don't want to tell them, just say, "I don't remember."

Not That Story Again!

If Uncle Jack is getting ready to tell that seemingly endless African story again, say: "Oh, this is that great story about how you interviewed the chief of the Zulus. That must have been quite an experience."

Then jump in with a new topic of conversation.

Stand By Me

Somebody verbally attacks your friend when your friend isn't present, and you know you will regret it if you don't speak up. Here are some ways to respond:

Wrong: "Look who's talking. You're the jerk who…" or, "That's a lie."

Better: "I'm not sure that's exactly the way it happened. Even if it is, I'm sure Tom had a good reason for reacting the way he did."

If the other person asks what kind of reason he could have, say

"I don't know. Why don't you ask him the next time you see him?"

Petitions

You are asked to sign a petition. If you don't agree with the thrust of the petition, say so without starting an argument that is not going to change anybody's mind: "I've given this issue a great deal of thought, and I'm afraid I can't support this petition. I hope you understand."

If the person persists, say: "I'm sorry. that's the way I feel."

If you are not familiar with the issue at hand, say: "I don't know enough about this issue to agree or disagree with the petition. I need some time to look into the matter."

Dirty Jokes

If that jerk Phil starts telling what is sure to be an obscene joke, you can say: "I don't think I want to hear this," and move away.

If you don't realize what kind of joke it is until it's too late, just look right at him without laughing, and respond with: "I didn't think that was the least bit funny."

One theme that has run though all of the issues and situations discussed in this chapter is human dignity—a sense of self-worth and a respect for others. It is the quality that allows us to deal with conflict without being diminished by it. It allows us to accept criticism without rancor. It allows us to give compliments generously and to receive them gracefully.

The Least You Need to Know

➤ When delivering criticism, use the "critical I." For example: "I've noticed that when you turn in your time sheets late in the day, our administrator gets annoyed. What can we do to solve this?"

➤ Criticism should be impersonal, specific, and as positive as possible.

➤ When being criticized, don't become overly defensive. Remember that people are most defensive when they know they are wrong.

➤ The best compliments are sincere, spontaneous, specific, and unqualified.

➤ When someone compliments you, the perfect response is to simply say thank you.

➤ When someone tells you bad news, don't try to cheer them up by telling them that it could be worse.

Chapter 19

Speak Up

In This Chapter

➤ Ways to deliver an effective speech

➤ Handling stage fright

➤ How to make small talk

➤ Keeping your conversation going and how to get away

The human brain starts the moment you are born…and never stops until you stand up to speak in public.

—Sir George Jessel

We'd rather be in the box than give the eulogy.

—Jerry Seinfeld

Everyone, sooner or later, has to speak before a group of people. You may be called upon to give a toast. As host, you must publicly welcome the guest of honor. You may be asked to speak at a club meeting or address the school board about a problem in your neighborhood school. On a larger scale, you may have to make a presentation before your superiors and colleagues that could have a profound impact on your career, or you may find yourself giving a speech before hundreds of strangers. Or you might be talking one-on-one with your boss about a raise or that managerial position that just opened up.

Guess what? No matter what kind of speech you give and to whom you deliver it, the ways you prepare and deliver a speech are all the same for every situation.

Similarly, there are preparations and techniques that will help you become a more comfortable and accomplished conversationalist.

Stage Fright

Everybody gets it. Everybody can get over it.

Third-degree stage fright manifests itself as a revved-up heart beat, elevated blood pressure, a flushed face, and trembling hands. You are experiencing a reaction shared by your cave-dwelling ancestors. Experts call it the flight-or-fight reaction. When the cave man saw a saber-toothed tiger, adrenaline was pumped into his blood stream, and his body prepared itself to scamper up a tree or, if necessary, do battle.

Some people have the same kind of reaction the first time they face an audience. Here are some physical and mental tricks you can use to control this reaction:

➤ Keep in mind that the audience is not a tiger. They are disposed to like you. They want to relax almost as much as you do. They want you to succeed because that means they will be entertained. In other words, the audience is on your side.

➤ Since your stage fright reaction is a "right brain" function—instinctive and emotional—counter it with "left brain" activity. Count or work a numbers problem in your head. Think about how your talk is organized and how the various points are marshalled.

➤ Breathe. Fitness guru Pat Croce recommends inhaling deeply through the nose and exhaling through the mouth.

➤ Smile.

Getting Ready

When preparing to give a talk or, for that matter, when preparing for an important one-on-one meeting, ask yourself four questions:

1. *Who am I?* Does this person (audience) know you? What is your relationship, if any? How do you want them to perceive you? What attire would be most appropriate to communicate your role?

2. *Where am I?* The physical space will determine how you should use your voice and gestures, and whether you will need a microphone. Check out what audio-visual equipment is available and who will be running it. Think about what you will do if the equipment fails to function as expected. (It so often does.)

3. *Who am I talking to, and what's in it for them?* Why are they here, and what are their expectations? Are there shared characteristics between audience members? Do they have a specific point of view concerning you or your topic?

Did You Know?

People's impressions of each other come in three ways: visually (how you look), 55 percent; vocally (how your voice sounds), 38 percent; verbally (what you say), 7 percent. First impressions are formed within the first four to seven seconds.

4. *What do I want?* To welcome, to instruct, to motivate, to persuade? Do I want to ask for a raise, explain my situation, praise another person?

The Delivery

Here are some insider tips on public speaking from experienced speakers:

➤ Speak while standing whenever possible.

➤ Adjust your language to the audience. That doesn't mean "talk down." But your language and your references will be different when speaking to engineers and when speaking to artists. A young audience has a shorter attention span, so you will need to sprinkle more spice into your talk—gestures, vivid images, jokes. Male audiences respond more to visual images, women to verbal images.

➤ People like people who are like them, so try to make a connection by mentioning early something that connects you to the audience:

"Some people think that, because we are volunteers and are not being paid, that our work is somehow easier or somehow less important. We all know just how wrong that is, don't we?"

➤ Remember that you are more important than the material. The people are in the audience because they want to hear what *you* have to say and how *you* present the information. Otherwise they could stay home and read the report.

➤ Decide what points you want to make. Don't try for more than four major points in a 20-minute speech. The usual technique is to make a point, give a descriptive example, then remake the same point.

➤ Speak with feeling. Try to communicate your enthusiasm for your topic to your audience. Keep your head up, and speak clearly.

Did You Know?
The average attention span of an audience is eight seconds. People forget 25 percent of what they hear within 24 hours, 50 percent within 48 hours, and 80 percent within four days. Variation in your visual, vocal, and verbal delivery is imperative to hold an audience's attention.

➤ Control voice volume. Inexperienced speakers have a tendency to shout or to get louder as they go along. Think in terms of projecting. You can project your normal tone of voice without shouting and without sounding like a sideshow barker.

➤ Take your time. Another common error of inexperienced speakers is a tendency to speak quickly, as if every second has to be filled with information.

➤ Avoid rambling and repeating.

➤ When you have finished, if there is no question-and-answer session, say thank you, and sit down. Don't wave or otherwise acknowledge applause.

➤ If there is to be a question-and-answer period, say so, and raise your hand briefly to indicate the protocol for asking questions. Restate and, if necessary, rephrase questions. Don't say "good question." This gives the impression you are judging the questions.

➤ Don't refer to the questioner by name unless you are prepared to address everyone in the room by name.

The Opening

This is the second most important part of your talk. First impressions are critical because this is where the audience is sizing you up, deciding whether they like you or not, whether they can learn from you, whether they are going to be bored or excited. Have the first few words and the first few ideas firmly in your mind. You may want to introduce yourself to the audience, even if the previous speaker has already done so. Some speakers open by complimenting the audience, making some startling or provocative statement, telling a joke, or quoting a prominent person.

Tip

Let's face it, some people just can't tell a joke, and shouldn't. If your humorous sallies are frequently met with quizzical looks or strained smiles, leave jokes out of your speeches, even if you think the joke is hilariously funny and your delivery cunningly droll.

The Closing

This is *the* most important part of your talk. This is the last impression the audience will have of you, and it will be the most lasting impression. We can be forgiven for weakness or lapses in the *body* of the presentation, but never for the opening or the closing.

If the talk has been of a rather light nature, you may want to end with a very good joke, or a humorous spin on the material already presented. More often, the closing takes the form of a call to action. Don't be afraid to employ some dramatic or emotional language here. You may want to use a portion of some great speech or use some lines of stirring poetry. Some experienced speakers have a whole arsenal of fiery or sentimental quotes they can use to close a speech.

Introducing a Speaker

Your job in this case is much easier. Your basic objective is to get the speaker to the podium without a lot of fuss or delay. Leave yourself out of it as much as possible. Don't go into a long story about what good friends you are.

Get hold of a biography, and pare it down. Hit the highlights, and emphasize what is of particular interest to this group. The tone should be warm and welcoming. If it is a family gathering, a retirement party, or something similar, you can be a little more sentimental than at a seminar, lecture, or business function. But, still, brevity is the best policy.

Making Conversation

There is nothing small about small talk. Just ask those who dread situations in which they must employ it, mainly because they think of it as uncomfortable, unnecessary, and trivial. Just ask those who know how truly valuable it can be and have learned to use it to their advantage.

You can overcome an aversion to small talk, and learn to use and even enjoy it. Anybody can. It's what the experts call "learned behavior," which means a silver-tongued genius will be better at it than most, but anybody can be good at it.

First Impressions

It takes only about four seconds for somebody to size you up and make a preliminary judgment. Research shows that Americans expect three things when they meet someone for the first time—a smile, eye contact,

Tip
Some people are uncomfortable about looking directly into the eyes of another. If you are one of them, try the "third eye" trick: focus on the space above the nose and between the eyes.

and a handshake. So, look directly at the person you are meeting. Smile sincerely. Shake hands firmly, but don't crunch.

Opening a Conversation

First, introduce yourself, and listen carefully to the other person's name, repeating it early in the conversation to lock it into your memory. If the person attaches any other information to the name, it may give you a conversational path to follow: "I'm with the volunteers from Aston," or, "This is my first meeting with…"

Don't worry about using cliches. You can find out a lot about a person with a topic as seemingly banal as the weather. For example, you can start by sharing something of yourself to learn something about the other person:

"I don't know about you, but I sure don't thrive in this heat. Some people do. Are you one of them? Did you grow up in a hot climate?"

"Not really. I'm not a heat lover. I grew up in Ohio."

"Oh. What was it like growing up in the Midwest?"

"It was pleasant. I felt really safe there. People were friendly, things were a little slower paced."

"What brought you to the East Coast?"

"I came to New York to be an actress."

"Are you an actress now?"

"No. I'm a corporate trainer."

Thus, simply by asking about the weather, you have learned that the other person:

➤ Hates heat

➤ Is from the Midwest

➤ Lives on the East Coast

➤ Wanted to be an actress

➤ Is a corporate career person

More importantly, from non-verbal cues such as tone of voice and gestures, you probably have an idea whether this is someone you want to know better and/or do business with.

Don't be afraid to say you're shy: "Big parties like this intimidate me," or, "I like meeting new people, once I get over being a little shy." Nothing encourages people to open up like a desire to get other people to open up.

Keeping it Going

Listen. When people say, "He's a good conversationalist," they usually mean, "He's a good listener." Don't lie in wait for one of those natural conversation breaks so you can jump in with your next prepared statement or question. Interrupting is the most common and among the most irritating errors people make in conversation.

Let people know that you are listening through eye contact, but don't stare fixedly at them.

Also, ask open-ended questions. "Why did you decide to volunteer?" or, "How did you become involved with our group?" Questions that result in "yes" or "no" answers stop the flow of conversation.

People like to be asked their opinions and impressions concerning major news events: "I heard this morning that the mayor resigned. Makes you wonder what's behind that, doesn't it?"

Every topic has its own natural life span, and if someone is going on endlessly about one thing, it is a good idea to cut in, as tactfully as possible. If, for example, the back and forth about the mayor is lively and quick, settle down and enjoy it. If it begins to sag under its own weight, try changing the topic. The easiest way is switching to a related topic. "Speaking of politicians (or speaking of retiring or public figures or our city)…"

When you're engaged in a conversation, keep in mind the following don'ts:

➤ Don't perform. This happens when you are concentrating too hard on the impression you want to make on the other person.

➤ Don't speed-talk. Sometimes people who are anxious to make a point try to spit it all out quickly, as if they're afraid they won't be permitted to finish the thought.

➤ Don't slow-talk. A sure sign that you're dragging things out is other people finishing a sentence for you or nodding to indicate they understand even before you have reached the point of your remarks.

➤ Don't watch other people moving around in the room while someone is talking to you.

➤ Don't hold a drink in your right hand, which leads to damp, cold handshakes. If your palm is sweaty, it's okay to give it a quick swipe on the side of your trousers or skirt before extending it for a handshake.

➤ Don't talk about your health, the cost of things these days, mean gossip, off-color jokes, or controversial issues—particularly when you don't know where the other person stands on the subject.

On the other hand, it is okay to disagree. Wait until the other person has had his say, then introduce your point of view without saying something judgmental like, "That's completely off base," or, "You couldn't be more wrong about that." Instead, say something like, "I disagree because…" or, "Well, another way of looking at it is…"

Body Language

Don't fold your arms, and do keep your hands away from your mouth. Both send negative signals. It is better to hold a drink in one hand and put the other in your pocket or, perhaps, on the strap of your handbag. The point is to look relaxed and receptive. Lean forward slightly when the other person speaks.

Getting Away

It is very important to close a conversation gracefully. As humans, there are two things we need when dealing with others—acknowledgment and closure.

We need people to acknowledge our presence. That's why it is less annoying waiting in line at the store when the clerk says, "I'll be right with you," or even just looks at you and nods so that you know he knows that you are waiting. This is also the reason that we are so annoyed when a receptionist says, "Please hold," and cuts us off before we can say anything.

By the same token, it is annoying when people just drift away after a conversation without some acknowledgment that a conversation has occurred. When you feel a conversation has run its course or it is necessary for you to move along, wait for a break in the conversation, then say:

"Well, I've got to say hello to our host (or George or my aunt, for example)."

Or say, "That food looks delicious. Think I'll have some."

Or say, "I'm going over to the bar for a refill." (Don't try this one while holding a full glass.)

Then say something like:

"It was good talking with you. I enjoyed learning about Ireland."

If others at a party interrupt, and it is not possible to end the conversation properly, make some sort of parting gesture, if it is only eye contact and a wave.

Giving a talk and holding a conversation have a lot in common. Both work better if you are relaxed and natural. In a way, both put you "on stage." If you try to put on a show or if you are not entirely sincere, your listeners will pick up on it. So, don' t say things you don't believe, even if it is something as trivial as complimenting someone on a hat or dress, or telling someone he looks terrific when you both know he doesn't.

The Least You Need to Know

➤ If you suffer from stage fright, remember that the audience wants to relax as much as you do.

➤ Before you speak, run over the four big questions: "Who am I? Where am I? Who am I talking to? What do I want?"

➤ The two most crucial parts of your speech are the closing and the opening.

➤ The most important aspects of a conversation are acknowledgment and closure: Greet people, and find out something about them; and end the conversation gracefully.

➤ When people say, "He's a good conversationalist," they really mean he knows how to listen.

Chapter 20

Giving and Receiving Gifts

In This Chapter

➤ The Gift Quiz

➤ Giving gifts in the workplace

➤ Children and gifts

➤ Gift ideas for special occasions and age groups

Even if you don't accept the precept that it is better to give than to receive, you must acknowledge that it is important to do both graciously.

Rule #1: Your mother was right. It's the thought that counts.

There are times when spending too much is taboo, and there are times when "a little something" is just not enough. But time given to the thoughtful selection of a gift, no matter who is receiving it, no matter what the occasion, is never wasted.

And receiving a gift with a graceful expression of gratitude will be appreciated in direct proportion to the time and thought given to the selection of the gift.

The Gift Quiz

Here are ten questions to ask yourself when giving a gift.

1. Why am I giving it?

2. Is it sincere?

3. Am I giving it without strings attached?

4. Does it reflect the receiver's taste—not mine?

5. Is it too extravagant?

6. Is it kind? (Beware of gag gifts.)

7. Is it appropriate? (No candy for a dieter.)

8. Can I present it in person?

9. Is it presented beautifully?

10. Do I feel good about giving it?

Let's expand a bit on number one, "Why am I giving it?" Often, we give a gift to say thanks to a business associate for an introduction, to someone who gave a lunch or dinner in our honor, to a couple for dinner at their home, to a person who gave us information that helped land business, or to someone who treated us to dinner.

Gifts also are given to congratulate someone on a promotion, an award, a marriage, a birth, an anniversary or a birthday. When choosing a gift, don't forget the reason you are giving it.

No matter what the occasion, keep these points in mind the next time you give someone a gift:

➤ If you are tempted to buy a youngster war toys, check first with the parents. Some have very strong feelings on the subject.

➤ Never give children pets unless you have cleared it with the parents beforehand.

➤ Joke gifts may get a laugh at the moment of giving, but can leave a sour aftertaste.

➤ The value of a gift is enhanced by the fact that it arrives on time and is nicely wrapped.

➤ Notes accompanying gifts should be hand-written. If you include a greeting card, there should be a written note to accompany whatever printed sentiment the card contains.

➤ A gift of money can be most conveniently given in the form of a check or cashier's check. Cash is more appropriate for a child. When giving cash, include a note mentioning the amount in case some is lost or mislaid and to help the recipient when it comes time to send a thank-you. The note can say something like: "I hope these ten dollars will fund your victory pizza after the game."

Generally, money is a gift given by older people to younger people. It's a good idea to try to learn if the recipient is saving for something special and to include a note saying the gift is to bring the person closer to that goal.

Gift Giving At Work

Some of the most difficult questions about gift-giving concern the workplace. It is an area of behavior in which careful thought and prudence are especially important.

Rule #1: Extravagance is bad manners and bad strategy.

Rule #2: Modesty and quality are the key words.

Once again, it is important that the recipient realize you gave some thought as to what would please him. This might mean talking to someone's spouse or secretary to learn what a person's hobbies are or what kind of music, books, or foods would be a special treat.

Faux Pas
Never send alcohol to a person's office. Most companies prohibit alcohol consumption on the job, and the mere presence of alcohol in the office is not very professional.

How Much Should I Spend?

Once you have an idea for a gift, consider how much to spend. Usually, $25 is an appropriate ceiling for gifts to employees and subordinates. That's the limit the government puts on such deductions.

However, if the employee has been working for a person for years and has become a personal friend or almost part of the family—as is the case with many executive assistants—the boss might want to spend up to $100, but no more. But watch out. What you give sets a precedent which must be matched or exceeded in the future. Etiquette does not dictate that a gift be matched or exceeded in the future, but the recipient will hope for this, and could be hurt

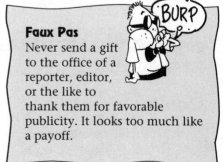

Faux Pas
Never send a gift to the office of a reporter, editor, or the like to thank them for favorable publicity. It looks too much like a payoff.

and confused if your next gift is little more than a token. It's best to keep a record of who got what and when.

On the other hand, an employee is under no obligation to give a superior a gift. There is always the danger of being suspected of apple-polishing. The truth is that you may be better advised to wait until there's a spontaneous reason to give a gift, and then bring along some flowers from the garden or a batch of cookies or brownies.

In all cases, the best way to present a gift is in person. Gifts must be wrapped beautifully to demonstrate that time and thought went into them. Shoving a nicely wrapped gift into a plastic shopping bag can ruin the entire effect. And, receiving a splendidly wrapped gift with a personal enclosure note in its own envelope is one of life's nicest experiences. This is especially true if the note shows a bit more thought than the usual platitudes.

Children and Gifts

If a child is giving a teacher a gift at Christmas or Hanukah, on a birthday, or at the end of the school year, the gift should not be extravagant. It is a good idea for the gift to come from the entire class. If, however, it is from a single child, a small token—perhaps something handmade—is appropriate. The gift should be wrapped and accompanied by a card.

Tip
Flowers are appropriate to send the morning of a party or the day after. If sending flowers to a home, make sure the recipient will be there to receive them. Women, remember that it is perfectly acceptable to send flowers to men.

And, like adults, children should send a thank you note if the giver has not been present to be thanked in person. In fact, it is a nice idea (and teaches a small lesson) to send a note to Uncle Danny, even if he has been thanked in person.

Parents should impress upon their children that, no matter how dumb or ugly they think a gift is, the giver must never know: "Uncle Danny likes you and respects you enough to go to the trouble and expense of getting you something he thinks you will like. Telling him it's dumb or ugly will hurt his feelings."

Ages and Occasions

Here are a few ideas for suitable gifts for special people and special occasions.

Babies

Baby gifts are often saved to be treasured as adults. Thus, small silver and gold objects can be considered. Pins, mugs, rattles, or bracelets, with the name and birth date, are good ideas. Consider a one-of-a-kind drawing created around the child's name and birth date.

Another idea is a photograph album with pictures of the baby and space for other pictures to be added through the years.

A gift that will be appreciated by the parents and, later on by the child, is a savings bond or a savings account opened with a suitable foundation to build on.

Gifts for contemporary use can include rattles, crib mobiles, a car seat, clothing, a baby blanket, or a music box.

Children

Books, toys, a telescope, magical tricks, simple and "parent-friendly" (non-messy) craft kits, computer games, and kaleidoscopes are all great gifts.

For Confirmation or bar/bat mitzvah, consider a sterling silver cross or a Star of David pin. Other possibilities include a subscription to a magazine like National Geographic, binoculars, an electronic dictionary, a nylon windbreaker, perhaps with the name of a favorite team on the back, roller blades, or a skateboard.

Teenagers

Money. Tickets to movies or a pop music concert will also be greatly appreciated. Other ideas include gift certificates to music and video stores, a camera, tickets to a sports event, sports equipment, or a portable CD player.

High School Graduation

This is one of the great turning points in life, a step from school kid into adulthood.

Money, of course, and savings bonds or stock and gift certificates are always appropriate and appreciated. A watch, a leather checkbook carrier, or a weekend travel bag can signal recognition of the graduate's new independent status.

If applicable, you can give things to take to college: luggage, clock radio, bed linens and towels, hair dryer, popcorn popper, a portable word processor, perhaps with a dictionary-thesaurus included. Also, gift certificates, cash, and tickets to movies or other events are always good ideas.

Tip
The trouble with gifts from gift shops is that they look like gifts from gift shops. An exception is the museum gift shop, particularly in the larger museums, where something interesting and/or classy can often be found.

235

College Graduation

Knowing the graduate's future plans can help with your selection. If they include graduate school, a gift certificate to the college book store will help. If an office job awaits, a monogrammed leather briefcase may be appropriate. Also consider buying beer or coffee mugs, luggage, engraved stationery, or a telephone answering machine.

Wedding Showers

Shower gifts are almost invariably things that can be used around the house, such as small appliances. Get together with the bride's friends, and confer. This will avoid duplication and also give you an idea of the price range. Bridal registries are also a possible source, although they're used mostly for wedding gifts. Showers may take different forms. Sometimes, guests are assigned to a specific "room" in the home of the newlyweds, and buy a gift appropriate to that room. Be practical. This is not a good situation in which to look for something "she wouldn't buy for herself." At one time, wedding showers were for women only. That is no longer the case.

If you decline an invitation to a shower, it is not necessary to send a gift.

Weddings

The bridal registry at local stores can save you lots of time and concern. You will be confident that you are purchasing something that the happy couple wants. Shopping early gives you a wider selection when you use the registry.

There is a whole new variety of stores where couples are registered these days, aside from the usual home and department stores. These include mega-hardware stores like Home Depot, electronic stores, records and CD stores. This opens up a whole new world of possibilities.

If, however, you do not wish to go the registry route, you must first set a budget figure. Then, consider the following categories:

Did You Know?
There is an old superstition, largely discarded now, that clocks are not appropriate wedding gifts because they are reminders that "time runs out."

➤ Money, in the form of checks, bonds, stocks

➤ Art objects, such as paintings, sculptures or antiques

➤ Silver flatware, candlesticks, salt and pepper shakers, chafing dishes, frames for wedding pictures, a box engraved with a facsimile of the wedding invitation.

➤ Crystal Stemware, candlesticks, vases.

➤ Furnishings, such as card tables, coffee tables, mirrors, table lamps.

Weddings are also occasions when treasured family heirlooms are passed along to the younger generation.

Anniversaries

For the most part, you will be giving gifts only on the occasion of special anniversaries, such as a silver or 25-year anniversary. Remember that the recipients are at a stage in their lives in which they are not interested in collecting possessions, particularly household items or knickknacks. A good strategy is to get together with a group of friends or relatives and jointly purchase a vacation trip or a big-screen television.

For very close friends or relatives, you may want to give anniversary gifts more often than every 25 years. If so, you might be interested in consulting the traditional and revised lists of gifts given for different years. The origins of the traditional list are lost in antiquity. The revised list, which is in more general use these days, was created in 1948 by the Jewelry Industry Council. The traditional list has no entries for the 16th through 19th anniversaries, so the entries for those years listed below are from the revised list.

Traditional/Revised Lists of Gifts by Anniversary

1st	Paper/clocks
2nd	Cotton/china
3rd	Leather/crystal, glass
4th	Books/electrical appliances
5th	Wood, clocks/silverware
6th	Candy, iron/wood
7th	Copper, bronze, brass/desk sets
8th	Electrical appliances/linen, lace
9th	Pottery/leather
10th	Tin, aluminum/diamonds
11th	Steel/fashion jewelry
12th	Silk, linen/colored gems, pearls
13th	Lace/textiles, furs
14th	Ivory/gold jewelry
15th	Crystal/watches
16th	Silver hollow ware
17th	Furniture
18th	Porcelain
19th	Bronze
20th	China/platinum
25th	Silver/silver

30th	Pearl/diamond
35th	Coral, jade/jade
40th	Ruby/ruby
45th	Sapphire/sapphire
50th	Gold/gold

Birthdays

There are no firm rules, except the usual ones regarding thoughtfulness and timeliness. Remember that a birthday is a magical time for a child; a little extravagance is permissible, and a lot of creativity is recommended. In the workplace, a card and/or an invitation to lunch are appropriate.

Birthday gifts involving birthstones are always welcome. The following is a list of birthstones by month:

January	Garnet
February	Amethyst
March	Bloodstone or aquamarine
April	Diamond
May	Emerald
June	Pearl or moonstone
July	Ruby
August	Sardonyx or peridot
September	Sapphire
October	Opal or tourmaline
November	Topaz
December	Turquoise or zircon

Housewarming

Stationery with the new address, a welcome mat (the practical kind), a plant that can survive some inattention, a coffee table book, and gift certificates to the local book store or wine merchant are all wonderful housewarming gifts.

Coming to Dinner

Don't bring things that need immediate attention from a person who may be frantically busy in the kitchen. Cut flowers, for example, cause the host or hostess to stop, find a vase, and add water. Instead, try wine or an easy-care plant.

> **Tip**
>
> If you are bringing wine or food to a dinner party, say something like: "We thought you might enjoy this later." This relieves the host of the pressure of having to deal with the gift immediately, and he knows that it was not necessarily intended to be part of the meal.

House Guests

When selecting a gift for the host and/or hostess, consider the nature of the friendship, the length of the visits, and the tastes of those being visited. If you want to bring something with you, consider a flowering plant, a wheel of Brie cheese, an art book; or you can offer to bring along that casserole which you are so famous for.

Many visitors like to observe the home and, after the visit, acquire a gift that will complement both the host and the house.

For the Traveler

Unless it's a shipboard bon voyage party, gifts for the traveler must be both practical and portable. For someone facing a long flight, for example, consider a compact tape player with tapes of music, poetry, or language instruction. Or, you can make your own tape, mixing music with personal messages, etc. If it's a driving vacation, the player will probably be unnecessary because most cars are equipped with tape players.

Some currency of the destination country might be helpful. Other ideas include a journal in which to record the highlights of the trip, a leather passport/ticket holder, one of those pocket-sized plastic rain ponchos, a small travel alarm clock, and a currency converter.

Retirement

Some people approach retirement with cheerful enthusiasm. Some, particularly if circumstances have forced retirement upon them, do not want the occasion celebrated. Check with the retiree's spouse or close friend before deciding on whether to give a gift.

Some ideas: A tool kit for the handyman, a home-brew starter kit for the beer lover, sporting equipment, a backyard hammock, piano lessons, a trial membership in a health club or spa.

When the party's over, and your grateful smile flickers and dims, it is time to consider returning gifts. It might be a book you have already read, clothes that don't fit, or something you just can't stand to have around. Remember, however, that you can't return things made especially for you or things that the giver might expect to find on your bookshelf or coffee table during a subsequent visit. You may be able to tell a very close friend that you will exchange a shirt for another size or color or a book for another title, but never ask the giver of a gift to exchange it for you unless you are physically unable to leave the house. Common sense in this area will bring you many happy returns.

The Least You Need to Know

➤ Gifts should be accompanied by a hand-written note and wrapped as beautifully as possible.

➤ Gifts of money are most conveniently given in the form of a check.

➤ For teachers, the gift ideally should come from the class, with all contributing. If giving a gift individually, it should be an inexpensive token.

➤ In general, $25 is an appropriate ceiling for gifts to employees, unless there are special circumstances.

➤ For the boss, flowers from the garden or brownies as a spontaneous response to a particular occasion will avoid giving the impression of apple polishing.

➤ Remember that gift-giving is not your golden opportunity to impose your taste on another person. Think about what would please the recipient, not you.

Part 6
Fun and Games

This part of the book begins with etiquette for the links, the slopes, and other energetic occasions and then moves on to ships (yachts and liners), trains, planes, and other modes of transportation.

Etiquette in the world of sports, whether it's working out at the health club or smashing a serve on the tennis court, takes on added importance because many of the rules of behavior are closely linked to safety. We will also talk about what to wear on the courts, the slopes, and so on.

Travel etiquette not only involves getting from here to there with style, but is also concerned with safety and comfort while on the road, tipping, luggage, packing, and other crucial matters.

Finally, we will deal with the pleasures and pitfalls of preparing for and surviving a wedding.

Chapter 21

Sports Etiquette

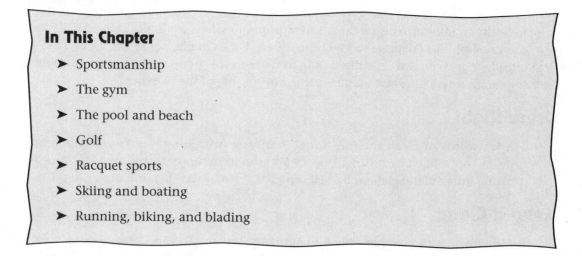

In This Chapter

➤ Sportsmanship

➤ The gym

➤ The pool and beach

➤ Golf

➤ Racquet sports

➤ Skiing and boating

➤ Running, biking, and blading

Sportsmanship is etiquette with an application of perspiration.

A good sportsman plays by the rules, gives opponents the benefit of the doubt, is concerned for everybody's safety, dresses appropriately for the situation, and is gracious in both victory and defeat.

Parents have always found that teaching their children to behave like good sports—being fair, trying hard to win but, win or lose, doing their best—gives them valuable, character-building tools that will help them throughout their lives.

While the overall rules of good sportsmanship apply to all athletic endeavors, there are special rules of etiquette and distinct consideration as we move from one arena of activity to another. There are, for example, things you should know about behavior on the golf course that are very much different from the etiquette considerations on the ski slopes. Let's look at some of these areas.

Gym Dandies

Some people seem to think it is not necessary to exercise common sense and good manners in places where people exercise.

The opposite is true.

When the fitness-minded get single-minded about their workouts, things can get pretty grim in the gym. People can lose all consideration for—or even awareness of—those around them. Maybe it's all those mirrors.

However, the very fact that gym activities are so "me" based makes courtesy an absolute necessity to minimize distractions and to promote safety. It's a place where bad manners can cause physical damage to you or to others. For example, never join an exercise group already in session: it will be distracting to those in the group, and you may have missed important safety information given at the beginning of the workout.

Dress Right

The key words are clean and functional. Scanty, sexy dressing is not only inappropriate, it is distracting and embarrassing. Don't walk around in flimsy footwear or stocking feet. Walking into a metal plate or barbell can give you a broken toe or foot.

Keep it Clean

Bring a towel with you, not only for your body, but also to wipe down weight machines. It is a mortal sin to leave these machines with your perspiration on the pads. Don't leave towels around where people can walk on or trip over them. Never leave a towel on a weight machine.

If you are carrying a water bottle or chart with you, keep them out of the way of others while you are exercising.

In the locker room, don't leave your bag or sweaty clothes on the floor, particularly in front of somebody else's locker. Clean up in the sink area after yourself as if you have been using the bathroom in someone else's house.

Making the Circuit

Here are some words of advice for those using free weights or weight machines, such as Nautilus.

➤ Don't jump ahead of someone because that machine or that set of weights is next in your routine. Wait. If there's any doubt about the availability of the equipment, ask.

➤ Don't dally. If you are going to rest a long while between sets of reps, give up the machine—particularly if the place is crowded. Don't leave your towel on the machine to hold it for yourself while you rest. If you are working out with a friend, don't stop to chat or compare notes between exercises. Keep each other's progress charts to keep the process moving.

➤ Shut up. Grunts and moans are unnecessary, theatrical, distracting, and unsafe. The professionals tell me that making these noises while straining increases pressure on your respiratory system and can push your blood pressure up. And don't count out loud when you are doing reps. It can throw off others around you who are counting reps to themselves.

➤ Unload. Always strip plates and clear your squat bars. If you borrow those little saddle weights that go on top of the weight stacks from another machine, return them when you are finished. Never leave plates or barbells where people can trip over them.

➤ Keep your chart with you, and be careful where you put it on the machine you are using. Generally it should be beneath the machine or on a hook if one is provided.

Trainers

Working with a personal trainer adds another layer of gym etiquette. The primary rule is to respect the trainer's expertise and time. Give 24 hours notice if you must cancel or reschedule an appointment, and be prepared to pay for the trainer's time if you don't give 24 hours notice.

Don't make it hard for the trainer to do the job by trying to take over or control the workout session. Sure, it's your body, but the trainer knows more about getting it in shape than you do.

The trainer is a physical, not emotional, therapist and shouldn't have to deal with your emotional ups and downs.

Don't talk to your trainer while she is with another client. Wait until the session is over.

Tip

Many people include a workout session when they are traveling. Here are some points to consider when you are planning to work out at a gym where you are not a regular.

➤ Find out what sort of place it is. Is it strictly a workout-sports gym or one of the "amenities" spas with a juice bar and carpeted walls?

➤ Ask what the guest policies are. What's the fee? Do you have to be a member or be sponsored by a member?

➤ Find out if there is a dress code.

The Pool

Generally the pool is used for three purposes, lap swimming, aqua-aerobics or just splashing around, and all of these people have an equal right to be in the pool.

Lap swimmers, of course, should stay in their lane. If the pool is a busy one, lanes may be reserved for specific times. When in doubt, check it out. If you are going to take a break of more than a few minutes, get out of the pool.

Others using the pool, either singly or in aerobics groups, can claim a lane of their own or use an unlaned area. If you are not in a group, try to find a lane or area that is not being used by lap swimmers. Parents should instruct children not to play in the lanes where the lap swimmers are chugging up and down.

In general, behaving cautiously is the best etiquette when it comes to swimming. If you can't swim, stay in the wading areas, and stop by your local YMCA, which probably has learn-to-swim classes all year round. It's great exercise and enjoyed by more people than any other sport.

If you are a guest at a swimming pool, private or otherwise, be sure to bring your own towel and swim attire. If you see a towel on a chair, it's a pretty good indication that somebody is using the chair and will return. Bring your own shampoo, makeup, hair dryer, and so on. As at the beach, use earphones, and try not to drip on people.

The Beach

Come equipped. Have cover-ups not only for going into nearby stores and restaurants, but for protection against the sun. And bring along sun block. The sun can be a dangerous enemy for the unprepared. Bring drinking water to protect against dehydration and repellent to protect against bugs.

Check out the rules before you make plans for picnicking, bonfires, and barbecues. And never leave trash behind. Also check out the signals used by lifeguards to indicate safety conditions. They can be written on a board or indicated by flags and markers.

If you want music, bring earphones. Don't drip on sunbathers.

If you are a guest at a private beach club, be guided by your host. Bring cash with you to pay for incidentals. Offer to pay for lunch, even though your host probably intends to do so. Make sure to ask about tipping protocol. Tipping is not permitted in many clubs.

No matter how well you swim, never swim alone—even in a pool. Every beach or swim club has posted rules. Read and obey. For instance, don't swim out beyond the posted limit. The rule applies even if you are an Olympic distance swimmer.

The Fair Way—Etiquette on the Links

Golf requires a level of personal integrity not found in other sports. The golfer himself declares his ball to be out of bounds. He keeps his own score and reports his scores to establish his handicap. (Handicapping allows two players of different degrees of accomplishment to compete equally. It gives the less skilled player a chance to beat a better player.)

It is important to know both the rules and the traditions of golf. The rules are published every year by the Royal and Ancient Golf Club of St. Andrews, Scotland, and the United States Golf Association, which is headquartered in Princeton, N.J. Even experienced players have a rule book handy, and it is a must for beginners.

The popularity of the game is increasing rapidly. Once considered a rich man's game, it is now most emphatically not just for the rich and not just for the men. More women are playing the game than ever.

As more and more golfers flock to the links, the need becomes greater for golfers to observe a consistent, companionable and comprehensive code of behavior.

Dress Code

Each club and course has its own standards, and if you play at someone else's club, it's important to do your homework before showing up. It's pretty safe to assume that an inordinate amount of exposed skin is not a good idea, from the point of view of both good health and proper decorum.

➤ Jeans are not considered appropriate, even when they are permitted.

➤ Women wear skirts (knee length) or long shorts or slacks, along with polo shirts. Either long or short sleeves are fine. In hot weather, sleeveless shirts are acceptable but might be inadvisable for those susceptible to sunburn.

➤ Men wear slacks and long shorts with polo shirts.

➤ Both men and women usually wear some kind of hat to shield them from the sun's glare.

➤ Golf shoes are cleated, and pros recommend wearing a leather golf glove and carrying protective rain gear when necessary.

A good pro shop will advise as to the proper attire. And, whether you plan to make a long-term, serious commitment to the game or to just play a few rounds with friends, you will want to wear the appropriate "uniform."

Carts

The emergence of the golf cart has not only contributed to the redesigning of golf courses to include narrow riding paths, it has necessitated a whole separate set of etiquette rules:

➤ Drive slowly and carefully.

➤ There should be no more than two persons per cart, and no more than two golf bags. Your bag should be on the side of the cart in which you are sitting.

➤ Children must not be permitted to drive the cart.

➤ Follow the directions on the course.

➤ Keep the cart out of sightlines of players in your group when they are hitting the ball.

➤ Don't drive too close to sand traps or greens or between them.

➤ Don't leave the cart in front of the green, but on the side nearest the next teeing-off location.

Safety

Make sure the players in front of you are well clear before hitting the ball. This may involve walking some distance to see over or around hills. If you think there is any chance of anyone being within range of your shot, yell "fore." Take a last look around before you settle down to take your swing to make sure everybody knows you are about to swing and is standing clear.

The Play

It's good manners to keep the game moving along. Make sure you are ready to hit the ball when your turn comes. Use the time while others are playing to decide which club to use and how to approach the next shot. You can concentrate and take your time and still play within the time frames set forth by the United States Golf Association.

If the party behind you is right on your heels, you might want to invite them to play through. Similarly, if the group in front is playing slowly, you can go ahead and ask them if you can play through.

The following are some additional rules of the green:

➤ Carry extra balls, and help your fellow players track down lost balls.

➤ Don't damage the course. Rake the sand after you hit out of a trap. Replace divots (chunks of turf torn loose by the club head).

➤ Littering on the course is a mortal sin. In fact, it is a bad idea to be eating or drinking anything at all on the course.

➤ If you lose a bet, pay up promptly.

Teeoff

Often, the men's tee is farther back than the women's, and men tee off first. If there is any question about who tees off first, flip a coin. There is no such thing as gender preference in this situation. After teeing off, the person whose ball is farthest from the hole plays first.

For the rest of the game, the golfer who won the last hole goes first. This rule applies to team play as well: the team that won the last hole goes first. The order of play within the team remains the same regardless of who had the best score.

Racquet Sports

At the exercise club or the tennis club, rules of preference or position cease to exist. Members and guests are on an equal footing, whatever their status outside.

Offer to help out or even instruct beginners if they need it. It's also okay to ask others for guidance. If you are unsure about the rules of the club, you will usually find them posted. If not, ask for a briefing. If you are unsure about the rules of a particular game, the club usually will have printed information. Tennis clubs follow the rules set forth by the United States Lawn Tennis Association.

➤ As for dress, white is usually safe for all racquet sports. Color variations are common at some places, but white is still the uniform at the stricter clubs. Find out in advance.

➤ No matter what you see professional tennis players doing on television, temper tantrums—verbal and non-verbal—are very bad form. In fact, players should be quiet on the courts. Obviously, it makes sense to exchange verbal signals with your partners when playing doubles. Beyond that, comments and exclamations are distracting to those you are playing with and those on other courts.

➤ Don't make a fuss about errors or bad play, even your own. And don't dish up excuses for a bad game such as the weather, your partner, your health, or your shoes. However, there's nothing wrong with saying, "I had a really bad game today."

➤ If you are a beginner and it looks as if you will be playing with a more experienced player, let him know what he's in for before you get on the court. And, if you are an experienced player up against a beginner, your job is to give advice and encouragement, not to see how thoroughly you can destroy him.

➤ No sneaky serves. If in doubt, say, "Ready?"

➤ Show up on time, and don't hog the court.

➤ If a ball comes into your court, return it when there's a break in the play. Don't expect others to interrupt their play to return your ball.

➤ Stay in your own court, and when you walk behind a court, wait until there is a break in the play before passing. Say, "Excuse me," on the way through.

➤ The wrong shoes can damage a court.

➤ Don't bring the pro shop with you onto the tennis court, or on any sports outing for that matter. Show up with just the equipment and accessories you know you will need. Extravagance is bad manners in most situations, and particularly in sports.

Skiing

This is another sport that is growing enormously in popularity, and in which the rules of etiquette are inextricably bound to safety.

Dress Right

No matter how adorable (or ruggedly casual) your outfit is, it will look stupid if it is not appropriate to the slopes. You need clothing that will not only keep you warm but will resist water and wind. The outfit must be snug while allowing you freedom of movement. Jeans are a bad idea because they don't dry out easily. They stay wet and cold and heavy.

Layering is essential. This means a cotton turtleneck, long underwear, sweater, ski pants, ski jacket and a hat or cap. Wear a pair of thin socks under heavy ski socks. Goggles are more durable than sunglasses. The reason outer ski wear is so colorful is so that it can been seen easily against the snow.

Don't forget the sun block. Even when the weather is cold, the sun is the sun.

Basic Rules of Manners

Basic rules of politeness include staying in your place in the lift line. If you are alone, offer to ride the lift with another single to avoid breaking up couples or groups. While in line, hold your skis upright in front of you to avoid whacking your neighbors. If it's your first experience with lifts, stand back and watch how the boarding procedure works before you get aboard. At the top, clear the lift area immediately so as not to cause a traffic jam.

Beginners should take some lessons before attempting the slopes. The sport only *looks* easy. In fact, the first experience with skis, boots, and poles can make even the most graceful individual feel like a klutz.

Experienced skiers should not boast or make remarks about the skill levels of the less experienced.

Rules of the Trails

Skiing is among the most dangerous of sports. Great care and attention to the rules are vitally important.

When hitting the slopes, remember these critical points:

➤ Regardless of your ability, never ski alone. Anyone can fall, get a cramp, or break a piece of equipment. If you get hurt or stuck and no one is around to assist you, it's just you and the mountain and the weather—a possibly deadly combination. And, if nobody knows where you are, no one can come to get you.

251

➤ Never ski on a closed trail. First, it might be closed because there is something treacherous there. Second, it could be closed in preparation for a special event. Third, the ski patrol only watches open trails.

➤ Ski only on trails that match your ability level. If you want the challenge of moving up to a more difficult trail, make sure you have an instructor or expert skier with you, and don't try it during peak hours. Novices on expert trails endanger themselves and the more skilled skiers. Experts on novice trails panic beginners by whizzing past them. Look for these trail markers:

Green circle for novices

Blue square for intermediates

Black diamond for experts

➤ The slower skier in front of you always has the right of way. If you are going to pass the slower skier, yell "track right" or "track left" depending on which side you will pass. This will warn the other skier against turning into your path.

➤ If you are climbing on skis or on foot, stay well over to the edge of the trail. The same applies if you decide to walk down.

➤ Mountains are large. It's a good idea to select a particular spot to check in with your friends periodically rather than relying on the chance of encountering each other randomly.

Accidents

If you come upon an injured skier, take off his skis, but never his boots. Mark the spot with crossed skis or poles. Don't attempt to move him. You may aggravate an injury. Wait for another person to come along before you go for help. Mark the spot well in your mind so that you will be able to lead the ski patrol to the victim.

Running

Running is the most inexpensive, effective and convenient form of cardiovascular workout. No wonder everybody seems to be doing it these days.

However, beginners should approach the sport with some caution. Learn how to stretch properly, or there's a good chance you will sprain something or do something else that will nip your running program in the bud. There are dozens of magazines for runners that provide solid basic information for runners—including the crucial consideration of getting the proper shoes.

A lot of runners start out by walking, which is itself an effective and highly recommended form of exercise.

Safety

It's a good idea to seek out designated running paths. It's a bad idea to explore unknown territory on your own. Never run in deserted or dark areas. Don't wear jewelry or carry a wallet. Let someone know where you will be running and what time you expect to return. Run where there is access to public telephones in case you need to make a call. You could, for instance, get a cramp and want to have someone come and pick you up.

Run against the traffic on the road. Pay attention to traffic signals. Don't expect drivers to watch out for you. Run during the day if at all possible. If you are out after sundown, wear a reflecting vest. Earphones can mask traffic noise, such as horns and sirens, and should not be played at high volumes, if at all.

Carry identification and a little change or a phone card for the telephone.

Biking

Biking is another fast-growing sport. Before you start, familiarize yourself with the rules of the bikers' road. You can find information and safety tips at any good bicycle store, and they also might be able to put you in touch with a local biking group.

If you are interested in pursuing the sport beyond a pleasant pastime, contact the League of American Wheelmen, and obtain a copy of its magazine, *Bicycle USA* (800-288-BIKE).

Did You Know?
You can be arrested and charged with drunken driving if you are caught operating a bicycle on a road or street while under the influence of alcohol or drugs.

On the road, your bike is a vehicle and subject to traffic regulations. Ride with the traffic, on the shoulder of the road where possible, use the proper hand signals, and give pedestrians the right of way. You must wear a helmet and, in the dark or at dusk, reflective gear. Other useful equipment includes goggles, gloves, proper shoes, and bicycle clips to keep your trousers from getting caught in the wheel.

Roller Blading

Roller blading is a relatively new and increasingly popular sport. It makes traditional "roller skating" seem tame.

The International In-Line Skating Association has these recommendations:

➤ *Skate politely.* Stay to the right, and pass on the left. Announce your intentions by saying, "Pass on your left." Yield to pedestrians. In general, try to be a good-will ambassador for in-line skating.

➤ *Skate smart.* Always wear protective gear—helmet, wrist protection, elbow and knee pads. Master the basics—moving, stopping, turning. Keep your equipment in safe condition.

➤ *Skate legally.* Obey all traffic regulations. Skaters have the same obligations as the operators of any wheeled vehicle.

➤ *Skate alertly.* Control your speed. Watch out for road hazards. Avoid water, oil, and sand. Stay away from heavy traffic.

Boating

Boating adventures come with a particular and distinct burden of etiquette. Considerate behavior and a knowledge of the rules (and traditions) are essential because of the close quarters and the very real dangers that ignorance can bring about for yourself and your shipmates.

Behavior

Whether you are going out for a few hours of sailing or a cruise of several days or weeks, the first rule is that the captain (or skipper) is the boss. When it comes to the ship, his word is law. If he orders you around on occasion, don't take it personally. He must put the welfare of the ship and the safety of those aboard before consideration for the feelings of people who might be in the way or who are needed to help out at any given moment.

Consideration for others is more important than ever in the compacted, isolated world of shipmates. Avoid complaining. Stay out of the way of those working the vessel. Keep your quarters and, for that matter, everything around you tidy. Sailors say "a taut ship is a happy ship."

Tip
On a boat, you have forward and aft, instead of front and back. The left side is port and the right side is starboard. You go below and topside when you go down or up.

Here are some tips that apply to both the greenest landlubber and the most seasoned salt:

➤ Help out in any way you can. Even a novice sailor can be of some use on board. You don't have to be navigating or hoisting the mainsail. It could be something like polishing brass or cleaning up in the galley.

➤ If you are staying up later than the others, keep the conversation, if any, muted.

➤ If you smoke, never smoke below decks. In particular, never smoke near the galley stove, which may be fueled by gas, alcohol, or kerosene.

➤ If you want to bring a gift with you, make it something that can be shared—food, beer, or wine.

➤ Take motion sickness medication with you. If you get sick, stay on deck in the fresh air. Don't be embarrassed. It's not your fault, and just about everybody has suffered some degree of motion sickness sometime in life.

➤ Use fresh water sparingly.

Dress Right

Keep it as simple as possible, and keep in mind that you may be encountering a variety of weather.

➤ Slacks and/or jeans

➤ Shorts

➤ Shirts, both short- and long-sleeved

➤ A warm turtleneck sweater and one or two lighter sweaters

➤ Swimsuit and cover-up

➤ Scarves and bandanas for women

➤ Knitted caps for cold weather and hats for protection from the sun

➤ Foul weather gear, if needed—ask your host if there will be foul weather gear aboard.

➤ Shoes—don't bring leather-soled shoes and, of course, no high heels. Sneakers are good, but non-skid Topsiders are better.

Ask in advance if you should bring towels and washcloths. If you end up using the host's, use them sparingly.

If the cruise includes a stop at a yacht club for a dinner and/or dance, check with the host about recommended attire. In most cases, men can get by with slacks, a jacket, dress shirt and tie, women with a silk dress or pantsuit and a shawl.

Use soft luggage rather than a suitcase for easier stowing.

Host/Captain

If you are the host or captain, remember that you are the boss, and guests and crew expect you to lay down the law about what happens on the vessel. On the other hand, they don't expect Captain Bligh. Here are some rules to follow:

➤ Never invite more people than can be comfortably accommodated, and have lifejackets for all.

➤ Brief guests about what to bring and what to wear. On board, make sure they understand the rules of behavior and the safety procedures.

➤ If guests are to be crewing, make sure they understand what's expected of them and what they should leave to you. Be patient with lubbers.

Glossary

Even the greenest landlubber should be familiar with the following terms:

Bunk — Bed
Chart — Map
Dinghy — A small rowboat
Galley — Kitchen
Halliard — A rope used to raise or lower a sail
Head — Toilet
Knot — A sea mile or 6076 feet
Ladder — Stairs
Lee — The side opposite the direction of the wind
Porthole — Window
Sheet or **line** — Rope used to work a sail
Stern — The rear of a boat
Swab — A mop and the act of mopping

The most crucial rules of etiquette when it comes to sports are those that relate to safety. Physical activity, even if not particularly strenuous, always involves some risk. This means following the rules is even more important than in social situations.

The Least You Need to Know

> ➤ Respect for others and safety are of utmost importance when participating in any sport. Always wear protective and proper clothing and equipment.

> ➤ In the gym, always return weights to where they belong, don't put charts or towels on the machines, move from one machine to another without delay, and don't walk into a group exercise session and join in.

> ➤ At the pool, stay out of the way of lap swimmers. At the pool or the beach, don't litter, kick sand, or drip on people, and if you want music, bring earphones.

> ➤ At the country club, wearing tennis whites is always a safe bet. Tantrums on the tennis court are strictly out of bounds.

> ➤ Never ski alone. Don't go on the slopes without warm, layered clothing, goggles, sun block, and lessons.

> ➤ Run against traffic in familiar terrain. Avoid dark or deserted areas. Do not use earphones.

On the Road

Travel can bring out the best and the worst in people. And no wonder. You find yourself dealing with masses of people, total strangers, in sometimes difficult and stressful situations—situations you probably have no control over. The people around you may be tired, edgy, anxious, excited, or gabby. You, yourself, may be any or all of the above.

Yet, pleasant travelers seem to be welcome everywhere. They get the best service and end up meeting the most intriguing people—and deservedly so. The pleasant traveler begins each journey armed with a positive attitude and a willingness to deal with new situations and meet new people. Each journey also should begin with a sure knowledge of the "Rules of the Road."

Are You Ready to Travel?

Rule Number One is "Be Prepared." People get into unnecessary travel trouble because they haven't prepared properly, and the pleasant traveler is the well-prepared traveler.

Appearance

Almost all of the people you will meet on your journey will be strangers, and their only way of judging you at first will be by your appearance. The fact that you may be in cramped seats for long periods and may have to spend a lot of time in the same clothes does not mean your attire should be sloppy or grungy. The way we dress is a symbol of who we are, what kind of person we are. If the way we dress sends out the signal that we are careless or unkempt, we don't have a prayer of successful, convivial traveling. People will also tend to shy away from us if we give the impression that we are poorly groomed. Close quarters demand scrupulous cleanliness.

Finances

In calculating how much money you will need, be realistic about meals, tips, admission charges, recreation, and other activities. Remember that if your plans include a stay in a luxury hotel, tips can add another 25 percent to the final tab. The reason is that there are more people waiting on you than at Motel 6, and if they "leave the light on for you," they want to be compensated for it.

If you are going to a different country, know the exchange rate, and if possible, carry a small exchange chart with you. Confusion over exchange rates and fumbling through different kinds of currency can be annoying to you and those around you. Make sure you have a small amount of local currency on hand when you arrive to take care of things like taxis and tips. If not, the currency exchange window should be one of your first stops at the airport. Hotels will exchange money, but they don't give the best rates. Banks are your best bet. The airport exchange window is often more expensive than banks and hotels.

Check to see if your ATM card can be used to get cash in local currency while you are away.

Packing

In general, less is better. You do not need to be prepared for every possible emergency. Some people pack as if every necessity of life will have to come from their suitcases. An over-abundance of luggage looks ostentatious and can make your trip unnecessarily complicated or burdensome. Remember that, almost anywhere you go, there will be places to buy small things if you find you need them.

> **Tip**
>
> Pack metal items in one particular bag, so that you can get through security metal detectors with a minimum of hassle.

Your luggage should have identification on the inside as well as the outside. Exterior labels sometimes come off during a trip.

Documents

Check to see if your passport is up to date well in advance of your trip. You will need about six weeks to obtain one. If you apply by mail or during the peak travel season, allow even more time.

To get a passport, you need proof of citizenship—an old passport, or birth or baptismal certificates will do. You also need two identical passport photos. If you are traveling with your family, every member of your family will need a passport. Most major cities have a passport office. Otherwise, your county courthouse or local Post Office can help.

Check at least six weeks in advance to see if you need a visa. You can find out from a travel agent or an airline ticket agent.

If possible, obtain an international driver's license. Your local auto club can help you. Whether you get an international license or not, carry your regular license with you, as well as other identification.

If you are attending any official functions during your trip, bring some documentation of that fact with you. For example, I arrived in London expecting to attend an international banking reception that evening on business. My luggage was lost, and the airline could not guarantee that I would have it in time for the event. As a result, the airline gave me a voucher and sent me off to Harrod's to purchase a dress suitable for the occasion.

> **Tip**
> The Citizens Emergency Center at the State Department in Washington can give you up to date information on health precautions for virtually any place you plan to visit. Call (202)647-4000.

Make sure you have copies of your eyeglass prescription and any medical prescriptions with you at all times when you travel. Keep them with your passport. Also, have records of your required inoculations. Check with your travel agent or board of health about this.

Some inoculations are mandatory, and some are merely recommended. Don't be so quick to disregard those "recommendations." I was not required to get typhoid shots before going to Egypt. So I didn't. You better believe I regretted my decision once I caught typhoid.

Did You Know?

It's a good idea to read the fine print on the back of your airplane ticket. You will find out how much liability the carrier accepts for things like lost possessions. You also can learn about circumstances under which the carrier will cease to honor your seat reservation. (You might arrive five minutes early for your flight and find your seat has been given to a standby.)

Tip

Here are some points to keep in mind about travel insurance:

➤ Your credit card may automatically provide travel and life insurance.

➤ Many people find trip cancellation insurance worthwhile. It reimburses you in the event you must cancel your trip because of a medical emergency or a death in the family.

➤ Check to see if your homeowner's policy covers loss of luggage and personal items while traveling.

Don't Leave Home Without It

If you do not have a printed itinerary from a travel agent, draw up one of your own to take with you and leave a copy of it at home with whatever telephone numbers you might have so that you can be contacted in case of an emergency.

Also, it's a good idea to list everything of value in your luggage. Take it with you (but not in your luggage) and leave a copy at home.

Travel Agents

Working with a travel agent can save you time and money. Their compensation comes from commissions paid by companies like airlines, hotels, and cruise lines. However, it is appropriate for a travel agent to charge you for out-of-pocket expenses incurred on your behalf, such as unusual long-distance telephone charges or messenger services.

Some travel agencies specialize and primarily handle cruises, hiking, and other special interest trips. Some are more knowledgeable than others about places and topics that are of special interest to you. The best way to shop for a travel agent is to ask friends who have interests similar to your own.

If you are consulting a travel agent and find he is not knowledgeable in areas that interest you, or you sense that the rapport or "chemistry" is not right, it is perfectly acceptable to say something like, "I'll get back to you," and try someone else.

Travel agents can arrange car rentals, chauffeur services, tour guides, theater tickets, and even meal reservations. They know about guided tours and group trips and can handle details as small as a one-shot AMTRAK ticket.

However, it is your responsibility to be clear about what your preferences are and about your budgetary limitations. And be reasonable. You can't accommodate Ritz Carlton tastes on an EconoLodge budget.

Hotels

Hotels can be so much more than places to sleep while traveling. They can be among the most interesting and memorable aspects of a trip. However, since hotels range from elegant luxury establishments to country inns to chain hostelries off the Interstate, they can be a bit confusing unless you know what to expect from them and what they may expect from you.

Luxury Hotels

It's usually a good idea to book rooms in luxury hotels well in advance. These hotels provide many extra amenities and services. You probably can count on bathrobes, hair dryers, and a mini-bar in your room. (Beware of mini-bars. They can get to be very expensive and confront you with a sobering surprise when it comes time to pay your bill.)

When you arrive, a doorman greets you, and a porter takes your bags. Tip the porter at least $1 per bag. If the doorman hails you a cab, tip him $1. If the service requires him to stand out in the rain, you might want to tip him more.

Proceed to the registration desk, and give the clerk your confirmation number. Married couples should sign in using both their names. If a woman uses her maiden name in business, she should include that in registering so that telephone calls can be fielded accurately. Unmarried couples should both sign in as well. These details may seem unnecessary, but they are important for security purposes and, practically speaking, for things like telephone calls.

The porter takes the bags to your room. Sometimes the desk clerk will direct you to the room and the porter will follow with the bags. The porter or bellman will open up the room, turn on the lights, adjust the air conditioning, put the luggage on stands, draw the curtains, show you the mini-bar and how the television works. If you don't like the room, ask the porter to call the front desk about a replacement. Remember that the porter cannot change your room on his own, and must clear the request through the front desk.

The next thing you should do, no matter what sort of hotel, motel, or inn you are staying at, is check out the emergency and fire exits. Check to see if you need more towels, pillows, blankets, hangers, or an iron. If you do, call housekeeping right away. Doing this late at night when there is a reduced staff can create difficulties and delays.

Luxury hotels have a concierge, in the European tradition. The concierge desk is generally located near the registration desk. Here you can obtain theater, concert, and sports tickets, have a look at local restaurant menus and make dining reservations, and find out about car rentals, sightseeing tours, baby-sitters, and even traffic and weather conditions. A good concierge is a miracle worker who seems to know everything about everything.

Commercial Hotels

These hotels, typified by those in the Marriott and Hyatt chains, are designed for the business traveler. They are clean, comfortable, and efficient. They also are cheaper and less frilly than the luxury hotels. Available for business travelers are conference rooms, computers, facsimile machines, copiers, and secretarial services.

Bring your own travel iron and hair dryer. You might be able to borrow these things from the hotel, but you might not be able to borrow them exactly when you need them. You can't afford to be held up for an appointment because you are stranded waiting for an iron.

Business people suggest you avoid doing business in your hotel room. And, if you are on a business trip, never share a room with a member of the opposite sex—colleague or not. This damages your credibility, as well as your company's.

Room Service

Especially if you are traveling on business, put in your breakfast order the night before, and allow yourself plenty of time. It's fine to greet the room service waiter in your robe. The waiter will set up the meal in your room. When you are finished, call room service to come for the tray or cart instead of leaving it in the hall. A service charge is added to the bill. If a tip is not included on the bill, the usual amount is 20 percent.

Security

Hotel guests, even guests in the most prestigious hotels, must be aware that they always have at least some responsibility for their security. Here are some basic rules to remember.

➤ Never keep cash or valuables in your room.

➤ Never open the door when someone knocks unless the knocker identifies himself. This is especially true at night. If the knocker says he is a hotel employee and you have any doubts, call the front desk to ask if this person has been sent to your room. If not, call hotel security, give them your room number, and tell them someone is at your door.

Faux Pas
Bathrobes, ash trays, wine glasses, and the like are not souvenirs. Neither are towels. If you like, you can arrange to purchase these things at the front desk. This approach is far superior to finding the items listed on your hotel bill because you have been caught in the act.

➤ Always double-lock your door. You may want to leave the television on to dissuade burglars.

➤ If the desk clerk announces your room number in a loud voice and this bothers you, as it should, quietly ask for another room, and explain that you are being cautious in case someone overheard.

➤ Don't flash a wad of bills in the hotel bar.

Checking Out

Confirm your departure the day before, and verify the checkout time. Usually, you can arrange a late departure if the hotel isn't full. Call the porter to collect your bags. Tip about $1 a bag. If you need to check your bags at the hotel for the day, the porter will take care of it and give you tickets to redeem them.

Motels

Motels may offer little more than a bed, bathroom, and television, or they may resemble mini-resorts, with pools, restaurants, and gyms.

The variety of possibilities is one of the advantages of motel travel. They are usually clustered at the convergence of major highways so that motorists have a wide range of options within the distance of a mile or so.

It's easy to make your own reservations, since the major chains have toll-free reservation numbers. Most offer discounts for members of auto clubs, holders of certain credit cards, and senior citizens. In some cases, these "senior" citizens can be as young as 50.

When you check in, the clerk may want identification, your driver's license number and a credit card, even if you are paying in cash.

You will carry your own bags. Ice, snacks, and some personal items like toothbrushes probably will be available at a vending center, usually one to a floor. Dress is casual, of course, but wear a cover-up at the pool, and avoid dripping all over the lobby. Don't leave children alone in the pool or Jacuzzi.

If you arrive late at night or leave early in the morning, be considerate of those still sleeping. If there is a disturbance late at night, don't elect to straighten it out yourself. Call the front desk, and do not open your door.

Tip the maid $2 or $3 for each night you stay.

The Bed and Breakfast

Antiques. A canopied bed. Tea or sherry in the afternoon. A convivial host. These are among the charms of the Bed & Breakfast.

For the price, often, of a good hotel, you can spend the night in a charming Victorian or colonial-era house, usually an interesting place with interesting owners who have an agreeably old-fashioned idea of comfort and hospitality.

And then there's breakfast. The variety of offerings may dazzle. Certainly, it's not the sort of breakfast you put together at home before dashing off to work.

The best ways to find out about B&Bs is from friends or from the many guidebooks that can be found in book stores and public libraries. Always call for reservations. Some require a stay of at least two days.

When you arrive, you will probably be greeted by the host, who will take your bags, help you get settled, and show you around. You will be shown the dining room and other spaces devoted to the guests. It is very bad form to stray into the host family's living quarters.

A good rule of thumb is to behave much like a house guest. Avoid loud conversations or television late at night. You may borrow books from the library to read in your room, but be sure to return them. Don't use the owner's private telephone without asking first.

Many such places have shared bathrooms, so don't luxuriate in the tub while someone may be waiting. And be sure to leave the tub and the rest of the room as clean as you can reasonably make it.

At breakfast, which is included in the price, introduce yourself and say "Good morning" all around. If you don't feel chatty in the morning, just smile and give minimal answers, and people will get the message. Be alert for such signals yourself.

Leave your room reasonably neat and say goodbye to the host before leaving. No tipping is required.

Travel Tipping

Tipping is so solidly ground into the fabric of the economy and culture, it is unavoidable. If you plan to travel, you must plan to tip.

Ship Lines

Shipping lines can provide you with a list of recommended tips. In general, it is a good idea to figure that tips on your cruise will amount to 15 to 20 percent of your cabin fare.

The porter who takes your bags at the pier gets $2 a bag, more if you have trunks. On board, it might be helpful to give your cabin steward and your dining room steward $20 or $30 at the beginning of the cruise. These stewards usually are tipped a total of $3 to $5 a day, more if you are in a suite. Bar and lounge stewards are tipped 20 percent of the bill. Wine stewards get 15 to 18 percent of the wine bill, just as they do at a fine restaurant.

For personal services—hairdressers, manicurists, and so on—tip as you would on land.

Don't tip officers or the cruise director. A thank you note will do.

On the last day of the cruise, put tips in envelopes with a note for each recipient. Hand them out personally or, if necessary, have the purser distribute them. It is worth the effort to write a note because the staff will appreciate your personal thanks.

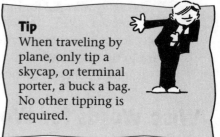

Tip
When traveling by plane, only tip a skycap, or terminal porter, a buck a bag. No other tipping is required.

Trains

In first class, the ticket covers the costs of meals and service. However, you may wish to tip $10 or $20 at the end of the trip if service was good. If meals are not included in the ticket price, tip as you would in a restaurant.

For overnight trips, tip the porter about $10 a day if he makes up your berth, wakes you, brings coffee and a newspaper, or performs similar services.

Redcaps, or baggage porters, get $1 or $2 per bag whether you are traveling first class or coach.

Tip
Tip a private driver, limousine or taxi, 18 to 20 percent of the total bill.

Buses

Someone will be designated to collect tips at the end of a bus tour. The usual rate is $3 to $5 a day for the tour guide and $2 to $4 a day for the driver. If you wish to contribute individually, put your tips in a sealed envelope with a note.

Hotels

The following are recommendations for tipping at a luxury hotel. Tip slightly less at less expensive hotels.

Doorman: $1 or $2 for hailing a cab

Porter: $1 a bag, more if unwieldy; $2 if a porter brings you something special, like a toothbrush, more if it involved leaving the hotel

Room service waiter: 20 percent of the bill, unless the tip is on the bill

Maids: $2 or $3 a night (If possible, give the maid the tip yourself. Too many people come and go in a hotel room to leave money lying around.)

Concierge: $5 a day if he or she does something for you that day

Parking valet: $2 for bringing the car around

Note: Some luxury hotels and spas include tips with the room charge. Even so, you might want to tip the maitre d' in the dining room $20 or $30 at the start of your visit, as a sort of insurance policy for good seating and service.

Wise Words for Women Traveling Alone

Women traveling alone have some special considerations with regard to safety and companionship. Fortunately, traveling alone in the United States poses no real difficulties culturally. Before going to another culture, however, it's a good idea to get a cultural perspective on the area. For example, I spent a long stretch of time in a Cairo hotel during which my husband was away frequently. Unfortunately, I felt forced to dine alone in my room, because a woman dining by herself is thought of as less than morally upstanding. Not very pleasant.

Even in the United States, certain social difficulties confront a woman traveling alone. In general, a good guide when it comes to talking to strangers, especially men, is to pay your own way even though you may be invited for drinks or a meal. At least, keep the rounds of drinks even as to who pays. Always make sure you are on equal footing.

Don't be afraid to talk to strangers. They might become the most interesting part of your trip. Just be wary of putting yourself in jeopardy because you are unaware of personalities and customs. Accepting an invitation to dinner often means—in some hosts' eyes—that you will be dessert.

You can communicate the fact that you are not interested in getting to know someone better by giving one-word answers, nodding, or saying you need to take a nap.

Women dining alone are still at a disadvantage these days. This is less so when the dinner hour is early, say 6 or 6:30 p.m. Traditionally, women are thought to eat less, drink less, and tip less than men. Do yourself a favor, and call first for a reservation. Tip the maitre d'. When you are perceived as knowing what you are doing, you will get better service. Don't be afraid to challenge a manager about discriminatory practices if you think it's warranted. Do so quietly and with no emotion in your voice.

Here are some other tips:

➤ If you agree to have dinner with a man you don't know, dine in the hotel dining room. Be sure to charge your meal to your room, thus averting any miscommunication about the nature of the date.

➤ If you have a drink in the bar alone, make sure you have a briefcase, files, or something diverting with you so that you don't look like a pickup. Sit at a table rather than the bar.

➤ If you are traveling on business and staying at a hotel (hotels are a better idea than motels for single women travelers), you may want to let the reception desk know that you are alone. Some women do, some don't. Better still, ask your travel agent to investigate which hotels are known for safe procedures when it comes to single women guests. Double locks on doors and windows, for example, are necessary, not optional.

➤ When you check in, make sure the clerk does not call out your room number to the bellman. If that happens, tell the clerk discreetly to give you another room and to be quiet about it.

➤ Make sure the bellman checks all the spaces in your room when he lets you in to be sure you are the only person there. Be alert when you approach your room for persons lurking in the hall nearby. Check your window locks, and make sure there are no other accesses to your room from outside.

➤ Never go into your room if you think something has been tampered with. Notify security immediately if you think there has been an unauthorized person in your room.

➤ Never admit anyone to your room whom you haven't invited or requested through the hotel—housekeeping, a repairman—without calling the front desk first.

People in the travel industry use the term, "good traveler." A good traveler is someone who doesn't expect things to be as they are at home, knows that things can go wrong, and doesn't panic when they do. The good traveler has good manners, particularly when it comes to dealing with the people whose very job it is to serve them, provide for their safety, and get them from one place to another.

The Least You Need to Know

➤ If you are not absolutely certain you will need it, don't pack it. If it turns out you need something you haven't packed, you can probably purchase it at your destination.

➤ Casual travel attire does not mean sloppy or grungy.

➤ Bring along some "local" money for tips, taxis, etc., on arrival. The best place to exchange your money is at a bank.

➤ Apply for a passport and visa *well* in advance.

➤ Be sure to factor travel tipping into your financial calculations. If you stay in a luxury hotel, for example, you can expect to spend up to 25 percent of your bill in tips.

➤ Women traveling alone often must be especially careful about meeting and dealing with strangers and dealing with security matters.

Chapter 23

Getting There—Planes, Trains, Ships and More

In This Chapter

➤ Airplane etiquette

➤ Ship etiquette

➤ Auto etiquette

Different modes of travel present us with different adventures, different problems, and different questions when it comes to behavior and the standards of etiquette that are required. Stress, proximity, and the occasional need to hurry lend a certain urgency to knowing what to expect and how to react. Also, there are traditions, particularly aboard ship, to be observed.

But, as always, when in unfamiliar circumstances, respect for others and a concern for what others are feeling and experiencing, will get you through most difficult situations. Let's begin with keeping your feet on the ground when you fly.

Airplanes

You can choose among four classes when you fly: Concorde, first class, business class, and coach.

Both a class and a type of plane, the Concorde provides the ultimate in service and cost. It's the class above first class, and only has limited availability. It flies from New York,

Washington, and Miami to London and Paris, and back. Tall persons may feel cramped because of the sleekness of the supersonic craft, but the trip, after all, takes less than four hours. There is only one class on the Concorde, and all meals and refreshments are free.

First class on regular flights means you have more space, more service, and more to eat and drink. Drinks, alcoholic and otherwise, are free, as are meals and snacks. Seats are larger and more comfortable. Video equipment and telephones are available, as are sleeper seats. Each airline is different, so it's a good idea to check which services are provided. In general, first class tickets do not carry any penalties for exchanging flights and have no minimum or maximum stay requirements.

Business class is available on most international and domestic flights. It is considerably more expensive than coach class. Seats are roomier than coach and more comfortable. Refreshments are more lavish, and service is upgraded. Most businesses no longer approve first class travel at their expense, but some find that, for long flights, business class is often worth the investment.

Coach class is the least expensive form of air travel. Seats are small, and space is limited, but the cost is so much lower that it compensates for such minor inconveniences. Sometimes a meal is served if you fly during mealtime, but usually only sparse snacks are available.

At the Airport

Here are some things to be aware of (and to beware of) when you arrive at the airport:

➤ Avoid the "bag lady" syndrome. Don't show up with both arms encumbered by plastic bags overflowing with newspapers, knickknacks, and snacks.

➤ Make sure your luggage ID tags are secure. Air travel is very hard on luggage. Most domestic flights have no weight restrictions on luggage and permit two carry-on bags, one for under the seat and one for overhead. A wardrobe/garment bag counts as one of the two.

➤ Remember that you may have to carry your own bags. If a porter is not available, look for a cart. A porter is tipped one dollar per bag. Don't expect porters to supply you with luggage ID tags.

➤ To take advantage of curbside check-in, you must have your ticket in your hand.

➤ Know where the metal objects in your luggage are when you go through the security checkpoint. It is irritating to have to wait for someone to go through an entire suitcase for a small silver mirror when it could have gone in a handbag.

➤ Alert security personnel if you have unusual items in your luggage. For example, I often travel with a formal place setting of silver when I'm on the road teaching dining etiquette. I save time and avoid being searched by letting security people know what I'm carrying. Your ticket will list items not permitted on the airplane such as lighter fluid, explosives, and poisons.

➤ Keep an eye on your luggage, and don't be quick to agree to watch someone else's luggage. You never know what could be inside, possibly a bomb or illegal substances. You may also need to move from your spot before the owner of the luggage returns.

On Board

Welcome aboard. Here are ideas to take with you as you board the plane:

➤ Be ready when your row is called. Have your overcoat or other outer garments removed before boarding so that you won't block the aisle doing this. People should get out of the aisle as soon as they can in the boarding process.

➤ If you intend to sleep during the flight, try to get a window seat so that others won't be inconvenienced by climbing over you and you won't be awakened by them doing so. Also, no matter how experienced a traveler you are, wait until you have heard the emergency instructions before putting earplugs and/or blindfolds in place for sleeping.

➤ Reserve an aisle seat if you have long legs or if you expect to be up and down a lot.

➤ Bring cash—small denominations—for in-flight purchases, such as beverages which are not complimentary and headphone rental for movies.

WDYS?

Your neighbor on a plane, train, or bus wants to chat, and you want to be left alone.

What do you say?

"I wish I had the luxury to talk, but I really have to catch up on my work" (or sleep, or reading).

You want to chat, but don't know whether your neighbor does.

What do you say?

"Is this a business or pleasure trip for you?" Take your cue from the tone of the answer.

➤ Flight attendants are there primarily for emergencies, not to chat and not to provide maid-valet service. Don't push the "call" button unless you have a very good reason. A very good reason might be that you need a drink of water, and you don't want to crawl over a row of sleeping passengers.

➤ Most airlines provide kosher, vegetarian, low sodium, low calorie, high protein, bland, and diabetic meals upon request, and there is no extra charge for this. These meals tend to be somewhat better than the usual airline fare, by the way, because they are not prepared in such great quantities. You must order one of these meals at least three days before your flight. Tell the flight attendant you are getting one such meal as soon as possible after boarding.

➤ Bathrooms should be left clean. Be efficient with your time while in there. This is no place for an overhaul. Women should leave home with enough of their face on so all that is needed is a touchup in flight, if necessary. Men should shave before boarding the plane, rather than trying to do so in the confined lavatory.

➤ Look behind you before you put your seat back in the reclining position, especially just before or after a meal. Moving the seat could spill a drink or dump a dessert into a lap.

➤ If working, keep your papers within the framework of your seat. It is polite to ask your neighbor if he minds your working on a laptop. Keep telephoning to an absolute minimum. Most passengers find these things irritating at best.

➤ If a delay means you have to dash to make a connection, tell the flight attendants before landing. They can assist you in deplaning quickly.

➤ When leaving the plane, stop and let people who are ready to enter the aisle do so in front of you. Don't get into the aisle until you are ready to proceed toward the door.

Delays

No airline ever created a blizzard, hurricane, thunderstorm, or tornado. No airline ever deliberately lost someone's luggage, especially yours.

Airlines do, however, "overbook." They do it to protect themselves from some travelers, certainly not you, who make more than one reservation for a trip and then fail to cancel the ones they don't use. These merry travelers are called, among other things, "no-shows."

Sometimes people with reservations, particularly those who arrive late, get "bumped." The airline generally tries to make up for this by upgrading your ticket, getting you onto the next possible flight, and giving you vouchers for meals and hotel if necessary.

When this happens, remember that getting angry will not get you a seat. In fact, the person who explains his problem quietly and politely could have a better shot at getting that last seat—if one becomes open—than the one doing all of the yelling, threatening, and name-calling.

If you see a swarm of indignant travelers besieging a hapless gate agent, instead of joining them, your time might be better spent calling other airlines about connecting flights. Or you can pick up a current copy of "The Official Airline Pocket Flight Guide." This annual guide lists all scheduled flights.

Tip

If you are treated rudely, write a letter to the customer service director of the airline. You can obtain the name of this person by calling the 800 number on your airplane ticket. The customer service director has the authority to decide what, if anything, the airline can do to make up for your getting "bumped." Keep the tone of your letter level, and report the facts without emotion.

Luggage

It *does* get lost. Most often, it is retrieved. Luggage with ID tags gets lost as easily as untagged luggage, but the bags with the tags get returned sooner.

As soon as you are certain that your luggage was not unloaded with the rest of your flight's, report it to the airline office, usually situated near the carousels for reclaiming luggage. This is where your itemized list becomes invaluable. It helps you identify your property. It also helps provide validity for any claim you might have for loss. Airlines carry very limited loss liability, so if you must carry anything of unusual worth in your luggage, let your ticket agent know when you check your luggage so that it can be noted.

Here, too, is where forethought in packing pays off. Always pack medicines, toiletries, pajamas, cash, jewelry, and a change of clothes (if possible) in your carry-on bags. It will get you through the night and get you to your meeting in the morning.

Children and Planes

Infants and babies up to age two do not need a ticket of their own. Be sure to tell the ticket agent when you purchase your ticket that you will be traveling with children. Request a bulkhead, which faces a wall instead of another seat.

Make sure you bring food, formula, diapers, wipes—everything you need. Recognize that flight attendants are not baby-sitters or nannies. It's fine to ask them to warm bottles or baby food, but not much else.

Only children older than five can travel alone. It is critical to have an Unaccompanied Minor form, which the airlines provide. Provide traveling children with the necessities of survival. These include games, snacks, cash, toys, and so on. Also, brief children before the flight. Talk about how planes work, the in-flight safety instructions, seat belts, meals, the importance of staying seated and obeying flight attendants.

Shipping Out

There is more travel by water than ever these days. Cruising to all parts of the world has become a primary mode of pleasure travel, and it's easy to understand why. Your cruise ship is a little self-contained city designed for your comfort and pleasure. It's a city with constantly changing dramatic vistas and a place in which the most challenging decision facing you is what to eat. Decisions about where to eat, where to stay, where to go, and how to get there have all been made for you.

The lure of the cruise experience involves the adventure of being on the high seas and visiting strange and, perhaps, exotic ports and the security of knowing that, once on board, everything you need for a pleasant journey is being taken care of. Your journey will be even more pleasant if you have a good knowledge of shipboard etiquette. But first, some details.

Extra Charges

The price of the cruise includes accommodations, meals, on-board entertainment, and the use of all shipboard sports facilities. There are extra charges for wine and liquor, port taxes and personal services such as beauty salon, barber shop, dry cleaning, massages. Another consideration is tipping, which can be costly and should be factored into your budget.

Getting Ready

Life is a breeze once on the ship, but preparation can be complicated. So it's a good idea to use the services of a travel agent, many of whom specialize in cruise travel. An agent will know what cruises are available and when, details about the style of the ship and the atmosphere created there, all costs, payment schedules for cruising and other logistical intricacies. The agent can even make beauty salon appointments in advance, which you can confirm later when on board. They will know dress guidelines on board, which can vary widely from ship to ship. They will see to your deck chair assignment as well as your dining seating preference.

The following is a list of tips to follow when preparing for a cruise:

➤ Get a diagram of the ship in advance so you will know where you are staying. The most expensive accommodations are the larger rooms, higher up and on the outside.

➤ Don't even think about having a bon voyage party on board. They are no longer permitted for security reasons. In fact, your friends can't come aboard at all unless they are passengers. You *can* have a party in your cabin for fellow passengers. The ship's purser is the person to arrange it.

➤ Pack light. Space is limited on the ship.

➤ If you are prone to motion sickness, see your doctor about medication before leaving. Also, herbal remedies are said to be effective, so you might want to check with a health food store. (If you become ill on board, of course, the ship's doctor will assist you.)

➤ Be sure your bags are tagged, and give them only to a porter wearing identification.

➤ Once you have made your plans and paid for the cruise, your travel agent will give you a packet of information. This packet, produced by the cruise line, will contain your ticket, onboard information, luggage tags, your personal ID tag, dining room reservation card, general information about the ship, and a complete itinerary with mailing addresses, information about ports of call, currency exchange, local customs, and so on.

Shipboard Etiquette

Address the captain as "Captain," and the other officers as "Mr.," "Mrs.," or "Ms."

If the captain has a reception, do not monopolize him in conversation. He is very busy and must do his best to meet everyone on board, in addition to his other duties. If you are invited to dine at the Captain's Table, consider it a high honor. Be on time. Introduce yourself to your dining partners, and wait for the captain to arrive before you order. Dinner at the Captain's Table is usually formal.

There are usually two dinner seatings on board. The earlier is usually for families. The second is considered more fashionable. You may be assigned to a table with strangers. You don't have to wait for everyone to be seated to order. If you are unhappy with your table, you may be able to ask the steward to assign you to another one. Do not request seating at an officer's table. That is considered a bestowed honor.

Ship Wear

Traditionally, formal dinner dress is required only for the Captain's Dinner. Most other nights, jackets and ties for men and cocktail dresses for women are appropriate. Generally, short-term cruising is more casual than trans-Atlantic travel or, say, a gala cruise around the world.

If you are traveling first class, dress will be somewhat more formal in the evenings than in, say, tourist class, where dressing for dinner or for special evenings is up to you. Even in first class, dressing is less formal than it used to be.

Since every cruise ship has its own flavor, it is wise to ask your travel agent and people you know who have sailed on that ship about appropriate attire.

Daytime dress is casual. Dress as though you were at a fine resort hotel. Shorts, slacks, and sweatsuits are fine for breakfast and lunch. Never wear a swimsuit without a good-looking cover-up. Men should bring at least one good business suit and a dinner jacket (tuxedo). Women will find a shawl or jacket very useful on chilly nights.

Tip
If the captain gives a reception, it will probably be dressy. Ask the purser.

On the QE2 (Queen Elizabeth II), the world's most famous luxury ocean liner, your cabin determines where you dine. The most expensive cabins dine in small dining rooms where formal dress is expected every night. Other accommodations do not require formal dress for dinner, although they request it when possible. Women should bring dressy cocktail dresses or suits.

Auto Etiquette

A considerate driver is a safer, as well as a more appreciated, driver. Cars are so much a part of our everyday lives that we take them for granted and usually forget that driving manners cannot be separated from safety.

Here are general and hopefully helpful tips for drivers and passengers:

Tip
The polite driver does not park in a handicapped zone, discard litter, use the horn unnecessarily, or take up two parking spaces.

➤ If it's your car and you are in the driver's seat, you are the boss. It's up to you to make sure your car is in good condition and is sufficiently fueled. You have every right to ask your passengers to wear their seat belts and to insist that very young children have child safety seats. Pets, too, should be contained properly when you are driving.

➤ Taking chances is not only unsafe, it is disconcerting to your passengers. Speeding, passing, dashing through yellow lights—all create tension.

➤ Never smoke in another person's car. The tobacco odor is nearly impossible to get rid of. Don't even ask if you can smoke unless the driver is smoking.

WDYS?
A back seat driver is really getting on your nerves.

What do you say?

"You know, your comments are really interfering with my concentration. Can you hold off until the car is stopped?"

➤ Don't use the cellular phone unless it is absolutely necessary, particularly in challenging traffic. Driving requires complete focus.

➤ Your trunk should be equipped with a first aid kit, flashlight, flares, blanket, ice scraper, and shovel.

➤ An investment in an emergency road service association such as AAA will pay off in peace of mind, even if you never have to use its services.

Safety Precautions

Remember that you are responsible for the safety of your passengers as well as your own safety. Here are some things to keep in mind:

➤ Park in well-lighted lots at night. Lock the doors, and use a steering wheel bar. When you return, check the back seat for intruders before you enter the car.

➤ If you are traveling with children, make sure all doors are locked, and be especially careful when closing doors. Kids just seem to have a way of getting fingers and feet in the way. Factor in frequent stops, and bring along snacks, toys, and games.

➤ Never stop when waved down by someone standing by a "disabled" car. Drive on to the next service station and tell the manager or attendant.

➤ Never stop for a hitchhiker.

When You're in Trouble

Lots of things can happen on the road. Here are some examples and some suggestions on how to react:

➤ If you are stopped by the police for a driving violation or for any other reason, don't try to schmooze the officer. It just annoys them. Be straightforward and polite, never argumentative.

➤ If you are involved in an accident, stay cool. Don't trade accusations with the other driver. Exchange identification. Be sure to get insurance data and write down the license number on the car.

➤ If you scrape somebody's fender, and they are not in the car, don't just take off. It's not how you would like to be treated, and besides, somebody is apt to get your license number, and then you'll be hit with a charge of leaving the scene of an accident. It's a situation in which good manners and self-interest coincide. Leave your name and telephone number under a windshield wiper blade.

➤ If you are really frightened by the way somebody is driving, just tell them to stop and let you out of the car. If the driver says, "Maybe you would like to drive," take him up on the offer.

Seating Etiquette

It is up to the driver to suggest where people sit. The seat of honor is the front passenger seat. It is polite to defer to older persons and give them that seat. In a business situation, the client or the highest ranking person gets that seat. If a couple has a single person in the car, it is best to offer the front seat to that person rather than to isolate him in the back.

(Note: Accommodating a passenger with long legs may have to take precedence over the above considerations.)

Chit Chat

For some reason, people seem to feel chattier in a small car. Large sedans often feel studied and formal. Generally, it is safest to hold a conversation with the person you are sitting next to, rather than to try to turn around or talk over a seat.

Driving is an activity that requires focus and good reflexes, so no one should feel uncomfortable about remaining quiet during a ride.

A driver can signal "no conversation" by turning on the radio.

The Limousine

The seat of honor is the curbside back seat. The guest of honor or senior executive is seated here. Junior executives take the jump seats or sit in the middle. A junior executive may also sit up front with the driver. This eliminates a chance to schmooze with the boss, but the driver is often a good source of information about the locale, information that might score points for you later. When in doubt, ask the senior executive or host where you should sit.

It is polite to have the seat divider lowered when a member of the party is sitting in the front seat.

The Rented Car

Try to speak with the actual office where you are renting. National reservation centers may be unaware of local or seasonal differences that may effect the rental. Specify exact times and, if you are running late, call the office to make sure your car is not given to someone else. Write down the confirmation number and the name of the person you spoke with.

Make sure you are comfortable with the car and everything in it before you leave the lot. They will expect you to return the car clean and in good condition, so make sure it is clean and in good condition when you accept it. Return the car with about the same amount of gas as when you rented it.

It's generally a good idea to rent a car that is similar in size and performance to your own. I have found that, when driving in "stay to the left" countries such as England and Ireland, small cars take some of the terror out of getting used to the system.

Some companies won't rent to persons under 25, and all require some sort of deposit. The easiest deposit is a credit card. You can pay in cash when you return the car to avoid charges on your card. On the subject of credit cards, many customers have a false impression that their credit card company will provide them with all of the insurance coverage they need. It's best to contact the card company and let them know what you intend to do with the rental car, and what sort of car you intend to rent. Most of these card companies provide only secondary coverage to your personal insurance. Some will not cover you at all if a third party is picking up the expense of the rental. Also some credit card companies have limits on the number of days you can rent a car and the value of the cars you can rent.

Even if you have what you consider adequate insurance coverage, you might want to consider the "collision damage waiver" and "loss damage waiver" offered by rental companies. Covering things as minor as flat tires, they provide peace of mind, and if you return the car damaged, they can save you the deductible and, perhaps, a subsequent increase in your car insurance rates.

Trains

Basically, there are two levels of AMTRAK travel—first class and coach.

For first class passengers, preferential treatment begins when you arrive at the station. The Metropolitan Lounges for first class passengers are similar to airline clubs. They provide a comfortable place to wait for trains, complimentary beverages, television, and a staff to help with confirmations, questions, and tickets. There are also telephones, fax machines, and sometimes conference rooms that may be rented for meetings.

Aboard, there is more room, better seats, good service, and meals. Overnight trips in first class include dining car meals. The dining etiquette here is the same as the rules that apply in an elegant restaurant. Dress is rather casual but certainly not careless. The tip in the dining car is generally 20 percent of your check.

Overnight accommodations do not always include private bathrooms. If you have no private bath, it is all right to wear a robe in the aisles. Use the bathroom facilities efficiently, and leave the room clean and orderly for the next person. Ask the sleeping car attendant to make up your bed at a reasonably early time—no later than 10 p.m. Tip the attendant about $3 per person, more if you have received excellent service or extra help.

Good manners are even more important in coach, where there are no reserved seats and conditions can be crowded. Also, people might be more edgy, tired, and irritable. Food is available for sale in coach, the cafe car or the dining car.

The same basic rules of courtesy as used on airplanes are applicable to train travel.

➤ Don't ask the conductors for favors.

➤ Bring blindfolds and earplugs for sleeping.

➤ If you want to close or open the shade, ask the person next to you if he minds.

➤ Keep the reading light off if you are not reading.

➤ Remember to dispose of litter in trash receptacles and not in the pouch in front of your seat.

➤ Smoke only in the designated areas, which are scarce.

➤ Keep quiet. Listen to the radio only with earphones and use the telephone minimally.

➤ Keep your children from running up and down the aisles.

Commuter Trains

Commuter trains are a culture unto themselves. Generally, passengers are not sociable, so don't expect them to be. As a matter of fact, commuters view train time as work time, and most of them want to use it productively. It seems the only time they talk to one another is when they have a mutual gripe about the train service.

Here are some important things to remember while traveling on commuter trains:

➤ Don't hog a seat with your briefcase, gym bag, or coat. If others do, it's perfectly okay to ask them to remove their things. But don't make a big deal out of it.

➤ Don't leave trash on the seat or the floor. Use the receptacle. Newspapers are an exception. If you have finished with it, you can fold it neatly and leave it on the seat for someone else to read.

➤ Keep the volume down when using headsets or cellular phones.

➤ If you are able bodied, giving up your seat to the elderly or disabled person is still the civil and decent thing to do. If other seats are at hand, you should move to allow people traveling together to remain together.

➤ If someone needs help heaving a bag onto an overhead rack, lend a hand if you are able.

➤ Have your ticket ready for the conductor, then smile and say "Thank you."

Busing It

Things that are annoying on buses include, but are not limited to:

➤ People hanging over your seat to talk or resting their arms on the back of your seat

➤ Loud radios or conversations

➤ Smelly food

Because bus travel is cheap, most travel agents don't deal with it. The commissions, if any, do not warrant their efforts. You make your own reservations, and any information you need, you will have to find out on your own.

Here are some tips:

➤ There is no reserved seating, but people tend to consider the seat they had when the trip began to be theirs for the entire trip. Some can get testy about this expression of the territorial imperative.

➤ Baggage limit is usually two per passenger, plus two carry-ons. This may vary, however, so check with the bus company in advance.

➤ Dress is casual, of course, but it is important to avoid even the appearance of grunge. Layering is advised in all weather because of drafts and uneven delivery of air conditioning.

➤ Persons with disabilities should notify the bus company in advance so that arrangements can be made.

➤ Bring a book or a headset to turn off chatty neighbors.

➤ Do not talk to the driver while the bus is in motion. You don't tip drivers on commercial bus lines, such as Greyhound. (On bus tours, drivers get a tip, usually in the form of a collection taken among the passengers.)

Children under eight must be accompanied by someone twelve or older. Over eight, children should have an Unaccompanied Child form and have identification that includes a telephone number and name of a person at home, along the way, and at the destination.

It is great to try new things, have adventures, and meet new people while on the road, but considerations of security supercede these. If you feel threatened, it is not discourteous to refuse to converse with someone, move away from them, or tell a crew member or security personnel that you are worried about a certain situation.

The Least You Need to Know

➤ If you intend to sleep, get a window seat, and bring earplugs and a blindfold.

➤ If there is even a remote chance that something in your luggage will cause a problem, alert security in advance.

➤ Tag your luggage. You'll be glad you did if it gets lost.

➤ Don't plan a bon voyage party for non-passengers aboard ship.

➤ Toiletries, a change of clothes, and other essentials should be in carry-on bags because luggage *does* get lost.

Chapter 24

Preparing for a Wedding

In This Chapter

➤ Getting engaged

➤ Showers

➤ The ring

➤ Announcements

➤ Invitations

➤ Who pays for what

Ah, love. It has been said that weddings have nothing to do with marriage. Weddings are a celebration of life and love, a grand party, a time when family and friends become closer. Weddings have also been called an ordeal and a costume party.

But, as long as there is love, there will be weddings. They can be as elaborate as a coronation or as simple and as solemn as a promise. But whatever form your wedding takes, it is important to know the basic, practical rules of wedding etiquette. Here, in broad brushstrokes, are guidelines, starting from the beginning.

You're Engaged

Before people get married, they become engaged. This is the period between making the commitment to each other to enter into marriage and the wedding ceremony itself. What happens during this period varies, depending upon the personalities of the two people involved. There are some basics, however.

Oh, Grow Up

First, tell you parents!

Whatever your circumstances, regardless of age, whether you think they will approve or their heads will explode, your parents have to know what's happening, and they have to hear about it from you.

It doesn't matter if they are divorced or if your relationship with them is strained at best. They must know, and you should tell them personally. It is better for all concerned, especially the happy couple, for the two of you to be together when you break the news.

Practice your speech beforehand.

Even if the announcement is greeted with great joy and a hearty approval, expect an eventual "but…" or two, or more. Usually, the first and most serious "but…" involves financial security. Most parents know the effect of financial difficulties on wedded bliss.

Have your arguments and explanations dressed and ready to be paraded. Don't make light of any issues, or try to laugh them off. Don't become defensive. Act like an adult. Acknowledge their concerns, and talk about your plans for dealing with problems, however conceptual those plans may be.

Once informed, there are certain ceremonies that parents are expected to perform. Traditionally, the groom's mother writes to the bride's mother to express her happiness about the betrothal and invites the bride's parents to visit. However, many parents are unaware that such traditions exist, so no one should be offended if this formality is overlooked.

Even if the groom's mother does not plan to invite the bride's parents for a visit, writing a note is a good idea. It should say something like:

Dear Matilda:

Robert just told us his good news, and I don't want to waste a minute before telling you how pleased we are. We've heard so much about you already, and are grateful for all the kindness you have shown our son. We feel pleased and privileged to welcome Paula to our family. Both of us are eager to meet you in person when we can toast the happy occasion together.

Fondly,

Helen Thomas

The couple should visit each set of parents individually. If you feel that your parents and your intended's parents will mix like oil and water, it's probably not a good idea to arrange a cozy sixsome. There probably will be an opportunity to introduce everyone at a less stressful time, such as a party some time before the actual wedding.

The Ring

There may or may not be an engagement ring. A ring or lack of it does not alter the fact that one is engaged once one has decided to marry.

There are some time bombs that come disguised as engagement rings. In an ideal world, every bride-to-be is thrilled with the selection of her intended ring and the couple lives happily ever after. If you think this is an ideal world, you are not ready for marriage.

Suppose you are presented with a ring you dislike intensely, but it has been in his family since the Bronze Age, and mother-in-law-to-be has her heart set on her little boy's bride wearing it.

Wear it. Smile. Do not change the setting. You can select a wide wedding band that will not comfortably accommodate the engagement ring. You can wear the engagement ring on your right hand for a while, and eventually stop wearing it. After all, it's clumsy when you're at the computer. You'll think of something.

The same guidelines apply if your dearly beloved presents you with a terrible ring of his own choosing. (Nobody's perfect.) The day after the second wedding anniversary, you can start talking about having the ring reset.

Did You Know?

The tradition of giving diamond engagement rings began in Venice in the 15th century. One of the earliest and smallest diamond engagement rings was made for the two-year-old Princess Mary, daughter of Henry VIII of England, on her engagement to the dauphin of France in 1518.

Not every couple does the formal engagement ring thing. It is a nice idea, however, to cement your engagement with a permanent gift, one that is not too practical, before the responsibilities of married life take over your resources. Some couples select gifts for one another that aren't rings—like bracelets, earrings, or pins.

Parties

The bride's family, the groom's family, or close friends might decide to honor the couple with an engagement party. The form of the party can vary widely from a cocktail party to a barbecue.

Invitations can be handwritten or printed or extended by telephone. Don't mention "engagement" on the invitations. The reason for this is to allay any concern people might have about giving engagement gifts. The purpose of the engagement party is to celebrate the good news. You don't have to worry about the obligations intrinsic to a wedding invitation list.

Showers

Bridesmaids or close friends of the bride usually give bridal showers. It is customary to ask the bride ahead of time what kind of shower she would like. Brides also should be very much aware that shower gifts are in addition to wedding gifts and constitute added expense. Thus, it is only fair and kind to be just that—fair and kind—in suggesting the sort of gifts you would like. Kitchen gadget parties and garden parties can be creative and fun and also easy on the budget.

No matter what, a shower should never ask for money, and a host should never ask guests to contribute to the cost of the party. Showers should be small, intimate gatherings for friends, not fund-raisers.

While the bride should be able to thank each person for the gifts, it is still gracious to send handwritten thank you notes. It's a good idea for the bride to have a friend unobtrusively taking notes during the shower, so that there will be no mistakes about which gift came from which person.

Tip
These days, showers are also given for the groom. In fact, this practice is becoming almost as popular as the somewhat jaded concept of the bachelor party. Bachelor parties won't ever really die out, but lifestyles are changing for the healthier.

Announcements

Many couples announce their engagement in the newspaper. It is best to call your local paper and ask for their requirements for this. They might have a standard form for you to complete and return with a photograph. If the bride and groom are from different towns, contact both local newspapers.

If there is no form, write it out yourself. The bride's parents announce the engagement of their daughter. If the parents are divorced and wish to use both names, the announcement would read:

> "Mr. William Keates and Mrs. Maura Keates (or Mrs. Daniel Johns if she had remarried) announce the engagement of their daughter, Eileen, to Alan Barts, son of Dr. and Mrs. Edward Barts of Great Neck, Long Island."

In the next paragraph, add information about where each went to school, honors received, and their current occupations. Add the wedding date at the end of the announcement. If you send a photograph, attach a caption to the back of it. Do not write on the back of the picture because it may interfere with the reproduction process. It is best to type the announcement, double-spaced.

Tip
When acknowledging the news that a couple is engaged, tradition dictates that we congratulate the man and wish the woman every happiness. The thinking behind this is that the man is to be congratulated for winning his prize after a long and difficult chase. Congratulating the woman would imply that she had been pursuing the man.

There is no guarantee that the newspaper will run your announcement, and the smaller the paper, the better your chances. Send the announcement to your local community papers as well as the big-city daily to have the best chance of getting a clipping for your scrapbook. Some papers may not run a wedding announcement if they have already used an engagement announcement, particularly if the wedding comes soon after the engagement.

Aghast in the Past

"Congratulations are sometimes too fervidly put. When, for instance, the bride is a little past the bloom of youth and brightness, it is well for her friends and acquaintances not to be too gushingly insistent with their congratulations. To be so is rather to suggest that she has been successful against terrible odds."

—Mrs. Humphry, *Manners for Girls*, 1909

Breaking Up

If you break your engagement, call your friends and family, and tell them. You do not owe anyone an explanation, and it is best not to delve into specifics or drift into character assassination, no matter how strong the temptation.

You must return any wedding gifts you might have received. It is best to do this simply by mail. Send a note saying something like:

"While I am very grateful for your gift and good wishes, I must return it because we have cancelled our engagement."

If formal wedding invitations have already been sent, you will need to send a formal cancellation.

Dr. and Mrs. Paul Mitchell

announce that the marriage of their daughter

Monica

to

David Peters

will not take place.

If you have sent informal invitations, send each person who received one an informal, brief note:

Dear Tom:

This is to let you know that Henry and I have broken our engagement.

Christine

Wedding Plans

When you begin serious planning for the wedding, some of the first questions you will encounter will involve who will pay for things, who should be invited, and what form the invitations should take.

Wedding Expenses

Let's start the wedding process with who pays for what. For many weddings, lots of people assume a share of the burden, and thus have some say in the proceedings.

Traditionally, however, the bride's family pays for invitations, announcements, photographs at the wedding and the reception, flowers for the wedding party, the cost of the ceremony itself (flowers, canopy, music, cars, and so on), and all the reception expenses.

The groom is responsible for the marriage license, bride's ring, his gift to the bride, the officiant's fee, gifts for his attendants, and the honeymoon. Sometimes the groom pays for the bride's bouquet and going-away corsage, the corsages for the mothers and grandmothers, and boutonnieres for his attendants and the fathers. The groom's family pays for the rehearsal dinner and hotel accommodations for the groom and his attendants.

But, tradition aside, the most practical and workable way to allocate wedding expenses is for the bride, the groom, and their families to sit down together and discuss the costs openly. This way, everyone will have the same picture of the event in their minds. Clear communication is essential from the start, especially about who should be billed for what and the billing and payment procedures.

Guest List

Since the wedding guest list dictates the cost and size of the wedding, it is a good idea to agree on some outer limits before you begin. Usually the two families—bride's and groom's—divide the number of guests equally between them.

Both families should determine their lists and then get together to combine the lists so that duplications can be eliminated. Be careful about assuming a certain number of no-shows. You could be in for some surprises. Friends from the past may consider this an opportunity to renew acquaintances, and distant relatives or friends may see the invitations as a chance to take that long trip they have been thinking about.

Invitations

Formal wedding invitations conform to a formula. They should be engraved on the top half of a piece of folded white or off-white paper. A loose piece of tissue paper protects the engraving, and the invitation is put into an inner envelope. The recipient's full name is written on the inner invitation in black ink by hand. This envelope then is put into another envelope of the same paper quality, and this is addressed and stamped by hand.

The formula:

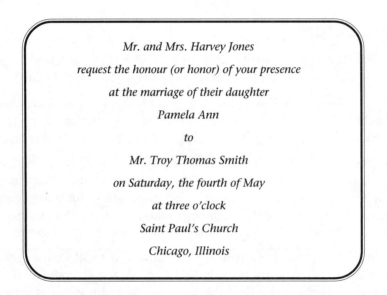

Mr. and Mrs. Harvey Jones
request the honour (or honor) of your presence
at the marriage of their daughter
Pamela Ann
to
Mr. Troy Thomas Smith
on Saturday, the fourth of May
at three o'clock
Saint Paul's Church
Chicago, Illinois

Although many persons simply add "and guest" when they inscribe the inside envelope, it is a good idea to ask the person if you can send an individual invitation to the person who will be accompanying him.

A formal engraved invitation sends the message that your wedding will be formal. If your wedding is to be less formal, your invitation can send that message as well. You may, for example, choose to have the invitation printed rather than engraved, on colored stock. You might eliminate the extra envelope and alter the wording of the invitation to suit yourself.

If you and your intended are responsible for the entire wedding, you might want to send the invitations in your own name. Thus:

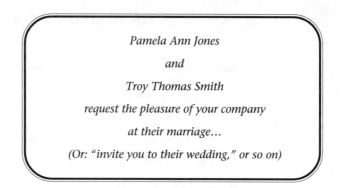

> Pamela Ann Jones
>
> and
>
> Troy Thomas Smith
>
> request the pleasure of your company
>
> at their marriage…
>
> (Or: "invite you to their wedding," or so on)

When the groom's family shares in the expense of the wedding, invitations are sent in the name of the groom's parents as well as the bride's:

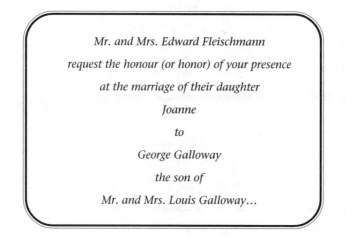

> Mr. and Mrs. Edward Fleischmann
>
> request the honour (or honor) of your presence
>
> at the marriage of their daughter
>
> Joanne
>
> to
>
> George Galloway
>
> the son of
>
> Mr. and Mrs. Louis Galloway…

Or:

> Mr. and Mrs. Edward Fleischmann
>
> and Mr. and Mrs. Louis Galloway
>
> request the honour (or honor) of your presence
>
> at the marriage of their children
>
> Joanne and George…

(Note: Middle names and initials are not necessary but are considered more formal.)

When the bride and groom share some of the expense of the wedding, the invitation might say:

> *Barbara Tamms*
>
> *and*
>
> *Jonathan Kreck*
>
> *join their parents*
>
> *Susan and Wayne Tamms*
>
> *and*
>
> *Helen and Walter Kreck*
>
> *in inviting you*
>
> *to share their happiness*
>
> *as they exchange marriage vows*
>
> *Saturday, the fourth of May*
>
> *Nineteen hundred and ninety-six*
>
> *at three o'clock in the afternoon*
>
> *Franklin Inn Club*
>
> *422 South Camac Street*
>
> *Philadelphia, Pennsylvania*

If you are inviting everyone to the reception who is invited to the wedding, you can include the words "and afterwards at" after the place of the wedding on the invitation. Another option is to include a separate engraved or printed card with the invitation. It should read:

> *Reception*
>
> *immediately following the ceremony*
>
> *The Philadelphia Club*

By all means, send maps with invitations to those coming from a distance.

If you have fewer than 50 guests, you should write out your own invitations in the form of a note. The phrasing is up to you. Mine read:

> Danny and I will be married at three o'clock on Sunday, the twenty-eighth of October. The wedding will be at our friend Mary Dungan's home, 2265 Cardinal Road, Washington Crossing, Pennsylvania. We hope you can join us.
>
> Please let us know if you can come.
>
> Yours,
>
> Mary

Replying to Invitations

There is no reason to reply or send a gift to a formal or informal wedding announcement unless you want to.

Although there is a correct form to reply to formal wedding invitations, few people know about it, much less actually use it. However, this is how it goes:

> *Mr. and Mrs. Peter Thompson*
>
> *accept with pleasure*
>
> *Mr. and Mrs. Warren Scott Tate's*
>
> *kind invitation for*
>
> *Saturday, the fourth of May*
>
> *at three o'clock*
>
> *at the Franklin Inn*
>
> *(Or:)*
>
> *regret they are unable to accept*
>
> *Mr. and Mrs. Warren Scott Tate's…*

Today, most invitations come with an enclosed reply card, stamped and addressed by the host. If not, a note saying you will attend will be appreciated. You don't have to write saying you will attend if the invitation is for the ceremony and not the reception. The reason is that your acceptance has no bearing on the plans being made by the wedding party.

Wedding Announcements

After a small wedding, it is appropriate to send engraved or printed wedding announcements to friends and acquaintances. It is also appropriate to send announcements after a large wedding to those who were not invited, those distant business and social people who are in our Rolodexes, but never make it to our dinner tables. The wording is:

Mr. and Mrs. Paul Edward Michaels

have the honour of announcing

the marriage of their daughter

Susan Marie

to

Mr. David Walter Reston

on Saturday, the fourth of May

Nineteen hundred and ninety six

Saint Thomas' Church

Philadelphia, Pennsylvania

It is not essential to mention where the wedding took place in the announcement. The announcement should complement the style of the invitation in terms of paper stock and printing or engraving.

When couples plan their own weddings, they often send their own announcements. They are printed or engraved. The wording is:

Susan Marie Michaels

and

David Walter Reston

have the honour (or honor) of announcing

have the honour to announce

with pleasure announce

(choose any of the above)

their marriage

on Saturday, the fourth of May...

For the newspaper announcement, call to see if there is a form. If not, give the following:

➤ The bride's maiden name and the groom's name

➤ Hour, date, and place of the ceremony

➤ Name of the officiating person

➤ Names of persons in the wedding party and their relationships to the bride and groom

➤ A description of the bride's dress and flowers and the bridesmaids' dresses

➤ Where the reception was held

➤ Names and occupations of the bride's parents

➤ Names of the bride's grandparents

➤ Where the bride went to school and college

➤ Where the bride is employed

➤ The same essential facts about the groom and his family

➤ Where the couple will live after the marriage

If the bride is keeping her maiden name, add this sentence to the announcement: "After the marriage, Ms. Michael will retain her maiden name."

Or: "After their marriage, Mr. Reston and Ms. Michael will use the surname Michael-Reston."

It should be noted here that the use of hyphenated surnames is becoming less and less common these days.

You may send a photograph along with the announcement. It may or may not get printed. Attach the caption to the back. Don't write on the back.

This chapter has dealt with the way people generally or traditionally prepare for a wedding. It is important to remember, however, that it is *your* wedding, and it should be planned and carried out in a way that *you* believe is appropriate. Remember, too, that your wedding is something that will always be a part of your memories, and deserves a great deal of serious thought and careful preparation.

The Least You Need to Know

➤ The engaged couple must tell their parents about their plans for marriage right away.

➤ Never reject someone's choice of an engagement ring. If you don't like it, there are other ways of dealing with the problem.

➤ Generally, but not always, the bride's parents announce engagements and weddings.

➤ It is essential that both families meet and decide in advance who will pay for what when it comes to the wedding.

➤ There is a well-defined and long-standing formula for formal wedding invitations, and it is not generally a good idea to deviate from it.

Chapter 25

The Big Day

In This Chapter

➤ The rehearsal

➤ Who's who

➤ What to wear

➤ The ceremony

➤ Kinds of weddings

So, the time has come. The big event. All of the planning, all of the hundreds of details have led up to this. From here on in, things will be happening fairly quickly, and you will be grateful for all of the time and effort you and others have devoted to the preparations.

The big event actually begins a day or two before the wedding, with the rehearsal and the rehearsal dinner.

The Rehearsal

In many cases, the entire wedding party comes together for the first time at the rehearsal. The atmosphere is informal and cheerful. The rehearsal takes place where the wedding will occur, and this helps the participants feel more relaxed when they show up for the actual ceremony.

There is a tradition that, at the rehearsal, the bride asks one of her attendants to walk down the aisle in her place, but otherwise, everyone goes through the same routine they will perform on the wedding day. This is also a chance to get an idea from the officiant about the nature of his remarks. Those who will be doing a reading should practice, and the sound system, if there is one, should be checked out.

The Rehearsal Dinner

The rehearsal dinner usually is held immediately following the wedding rehearsal. The circumstances vary widely, but the dinner is most often hosted by the parents of the groom. When the groom's family is from out of town, the bride and her family should provide support with organizing the details.

These occasions are generally informal, and invitations are telephoned, although written invitations are gracious. It is an opportunity for the two families to meet and get to know each other a little better before the wedding. Besides the wedding party and the two families, the dinner sometimes includes out-of-town guests who have come in early for the wedding.

The rehearsal dinner is the time for the bride and groom to give their attendants their gifts. These gifts are to commemorate the wedding. They are not elaborate and often are engraved with the wedding date. Traditional gifts include bracelets and other jewelry for the bridesmaids, cuff links and silver shot glasses for the groomsmen.

The Cast of Characters

The bride, of course, is the star of the wedding. The groom's function is principally decorative. Here are the other participants with the roles they play:

➤ *The best man*: He assists the groom, escorts him to the church, and hands over the wedding ring at the appropriate moment. He safeguards the necessary money for church donations and other details, takes care of the groom's car, sees that he has his travel tickets, and so on. The best man also makes the toast at the wedding reception. If there are any congratulatory telegrams for the couple that they would like read aloud, and if he wishes to do so, he reads them at the reception.

➤ *Maid/matron of honor*: She fusses over the bride as she prepares for the ceremony and helps her get ready to go off on her honeymoon. She holds the bride's bouquet during the ceremony. She also supervises the other bridesmaids and the child attendants.

➤ *Father of the bride*: He accompanies the bride to the church, walks her up the aisle, and hands her over to the groom at the altar. He also toasts the happy couple at the reception.

If for any reason this function is not done by the father of the bride, a relative or close family friend will be chosen for these duties. If the bride's father is deceased, and her mother has remarried, the mother's husband may take this role, providing he and the bride are on good terms. If there has been a divorce, and the bride has been raised by a stepfather, she may still want her biological father to participate. These decisions are, of course, up to the bride, and she must follow her heart and her conscience.

Tip

The bride and groom must be fairly sure of a positive response when they ask people to be the maid/matron of honor and best man. These jobs involve a considerable commitment. And, if you are asked to serve, remember that it is an honor to be asked and refusing can be very hurtful to the bride or groom or both.

➤ *Ushers*: These men greet the guests and help seat people at the church. The usher offers his inside arm to escort the women down the aisle. Men follow behind the usher. If a group of women arrive at the same time, they can choose to wait while the usher escorts them one by one, or the usher can escort the one he knows best or the most senior among them, and the others can seat themselves.

The bride's family sits on the left in the front pews, and the groom's family sits on the right. If there are no assigned seats, guests are seated on a first-come, first-served basis.

The mother of the bride is the last to be seated and sits in the first pew on the left side. When she is seated, that is the signal that the wedding is about to begin.

If there is an obvious imbalance of guests on the side of either the bride or groom, the ushers should endeavor to fill up the church in a balanced way. It's a good idea to have ushers from both families to minimize the "bride or groom" questions.

What To Wear

Winter brides traditionally choose velvet, satin, brocade, or other heavy formal fabric. Spring brides favor taffeta and lace, while summer suggests chiffon, organdy, or cotton.

Tradition dictates that the bride's wedding dress be white or off-white. The number of non-traditional brides is growing at the moment, however, and brides are opting more and more for colored dresses and prints. Basically, a bride should feel comfortable and at ease in whatever she wears because she is the star of the show.

If it's a formal wedding, the bride may wear a long veil reaching to her waist or a short face veil. Many brides opt to disregard the veil entirely in favor of a hat or simple flowers in the hair. When a groom wears a dark suit for his wedding, the bride sometimes opts for wearing a long white dress without train and veil.

Bridesmaids

The bride chooses her attendants' dresses. The cost of the dresses is borne by the attendants themselves, and this is a factor that the bride must take into consideration in making her decision.

Usually, bridesmaids' dresses are identical. The maid/matron of honor wears either the same dress as the bridesmaids or a dress that complements those dresses but in a slightly different style and/or color. It is also important for color harmony that any shoes that need to be dyed are dyed at the same place, so that the colors match.

At a small wedding, there may be only one attendant. The bride and her attendant should agree on the attendant's dress, and initial suggestions might come from the bride, but ultimately, the attendant should be able to choose her own dress. It's important that the bride has an opportunity to see her dress and make sure their outfits are compatible, but she shouldn't be autocratic about it.

The Groom

For traditional, formal daytime weddings, the men in the wedding party wear cutaway jackets, gray waistcoats, and dark striped trousers.

For a more informal wedding, men wear gray sack coats, gray waistcoats, and dark striped trousers.

Evening weddings (after 6 p.m.) are the most formal occasions. Traditionally, men wear white ties and tails.

However, grooms are becoming somewhat more flamboyant and creative in their attire, and now often stand out from their attendants as the bride does from hers.

> **Tip**
>
> One easy and risk-free alternative for male members of an informal wedding is navy blue blazers with gray trousers. Another attractive factor is that this outfit is already a part of many men's wardrobes.

The Mothers

The mothers of the bride and groom do not have to dress similarly, particularly if they do not have the same tastes. There is no law, for example, that says both have to wear short or long dresses. They should consult with one another and the bride to be sure they don't clash, but they each should be comfortable in what they wear. Of course, they should not outshine the bride.

Guests

The time of day dictates the sort of attire guests wear.

For a formal daytime wedding, women guests wear a cocktail dress or long skirt and festive blouse or sweater. Men wear suits for a formal daytime wedding, as well as an evening wedding. If an evening wedding is very formal, men wear dinner jackets, and women wear dressy cocktail suits or dresses or long dresses.

Black is a fine color to wear at a wedding, although there are so many other color choices that it seems pointless to court criticism. Pants are inappropriate for women to wear, whatever the color. It is also fine to wear white or off-white to a wedding if you are a guest.

Presents

If you accept someone's invitation to attend their wedding, you are obliged to give a gift. If you do not attend, there is no need to give a gift, although it is gracious to give something modest when you decline if the couple are friends.

There is a one-year "grace" period in giving wedding gifts. As long as you get it there before the couple's first anniversary, you're fine. Traditional gifts are silver, china, crystal, and items of lasting value. However, today's wedding gifts also include electronic equipment and practical items.

Wedding gifts should be sent to the bride's home.

Bridal registries can be useful in making sure you are selecting something the bride and groom want and like. Personally, I think they are cold-hearted, and I avoid them.

The Ceremony

There are as many variations within the wedding ceremonies as there are weddings. There are, however, some elements that are typical of all or most weddings.

Here is what may be expected when it comes to entering and leaving the church, and approaching and withdrawing from the altar:

➤ *Seating*: At a traditional church wedding, ushers escort guests to their seats, the bride's guests to the left and the groom's to the right. The mother of the bride is the last to be seated, and that begins the wedding ceremony. At small, informal weddings or ones that take place at home or outdoors, guests form a semi-circle.

If there are no ushers, guests seat themselves, leaving the first few pews for the couple's families. There is no need to divide the ranks left and right in this case.

➤ *The Processional*: In a formal wedding, the bride walks down the aisle on the arm of the man giving her away, usually her father (see "Cast of Characters").

The bridesmaids lead the processional, followed by the maid or matron of honor, the flower girl or ring bearer, and the bride, in that order. The bride meets the groom, best man, and clergyman at the altar. Generally, these three enter from a side door at the front.

After seating the guests, the ushers take their places in the processional, either walking down the aisle in pairs or accompanying the bridesmaids. After the ceremony, the ushers join the recessional, again walking in pairs or as escorts for the bridesmaids.

The clergyman asks, "Who gives this bride in marriage?" and the father says, "I do," or, "Her mother and I do." There are variations on this. If, for example, the bride objects to such sexist language, she may leave the father at the first pew and walk the last few steps to the altar on her own. Or, sometimes, the couple walks up the aisle together holding hands, particularly if they have been together for some time.

➤ *Recessional*: Traditionally, the bride takes the groom's right arm and walks away from the altar, followed by the flower girl and the maid of honor on the arm of the best man. If there is both a maid of honor and matron of honor, one will be accompanied by an usher. (The matron of honor outranks the maid of honor in the wedding party hierarchy.) Next come the bridesmaids, usually accompanied by ushers. If not, they precede the ushers walking single file out of the church.

If it is a small wedding with no recessional, the wedding ends with the groom kissing the bride. The clergyman congratulates the couple, and then the immediate family does so. At this point, an informal receiving line usually forms and guests give their good wishes to the couple.

➤ *Receiving line*: This can form in the church vestibule or at the start of the reception. The receiving line always includes the bride and groom, the two mothers, and the matron or maid of honor. If there are both, the maid of honor can choose to be part of the line or not, since the matron of honor outranks her. Fathers and bridesmaids are optional.

Guests going through the receiving line shake hands with its members, wishing the couple every happiness, congratulating the groom, and telling the bride she is beautiful. Don't tarry for a chat. Give your name, state your relationship with the couple (if necessary), say what a wonderful wedding it was, and move along.

Never go through a receiving line with a drink in your hand.

Kinds of Weddings

In some ways, all weddings are the same. In other ways, they may be profoundly different. Below are some examples of different sorts of weddings and some ideas about what to expect.

Civil Ceremonies

These are usually small, although frequently a civil authority officiates at a large wedding in a public hall. When this happens, follow the guidelines for a formal wedding, creating the stage by setting up rows of chairs on both sides of a central aisle.

When a civil ceremony takes place in a private home or judge's chambers, follow the guidelines for an informal wedding. If you go to a justice of the peace, dress in keeping with the dignity of the occasion, even though the ceremony might be short and rather impersonal.

The only persons who absolutely must be present for a civil ceremony are the bride and groom, the civil official, and the legal witnesses, who need not even be friends of the couple.

Beyond that, the couple may be attended by a bridesmaid or bridesmaids, best man, groomsmen, maid or matron of honor, someone to give the bride away, ushers, possibly child attendants (flower girls or ring bearers), friends, and relatives.

Roman Catholic Weddings

Roman Catholics are married in the presence of a priest. They may or may not have a nuptial Mass. The bride's father walks the bride down the aisle and "gives" her to the groom, who walks out a few steps to meet her. The father then assumes his seat in the front pew on the left.

If there is a nuptial Mass, the bride and groom and the wedding party receive Communion, and the guests frequently do as well. Of course, guests who are not of the faith will remain in their pews during Communion. That little bench at your feet is a kneeler, used during prayer; it's not a footrest.

Often, there are scriptural readings that are given by family members or close friends.

Jewish Weddings

Jewish wedding ceremonies vary from Orthodox to Reformed. However, there are some components of the wedding service that are found in all of the services.

The huppah, or wedding canopy, covers the bride, groom, and rabbi during the ceremony. Originally, the huppah was the bridal chamber itself. In our times, the word symbolizes the couple's entering into the chamber.

The wedding ring must be plain gold, without any stones. The groom places it on the bride's finger as he says, "You are sanctified to me with this ring according to the religion of Moses and Israel."

He and the bride sip wine from the same glass, over which blessings have been said. The groom steps on the wine glass, crushing it, to symbolize Jewish mourning for the destruction of the Temple. The wine glass is covered with cloth before it is crushed to prevent splinters and cuts.

Jewish weddings are forbidden on holy days, such as the Sabbath. However, the holy days end at sundown, so there are often weddings on Saturday nights.

Men cover their heads in the synagogue as a sign of respect for God. Guests are given skullcaps, called yarmulkes, for this purpose.

Islamic Weddings

Generally, Islamic weddings are not elaborate. The bride and groom exchange their vows in the mosque in the presence of family, friends, and the Imam, or religious leader. There are no restrictions as to color of clothing, but modest clothing is expected. Everyone removes shoes before entering and places them on racks. This is not a religious custom, but a sanitary one, since worshippers often pray touching the floor. At the end of the ceremony, those present often say "salaam aleikum" (peace be with you) to one another.

There is generally a reception following the ceremony in a hotel or hall. These are very much like wedding receptions anywhere, except that no alcohol is served and the food conforms to the Islamic dietary laws.

Quaker Weddings

Quaker weddings are warm, personal, and intimate. No clergy preside at Quaker weddings because Quakers believe that the divine spirit is present in all of us, and that we all are ministers, in a sense.

Guests enter the meeting house and sit wherever they feel comfortable. When all are seated, someone will stand and explain what to expect during the service. There will then be a period of silence, perhaps lasting several minutes. When they are ready, the bride and groom stand and exchange their vows. They then sit down, and another period of silence ensues.

During this period of silence, those present may rise when they wish and give their blessing to the couple. When the blessings are finished, the same person who spoke at the beginning of the meeting will "break" the meeting by rising and shaking the hand of someone nearby.

After the wedding, those present are invited to sign the marriage certificate. You need not be a Quaker to sign the certificate.

The reception following the wedding will be considerably less elaborate than the usual wedding reception. Probably, it will also be more personal and homey.

Military Weddings

A groom who is a member of the armed forces may opt to be married in uniform. When the groom is in full dress uniform, it automatically makes the wedding formal; thus, the bride wears a long dress.

Usually, the groom's attendants are largely in uniform, although some of the ushers may wear civilian dress. Men in uniform do not wear boutonnieres. They do wear military decorations.

At the end of the ceremony, the ushers form the traditional arch of steel under which the bride and groom walk as they leave the church. The saber or sword, as it is called in the Navy, is only worn by commissioned officers on active duty.

Sometimes, if the church permits, the arch is formed immediately after the bride and groom turn to face the assembled guests inside the church. In this case, the head usher calls "center face," and the ushers form two lines facing each other on the steps beneath the altar. The next command is "draw swords" or "arch sabers," and the ushers raise their swords, cutting edge facing up. The bride and groom pass under the arch.

The ushers then join the bridesmaids and leave with them. However, they may walk down the aisle with the bridesmaids, then leave through a side entrance to reassemble outside the church to form another arch. When this happens, the others in the wedding party wait in the vestibule of the church until the second arch is formed. Civilian ushers can choose to stand beside the military men forming the arch or not.

All of the traditions, details, and variations in this chapter must never obscure the intrinsic truth of every wedding. It is a joyful occasion and a celebration of love. Everyone involved, from the bride and groom to the last guest has an obligation to remember this. Smile through the inevitable glitches. Put aside any criticisms or feelings of annoyance. Be helpful, be courteous, and most of all, be happy.

The Least You Need to Know

➤ Traditionally, the bride's family bears most of the cost of the wedding. The groom's family is responsible for the rehearsal dinner and other incidentals.

➤ If you attend a wedding, you must give a gift. If you are invited and do not attend, a gift is not necessary.

➤ Evening weddings are more formal than day weddings. If in doubt about what to wear, check with the mother of the bride or others who will be attending.

➤ The bride's friends and family sit on the left in church, the groom's on the right. That little bench at your feet is a kneeler, not a footrest.

➤ No two weddings are alike. They are made more interesting and more special through the influence of secular and religious traditions.

Index

When You're Smart Enough to Know That You Don't Know It All

For all the ups and downs you're sure to encounter in life, The Complete Idiot's Guides give you down-to-earth answers and practical solutions.

Personal Business

The Complete Idiot's Guide to Terrific Business Writing
ISBN: 0-02-861097-0 ▪ $16.95

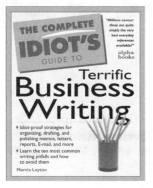

The Complete Idiot's Guide to Getting the Job You Want
ISBN: 1-56761-608-9 ▪ $24.95

The Complete Idiot's Guide to Managing Your Time
ISBN: 0-02-861039-3 ▪ $14.95

The Complete Idiot's Guide to Speaking in Public with Confidence
ISBN: 0-02-861038-5 ▪ $16.95

The Complete Idiot's Guide to Winning Through Negotiation
ISBN: 0-02-861037-7 ▪ $16.95

The Complete Idiot's Guide to Managing People
ISBN: 0-02-861036-9 ▪ $18.95

The Complete Idiot's Guide to a Great Retirement
ISBN: 1-56761-601-1 ▪ $16.95

The Complete Idiot's Guide to Starting Your Own Business
ISBN: 1-56761-529-5 ▪ $16.99

The Complete Idiot's Guide to Protecting Yourself From Everyday Legal Hassles
ISBN: 1-56761-602-X ▪ $16.99

The Complete Idiot's Guide to Surviving Divorce
ISBN: 0-02-861101-2 ▪ $16.95

You can handle it!

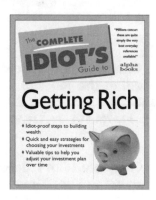

The Complete Idiot's Guide to Learning French on Your Own
ISBN: 0-02-861043-1 ▪ $16.95

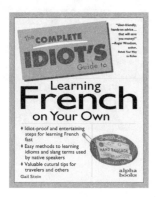

The Complete Idiot's Guide to Dating
ISBN: 0-02-861052-0 ▪ $14.95

The Complete Idiot's Guide to Cooking Basics
ISBN: 1-56761-523-6 ▪ $16.99

The Complete Idiot's Guide to Hiking and Camping
ISBN: 0-02-861100-4 ▪ $16.95

The Complete Idiot's Guide to Learning Spanish on Your Own
ISBN: 0-02-861040-7 ▪ $16.95

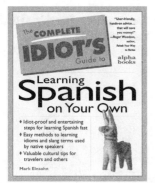

The Complete Idiot's Guide to Gambling Like a Pro
ISBN: 0-02-861102-0 ▪ $16.95

The Complete Idiot's Guide to Choosing, Training, and Raising a Dog
ISBN: 0-02-861098-9 ▪ $16.95

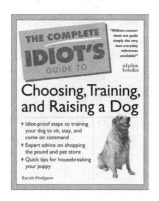

Y o u   c a n   h a n d l e   i t !

The Complete Idiot's Guide to Trouble-Free Car Care
ISBN: 0-02-861041-5 ▪ $16.95

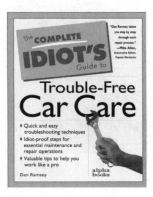

The Complete Idiot's Guide to the Perfect Wedding
ISBN: 1-56761-532-5 ▪ $16.99

The Complete Idiot's Guide to Getting and Keeping Your Perfect Body
ISBN: 0-286105122 ▪ $16.99

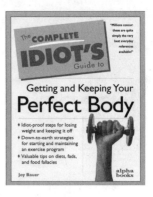

The Complete Idiot's Guide to First Aid Basics
ISBN: 0-02-861099-7 ▪ $16.95

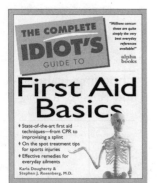

The Complete Idiot's Guide to the Perfect Vacation
ISBN: 1-56761-531-7 ▪ $14.99

The Complete Idiot's Guide to Trouble-Free Home Repair
ISBN: 0-02-861042-3 ▪ $16.95

The Complete Idiot's Guide to Getting into College
ISBN: 1-56761-508-2 ▪ $14.95

You can handle it!